ISRAEL'S MESSIAH

IN THE BIBLE *and* THE DEAD SEA SCROLLS

ISRAEL'S MESSIAH

IN THE BIBLE *and* THE DEAD SEA SCROLLS

Edited by
Richard S. Hess and
M. Daniel Carroll R.

WIPF & STOCK · Eugene, Oregon

Wipf and Stock Publishers
199 W 8th Ave, Suite 3
Eugene, OR 97401

Israel's Messiah in the Bible and the Dead Sea Scrolls
By Hess, Richard S. and Carroll R., M. Daniel
Copyright©2003 by Hess, Richard S.
ISBN 13: 978-1-61097-145-4
Publication date 5/1/2011
Previously published by Baker Academic Press, 2003

Contents

Part 4: The Messiah in Latin American Theology

Contributors

Gerardo A. Alfaro González, Ph.D.
Professor of Systematic and Contemporary Theology
El Seminario Teológico Centroamericano, Guatemala City, Guatemala

Daniel I. Block, Ph.D.
Associate Dean and John R. Sampey Professor of Old Testament Interpretation
The Southern Baptist Theological Seminary, Louisville, Kentucky

Craig L. Blomberg, Ph.D.
Distinguished Professor of New Testament
Denver Seminary, Denver, Colorado

M. Daniel Carroll R. (Rodas), Ph.D.
Professor of Old Testament
Denver Seminary, Denver, Colorado
and Adjunct Professor
El Seminario Teológico Centroamericano, Guatemala City, Guatemala

Craig A. Evans, Ph.D.
Professor of New Testament
Acadia Divinity College, Wolfville, Nova Scotia

J. Daniel Hays, Ph.D.
Chair, Department of Biblical Studies and Theology
Ouachita Baptist University, Arkadelphia, Arkansas

Richard S. Hess, Ph.D.
Professor of Old Testament
Denver Seminary, Denver, Colorado

Karen H. Jobes, Ph.D.
Associate Professor of New Testament
Westmont College, Santa Barbara, California

William W. Klein, Ph.D.
Professor of New Testament
Denver Seminary, Denver, Colorado

Editors' Preface

No theme is more central to the study of the Bible than that of the messiah. The definition and the expectation of this figure fill the pages of the Old Testament with hope. The ongoing anticipation of the messiah's coming is evident in the writings of the Dead Sea Scrolls and is the subject of debate and controversy. For the Christian believer, the realization of that longed-for king and redeemer is found in the events of the Gospels and in the reflections of the epistolary literature of the New Testament.

The chapters of this book present the papers delivered at the second annual biblical studies conference hosted by the Denver Institute for Contextualized Biblical Studies of Denver Seminary from February 2 to 3, 2001. The goal of these conferences is to offer a venue, within an Evangelical framework, for considering the biblical text within both its original context and the modern world. Conferences and publications tend to focus on one of these two poles. A more comprehensive understanding of the Word of God, however, will grapple with its meaning in ancient Israel and the first-century world of Jesus and the apostles, as well as appropriate the illuminating insights that can be generated from contemporary minority and international perspectives.

The essays reflect this commitment to serious up-to-date scholarship grounded in textual fidelity and hermeneutical diversity. The contributions of Daniel I. Block, Craig A. Evans, and Craig L. Blomberg provide the reader with comprehensive surveys of the descriptions and expectations of messiah in the Old Testament, the Dead Sea Scrolls, and the New Testament, respectively. But the messiah of the Bible and Qumran cannot be limited to a topic of purely antiquarian interest. Accordingly, Gerardo A. Alfaro González, an El Salvadoran now teaching in Guatemala, explores the portrait of the biblical messiah developed in Central America today by liberation theologian Jon Sobrino. The interchange of ideas and the critiques voiced in the responses by J. Daniel Hays, M.

Daniel Carroll R., Richard S. Hess, William W. Klein, and Karen H. Jobes are at once respectful and lively. Obviously, the interpretation and the application of the relevant biblical texts continue to foster healthy debate. This collection provides a unique survey of the discussion of messiah. It summarizes and evaluates the best of modern biblical scholarship and applies this material to a mature and fully developed understanding of the figure that stands at the center of the Christian faith.

We thank Denver Seminary for hosting this conference. We appreciate the efforts of Marilyn Carroll for her editorial work in preparing the papers for publication. We especially thank the contributors for the serious effort that these papers reflect and for their willingness and courage in accepting a difficult and wide-ranging assignment. Finally, we thank the publishers, Baker Books, and Jim Kinney, for accepting this volume for publication.

The Editors
The Feasts of the Conversion of St. Paul
(Western church)
and of the Prophet Isaiah
(Eastern church)
January 25, 2002

Abbreviations

AB	Anchor Bible
ABD	*Anchor Bible Dictionary*, ed. D. N. Freedman, 6 vols. (New York: Doubleday, 1992)
AUSS	*Andrews University Seminary Studies*
b.	Babylonian Talmud
BAR	*Biblical Archaeology Review*
BBR	*Bulletin for Biblical Research*
BECNT	Baker Exegetical Commentary on the New Testament
Bib	*Biblica*
BNTC	Black's New Testament Commentaries
BolTeol	*Boletín Teológico*
BRT	*Baptist Review of Theology*
BSac	*Bibliotheca Sacra*
BST	Bible Speaks Today
BZ	*Biblische Zeitschrift*
CBQ	*Catholic Biblical Quarterly*
ChrSchR	*Christian Scholars Review*
CJAS	Christianity and Judaism in Antiquity Series
ConBot	Coniectanea biblica: Old Testament Series
CTR	*Criswell Theological Review*
DSD	*Dead Sea Discoveries*
DSSRL	Dead Sea Scrolls and Related Literature
EBib	Etudes bibliques
EDSS	*Encyclopedia of the Dead Sea Scrolls*, ed. L. H. Schiffman and J. C. VanderKam, 2 vols. (Oxford: Oxford University Press, 2000)
ErIsr	*Eretz-Israel*
EvQ	*Evangelical Quarterly*
HALOT	L. Koehler, W. Baumgartner, and J. J. Stamm, *The Hebrew and Aramaic Lexicon of the Old Testament,* trans. and ed. M. E. J. Richardson, 4 vols. (Leiden: Brill, 1994–99)
HBT	*Horizons in Biblical Theology*
HKAT	Handkommentar zum Alten Testament
HSS	Harvard Semitic Studies
ICC	International Critical Commentary
Int	*Interpretation*
IVPNTCS	IVP New Testament Commentary Series

JAOS	*Journal of the American Oriental Society*
JB	Jerusalem Bible
JBL	*Journal of Biblical Literature*
JBLMS	Journal of Biblical Literature Monograph Series
JBT	*Jahrbuch für biblische Theologie*
JETS	*Journal of the Evangelical Theological Society*
JJS	*Journal of Jewish Studies*
JRT	*Journal of Religious Thought*
JSJSup	Supplements to the Journal for the Study of Judaism
JSNT	*Journal for the Study of the New Testament*
JSNTSup	Journal for the Study of the New Testament: Supplement Series
JSOT	*Journal for the Study of the Old Testament*
JSOTSup	Journal for the Study of the Old Testament: Supplement Series
LBI	Library of Biblical Interpretation
LDSS	Literature of the Dead Sea Scrolls
LXX	Septuagint
MT	Masoretic Text
NA²⁷	*Novum Testamentum Graece,* ed. Barbara Aland, Kurt Aland, Johannes Karavidopoulos, Carlo M. Martini, and Bruce M. Metzger, 27th ed. (Stuttgart: Deutsche Bibelgesellschaft, 1993)
NAB	New American Bible
NAC	New American Commentary
NASB	New American Standard Bible
NCBC	New Century Bible Commentary
NICNT	New International Commentary on the New Testament
NICOT	New International Commentary on the Old Testament
NIDNTT	*New International Dictionary of New Testament Theology,* ed. C. Brown, 4 vols. (Grand Rapids: Zondervan, 1975–85)
NIDOTTE	*New International Dictionary of Old Testament Theology and Exegesis,* ed. W. A. VanGemeren, 5 vols. (Grand Rapids: Zondervan, 1997)
NIGTC	New International Greek Testament Commentary
NIV	New International Version
NIVI	New International Version, Inclusive Language Edition
NovTSup	Novum Testamentum Supplements
NRSV	New Revised Standard Version
NTC	New Testament Commentary
NTS	*New Testament Studies*
OBO	Orbis biblicus et orientalis
OBT	Overtures to Biblical Theology
OTG	Old Testament Guides
OTL	Old Testament Library
OTM	Oxford Theological Monographs
PNTC	Pillar New Testament Commentary
PSTJ	*Perkins (School of Theology) Journal*
REB	Revised English Bible
RevQ	*Revue de Qumran*
RILP	Roehampton Institute London Papers
RSV	Revised Standard Version
SAA	State Archives of Assyria
SBLRBS	Society of Biblical Literature Resources for Biblical Study
SBLSymS	Society of Biblical Literature Symposium Series

SBLWAW   Society of Biblical Literature Writings from the Ancient World
SBT   Studies in Biblical Theology
SP   Sacra Pagina
STDJ   Studies on the Texts of the Desert of Judah
TDNT   *Theological Dictionary of the New Testament*, ed. G. Kittel and G. Friedrich,
           trans. G. W. Bromiley, 10 vols. (Grand Rapids: Eerdmans, 1964–76)
TDOT   *Theological Dictionary of the Old Testament*, ed. G. J. Botterweck, H. Ring-
           gren, and H.-J. Fabry, trans. J. T. Willis, G. W. Bromiley, D. E. Green, and
           D. W. Stott, 12 vols. (Grand Rapids: Eerdmans, 1974–)
TLOT   *Theological Lexicon of the Old Testament*, ed. E. Jenni, with assistance from
           C. Westermann, trans. M. E. Biddle, 3 vols. (Peabody, Mass.: Hendrickson,
           1997)
TNIV   Today's New International Version
TNTC   Tyndale New Testament Commentaries
TOTC   Tyndale Old Testament Commentaries
TPINTC   TPI New Testament Commentaries
TS   *Theological Studies*
UBS⁴   *The Greek New Testament*, ed. Barbara Aland, Kurt Aland, Johannes Karavi-
           dopoulos, Carlo M. Martini, and Bruce M. Metzger, 4th rev. ed. (Stuttgart:
           Deutsche Bibelgesellschaft, 1994)
UF   *Ugarit-Forschungen*
VTSup   Vetus Testamentum Supplements
WBC   Word Biblical Commentary
WTJ   *Westminster Theological Journal*
y.   Jerusalem (Yerushalmi) Talmud

Part 1

THE MESSIAH IN THE OLD TESTAMENT

ONE

My Servant David: Ancient Israel's Vision of the Messiah

Daniel I. Block

It is understandable that believers on this side of the cross should have a special fascination with the messiah in the Old Testament. After all, followers of Jesus are called "Christians" or, if one prefers the Jewish term, "Messianists." But what does this mean to us? More importantly, what did it mean to the writers and original readers of the Old Testament? And how does the New Testament portrayal of the messiah compare with the Old Testament anticipation? Unfortunately, as we begin to explore these issues, we discover that the difficulty in answering these questions is directly proportional to their importance.

Formidable challenges face any attempt to investigate ancient Israelite perceptions of the messiah. (1) How can we determine which texts are to be interpreted messianically and which are not? And what rules do we follow in making this determination? (2) What are the origins of Israelite messianism? (3) What roles did the ancient Israelites expect the messiah to play and what responsibilities would he bear? (4) What is the relationship between the kingship of Yahweh and the rule of the messiah? (5) Should we distinguish between "messianism" and "messianic hope"? (6) How eschatological was the Israelites' messianic hope? (7) How are

we to understand the relationship between messianic prophecy and fulfillment, or between New Testament appropriation of Old Testament
texts and the original contextual meaning? (8) Who is the messiah?
So many questions! So many disputed answers! I commend the organizers of this conference for devoting a weekend to the investigation of
this extremely important biblical theological theme. If our search for
the answers does not yield a clearer understanding of the messiah in the
Old Testament, at least we will have gained an appreciation for the complexity of the problem that modern Western readers face when confronted with an ancient Eastern idea.

Although the secondary literature on ancient Israelite messianism is
vast and growing,[1] the primary Hebrew sources that might contribute
to the subject are constant and limited to the Old Testament.[2] However,

1. Full-scale treatments of the subject include J. C. K. von Hofmann, *Weissagung und
Erfüllung im Alten und im Neuen Testamente*, 2 vols. (Nordlingen: Beck, 1841–44); E. W.
Hengstenberg, *Christology of the Old Testament and Commentary on the Messianic Predictions of the Prophets*, trans. R. Keith (London: Francis and John Rivington, 1847); avail-
able in an abridged reprint edition with a foreword by Walter C. Kaiser Jr. (Grand Rapids:
Kregel, 1970); Franz J. Delitzsch, *Messianic Prophecies in Historical Succession* (Edin-
burgh: Clark, 1891); Eduard König, *Die Messianischen Weissagungen des Alten Testa-
ments* (Stuttgart: n.p., 1923); Hugo Gressmann, *Der Messias* (Göttingen: Vandenhoeck &
Ruprecht, 1929); A. Bentzen, *King and Messiah* (ET; London: Lutterworth, 1955); S.
Mowinckel, *He That Cometh*, trans. G. W. Anderson (New York: Abingdon, 1959); Henri
Cazelles, *Le Messie de la Bible: Christologie de l'Ancien Testament* (Paris: Desclée, 1978);
Gerard van Groningen, *Messianic Revelation in the Old Testament* (Grand Rapids: Baker,
1990). For recent collections of essays on the messiah, see J. H. Charlesworth, ed., *The
Messiah* (Minneapolis: Fortress, 1992); Ingo Baldermann et al., eds., *Der Messias*, JBT 8
(Neukirchen-Vluyn: Neukirchener Verlag, 1993); Philip E. Satterthwaite, Richard S.
Hess, and Gordon J. Wenham, eds., *The Lord's Anointed: Interpretation of Old Testament
Messianic Texts* (Carlisle: Paternoster, 1995); John Day, ed., *King and Messiah in Israel
and the Ancient Near East: Proceedings of the Oxford Old Testament Seminar*, JSOTSup
270 (Sheffield: Sheffield Academic Press, 1998). For a recent survey of scholarship on the
subject, see Magne Sæbø, "Zum Verhältnis von 'Messianismus' und 'Eschatologie' im Alten Testament," in *Der Messias*, 25–35.

2. Although deliverance terminology such as *nāṣal* and *yāšaʿ* occurs frequently in epigraphic texts dating from Old Testament times, especially in personal names, to date no
references or even allusions to the messiah have surfaced. The Hebrew epigraphic texts
have been conveniently published in transliteration and translation in Sandra Landis Go-
gel, *A Grammar of Epigraphic Hebrew*, SBLRBS 23 (Atlanta: Scholars Press, 1998), 385–
494. Inasmuch as the apocryphal and pseudepigraphic compositions and the documents
from Qumran postdate the Old Testament texts (including Daniel, by my dating), they are
excluded from consideration. The subject of messianism in early Judaism, which de-
serves investigation in its own right, has been examined in several important recent
works. See, for example, John J. Collins, *The Scepter and the Star: The Messiahs of the
Dead Sea Scrolls and Other Ancient Literature* (New York: Doubleday, 1995); Johannes
Zimmermann, *Messianische Texte aus Qumran: Königliche, priesterliche und prophetische
Messiasvorstellungen in den Schriftfunden von Qumran* (Tübingen: Mohr Siebeck, 1998).

because the Old Testament sources span a period of one thousand years, derive from a wide geographic range, and come in a variety of literary forms (e.g., narrative, prophetic oracles, poetic verse), one doubts whether we may even speak of *an* Old Testament messianic vision, as if there were a single, universally accepted view of the messiah. Each supposedly messianic text needs to be interpreted within its own historical and cultural context and according to rules appropriate for that genre.

Some scholars suggest that the fundamental, even if not primary, message of the Old Testament canon is messianic.[3] Others go even farther. Based largely on Luke's account of Jesus' postresurrection discussion with two of his disciples on the road to Emmaus (24:13–35), many seek to find Christ, that is, the Messiah, on every page of the Old Testament. Our participation in this conference demonstrates our conviction that the Messiah is indeed *an* extremely important theme of the Old Testament, but we exaggerate Luke's interpretation of the significance of Jesus' speech on two counts if we assume that this is *the* theme of the Bible and look for the Messiah on every page.

First, with respect to grammar and syntax, our English translations all agree in their interpretation of v. 27. The NRSV, for example, reads, "Then beginning with Moses and all the prophets, he interpreted to them the things about himself in all the scriptures."[4] With this statement Luke does not declare that Jesus saw references to himself in every verse or on every page of the Hebrew Bible (the Scriptures). And even if he did, it does not mean that Jesus saw references to himself *as messiah* in every verse. We do have two other options. Many have interpreted the statement to mean that Jesus drew on the general teaching of the Old Testament, which presents a consistent divine purpose, and thereby declared himself to be the fulfillment of God's plan of salvation, which he accomplished through his sufferings and his subsequent glorification.[5] But this interpretation is doubtful on grammatical grounds. It seems more likely that, beginning with Moses and the prophets, Jesus drew

3. On this view of the canon, see most recently John Sailhamer's Evangelical Theological Society presidential address, "The Messiah and the Hebrew Bible," delivered on November 15, 2000, and published in *JETS* 44 (2001): 5–23. See especially his concluding comments on p. 23.

4. See, similarly, RSV, NIV, NASB, REB, NAB, JB. The Greek reads, καὶ ἀρξάμενος ἀπὸ Μωϋσέως καὶ ἀπὸ πάντων τῶν προφητῶν διερμήνευσεν αὐτοῖς ἐν πάσαις ταῖς γραφαῖς τὰ περὶ ἑαυτοῦ.

5. Leon Morris (*Luke*, rev. ed., TNTC [Grand Rapids: Eerdmans; Leicester: Inter-Varsity, 1988], 370) declares, "We should perhaps understand this not as the selection of a number of proof-texts, but rather as showing that throughout the Old Testament a consistent divine purpose is worked out, a purpose that in the end meant and must mean the cross." For a similar perspective, see Joel Green, *The Gospel of Luke*, NICNT (Grand Rapids: Eerdmans, 1997), 848–49.

from the entire Scriptures those statements and texts that referred to him *as messiah*, that is, as the anointed Son of David and incarnate Son of God, and for the benefit of the disciples, he interpreted these in the light of his own mission—his life, death, and resurrection.[6] But how I wish the Gospel writers had preserved that speech for us! It would have saved us a lot of headache and speculation about which texts we may legitimately interpret as messianic.[7]

Second, with respect to the nature of the Old Testament itself, given the prevalence of messianic expectation in the intertestamental and early New Testament periods, it would be surprising if those responsible for the structure and arrangement of the canon were not driven to some extent by messianic hope.[8] However, we do well to recognize that the Old Testament consists of a collection of compositions deriving from a specific ancient Near Eastern cultural context and addressed to specific historical and religious circumstances. The purpose of the Law (Torah), for example, was to preserve a written record of Yahweh's revelation of himself, thereby keeping alive the Israelites' memory of his gracious acts of election, salvation, providential care, and revelation, and to provide God's people with an authoritative written record of the divine suzerain's expectations of his people in response to his gracious acts. The historiographic

6. Compare the comment of I. Howard Marshall on this text in his *Gospel of Luke*, NIGTC (Grand Rapids: Eerdmans, 1978), 897: "The verb [διερμηνεύω] signifies that the speaker chose out those passages which might be regarded as 'messianic' and then proceeded to show how they should be understood, so that they could now 'speak' to the disciples." Darrell Bock (*Luke*, BECNT [Grand Rapids: Baker, 1996], 1918) adopts a mediating stance in seeing Jesus' statement as referring both to texts referring to Jesus that are directly prophetic and to "typico-prophetic texts" that reflect Old Testament patterns reenacted by Jesus and that he escalated to a new level by his own eschatological fulfillment/inauguration of them.

7. In either case, "messianism" should not be adopted as a fundamental hermeneutical stance or method. The search for Jesus on virtually every page of the Old Testament is legitimate only to the extent that we recognize Jesus' identification with Yahweh, the Creator of the universe and universal God of Israel, who is indeed mentioned on nearly every page. But then we are no longer dealing with "messianism" in the strict sense.

8. The placement of Ruth, which ends with the genealogy of David, before Psalms in *b. Baba Bathra* 14b (the earliest Jewish witness to canonical order) seems to reflect a messianic hope, but most see this agenda eclipsed in the tradition associated with Josephus and the Septuagint (which have Ruth attached to Judges, presumably for chronological reasons; Ruth narrates events dated to the period of the judges) and in the liturgical Tiberian Masoretic tradition (which places Ruth at the head of five small scrolls used in the festivals, and after Proverbs 31, linking the character of Ruth with that chapter's celebration of wifely nobility). On the other hand, it can also be argued that the attachment of Ruth to Judges, which places it immediately before Samuel (that is, the story of David, the Old Testament messiah par excellence), reflects a messianic hope. For presentation and discussion of the various canonical orders in early traditions, see Roger Beckwith, *The Old Testament Canon of the New Testament Church and Its Background in Early Judaism* (Grand Rapids: Eerdmans, 1985), 181–234, and appendix 2, 449–68.

writings are rightly characterized in the Hebrew canon as the Former Prophets, representing divinely inspired interpretations of Israel's performance and paraenetic appeals to a later readership to recognize and avoid the sins of the past. The Latter Prophets have a similar purpose, though in the collections of oracles, the paraenetic appeals tend to overwhelm the historical description. The Writings consist of a wide variety of compositions, some historiographic (Chronicles, Ezra-Nehemiah, Ruth, Esther), some sapiential (Proverbs, Ecclesiastes, Job), some inspirational (Daniel), and some for use in corporate and private worship (Psalms), but all intended to describe for the ancient Israelites the national and personal implications of life as the people of God.

In its canonical shape the Old Testament may function as a road map pointing to the messiah, but it is much more than messianic history written *ante eventu*. In the past, its multifarious compositions provided Israel with a vision of God and a guide to life past, present, and future, but especially present. The New Testament recognizes the same function of the Old Testament for the church. In 2 Tim. 3:16–17, Paul declares unequivocally his understanding of the theological and ethical significance of the Old Testament for Christians: "All Scripture is breathed by God, hence beneficial/effective for teaching, reproof, correction, and training in righteousness, so that the person who belongs to God may be capable and equipped for every kind of good work."[9] This statement certainly is much more comprehensive than Luke's comment concerning the messianic significance of the Old Testament in Luke 24:27.

As a matter of fact, the books that make up the Old Testament are not obviously preoccupied with the messiah.[10] Within this variegated record of divine action and revelation, the messianic hope is embedded like a diamond, precious not only because of its intrinsic value, but in the He-

9. The primacy of concern for the Torah over messianic interests is reflected in the "Torathite" stitching evident between major sections of the canon in virtually all canonical traditions: the Former Prophets open with an appeal to meditate day and night on the Torah (Josh. 1:7–9); the Latter Prophets close with an appeal to return to Moses and the Torah (Mal. 3:22 [Eng. 4:4]), which is mirrored in Psalm 1 at the beginning of the Writings. The ethical interest of these traditions may be reflected in the liturgical Tiberian tradition, which places Ruth (as the head of the five Megilloth) immediately after Proverbs, whose ending consists of an alphabetic acrostic of wifely nobility. Boaz's characterization of Ruth as an *ʾēšet ḥayil* in Ruth 3:11 answers to Prov. 31:10, where this same expression appears in the heading of the literary unit. Whatever we say about the agendas driving the various canonical arrangements, the evidence of the Dead Sea Scrolls suggests that even within New Testament times there was no fixed canonical order for the Old Testament. On this subject, see Eugene Ulrich, *The Dead Sea Scrolls and the Origins of the Bible* (Grand Rapids: Eerdmans, 1999), 51–78, esp. 59.

10. In his paper delivered at this conference, Craig Evans made the same observation with respect to Qumran.

braic sense also because of its rarity. Inasmuch as the Old Testament is a record of God's gracious reach to fallen humankind within history, it is indeed filled with hope, but to characterize this as an overtly and pervasively messianic hope is to overstate the case. Explicit references to the messiah in the Pentateuch can be counted on a single hand, and their relative frequency increases only slightly as we move through the Former Prophets to the Latter Prophets, and then the Writings.

The purpose of this paper is to explore the Old Testament portrayal of the messiah, with the hope of coming to a realistic understanding of how the ancient Israelites viewed this intriguing figure. Specifically, I will try to answer this question: What kind of person did the Israelites of the Old Testament expect the messiah to be, and what future role(s) did they expect him to play? The traditional answers to this question range widely. In the written records of the Judaisms of Palestine around the time of Jesus, we learn of different messianic types: an ideal king, a Davidic ruler, a branch, an Aaronic priest, a teacher of righteousness, an eschatological prophet, a son of God, a son of man.[11] This catalog of epithets is similar to titles attributed to the messiah by Evangelical scholars in our own day. For example, Walter C. Kaiser lists, among others, triumphant king, second David, branch of the Lord, faithful/high priest, teacher, prophet, son of man.[12] Many abbreviate the list to three titles: prophet, priest, and king.[13]

But did the Israelites of the Old Testament actually understand the messiah in these terms? It seems to me that in answering these questions we have sometimes played loose and free with the evidence and imposed on texts meanings and/or significance that go beyond authorial intent. In this paper I will try to answer the question: How did the writers (and original readers) of the Old Testament perceive the messiah?[14] I will begin by examining briefly how the root of the verb *māšaḥ*, "to anoint," was used in the Old Testament, but the major portion of this paper will be devoted to determining whether or not persons in Old Testament times actually looked forward to the coming of a messiah who would hold the offices of prophet, priest, and king.

11. For detailed discussions of these images of the messiah in Judaism, see Collins, *The Scepter and the Star;* Zimmermann, *Messianische Texte aus Qumran;* Michael Wise, *The First Messiah: Investigating the Savior before Jesus* (San Francisco: HarperCollins, 1999); and the collection of essays in J. Neusner, A. S. Green, and E. S. Frerichs, eds., *Judaisms and Their Messiahs at the Turn of the Christian Era* (Cambridge: Cambridge University Press, 1987).

12. Walter C. Kaiser Jr., *The Messiah in the Old Testament* (Grand Rapids: Zondervan, 1995), appendix 2, 240–42.

13. For the basis of this "messianic" triad, see van Groningen, *Messianic Revelation in the Old Testament*, 32–38.

14. Cf. the question that Jesus raised to his disciples in Mark 8:27; Matt. 16:13; Luke 9:18.

The Messiah as the Anointed One

A consideration of the ancient Israelite view(s)[15] of the messiah begins naturally with the word "messiah" itself. In modern usage, the technical term "messiah" refers minimally to "a future figure who will play an authoritative role in the end time, usually the eschatological king."[16] The term "messiah" entered the English language from the Latin *messias*, which was borrowed directly from the Greek *messias*,[17] which in turn represents an imprecise transliteration of Hebrew *māšîaḥ* (Aramaic *mĕšîḥā*). Like numerous other designations for classes of people,[18] Hebrew *māšîaḥ* is a passive *qāṭîl* form, being derived from the verb *māšaḥ*, "to smear, to anoint," hence the meaning "anointed one."[19] There is no need in this context to repeat the detailed analyses of the term readily available elsewhere.[20] It will suffice to reiterate that anointing with oil was a common ancient Near Eastern custom by which indi-

15. This paper employs the term "Israelite" the way the prophets used it, that is, of any citizen of the nation, whether by birth in one of the twelve (thirteen) tribes or as a proselyte. Since images of the messiah varied from place to place and from time to time, to be precise we should analyze separately the messianic visions (if any) of (1) the patriarchs, (2) premonarchic Israel, (3) Israel under the united monarchy, (4) the northern kingdom of Israel, (5) the southern kingdom of Judah, (6) the exilic communities in Egypt and Babylon, (7) the postexilic community in Judah, and (8) postexilic Diaspora Israelites. Limitations of space and time preclude separate discussions based upon these distinctions.

16. Collins, *The Scepter and the Star*, 11. Compare the definition of Wolter H. Rose (*Zemah and Zerubbabel: Messianic Expectations in the Early Postexilic Period*, JSOTSup 304 [Sheffield: Sheffield Academic Press, 2000], 23), who sees the messiah as "a future royal figure sent by God who will bring salvation to God's people and the world and establish a kingdom characterized by features like peace and justice."

17. *Messias* occurs only twice in the New Testament (John 1:41; 4:25), being followed in each case by a translation, *Christos*. The first vowel derives from the Aramaic; the doubled *s* captures Semitic *sh*; the final *s* renders the term declinable (cf. *Iēsous*).

18. *Nāgîd*, "promoted one, ruler"; *nāśî*, "raised one, prince"; *nāzîr*, "consecrated one, Nazirite"; *pāqîd*, "appointed one, overseer"; *śākîr*, "hired one, hireling"; *nābî'*, "called one, prophet." For a defense of this interpretation of *nābî'* and a discussion of such forms, see John Huehnergard, "On the Etymology and Meaning of Hebrew *nābî'*," *ErIsr* 26 (1999): 88*–93*.

19. See J. Barth, *Die Nominalbildung in den semitischen Sprachen* (Leipzig: Hinrichs, 1894), 184; C. Brockelmann, *Grundriß der vergleichenden Grammatik der semitischen Sprachen*, 2 vols. (Berlin: Reuther & Reichard, 1908–13), 354.

20. Especially Richard S. Hess, "The Image of the Messiah in the Old Testament," in *Images of Christ Ancient and Modern*, ed. S. E. Porter, M. A. Hayes, and D. Tombs, RILP 2 (Sheffield: Sheffield Academic Press, 1997), 22–33. See also J. A. Soggin, "מֶלֶךְ *melek* king," *TLOT* 2:676–77; J. N. Oswalt, "משׁח," *NIDOTTE* 2:1123–27; K. Seybold, "מָשַׁח *māšaḥ*," *TDOT* 9:43–54. On the meaning and significance of anointing, see especially Ernst Kutsch, *Salbung als Rechtsakt im Alten Testament und im Alten Orient* (Berlin: Töpelmann, 1963); T. N. D. Mettinger, *King and Messiah: The Civil and Sacral Legitimation of the Israelite Kings*, ConBOT 8 (Lund: Gleerup, 1976), 185–232.

viduals were ritually purified[21] and that conferred special power, authority, honor, and glory.[22]

According to the usage of the root *mšḥ* in the Old Testament, in general, a messiah was anyone inducted into an office through anointing with oil. The verb *māšaḥ*, "to smear, to anoint," occurs seventy-plus times in the Old Testament. The idiom involving *māšaḥ* followed by the preposition *lĕ* plus a title highlights the purpose of a specific anointing. Individuals were anointed *lĕmelek*, "to be king";[23] *lĕnāgîd*, "to be ruler";[24] *lĕkōhēn*, "to be priest";[25] *lĕnābîʾ*, "to be a prophet."[26] The noun *māšîaḥ*, "anointed one," occurs thirty-eight times in the Old Testament.[27] However, the unaugmented absolute form occurs only twice, both in Dan. 9:25–26, and the articular adjectival form only four times, in each case with reference to the anointed high priest.[28] Elsewhere the word always appears in a genitival context, either in a construct relation with divinity[29] or as a suffixed form.[30] Obviously, not every anointed person was a messiah by the modern technical understanding of the term.

Although the Latter Prophets (according to the Jewish canon) tell us a lot about the prophets' understandings of the messiah, it is remarkable that the noun *māšîaḥ* occurs only in Hab. 3:13 and Isa. 45:1. But neither text may be construed as a technical reference to the anointed one. Appearing as a correlative to "your people" (*ʿammekā*), in the former text

21. Kutsch, *Salbung als Rechtsakt*, 16–33.

22. To the clear evidence of the practice in Egypt and among the Hittites (for citation and discussion, see Kutsch, *Salbung als Rechtsakt*, 37–70) we may now add the evidence from Emar. For the full investigation, see especially Daniel E. Fleming, *The Installation of Baal's High Priestess at Emar: A Window on Ancient Syrian Religion*, HSS 42 (Atlanta: Scholars Press, 1992); for the practice of anointing in particular, see Gerald Klingbeil, "The Anointing of Aaron: A Study of Leviticus 8:12 in Its OT and ANE Context," *AUSS* 38 (2000): 231–43, esp. 237–40.

23. Judg. 9:8, 15; 1 Sam. 15:1, 17; 2 Sam. 2:4, 7; 5:3, 17; 12:7; 1 Kings 1:34, 45; 5:15 [Eng. 1]; 19:15, 16; 2 Kings 9:3, 6, 12; 1 Chron. 11:3; 14:8.

24. 1 Sam. 9:16; 10:1; 1 Chron. 29:22.

25. 1 Chron. 29:22.

26. 1 Kings 19:16.

27. Excluding 2 Sam. 1:21, which has a passive participle form.

28. *Hakkōhēn hammāšîaḥ* (Lev. 4:3, 5, 16; 6:15 [Eng. 22]). According to Kutsch (*Salbung als Rechtsakt*, 22–25), the anointing of the high priest did not signify the conferring of power and authority, but the purification of the individual by which he was liberated and separated from the people for the service of Yahweh.

29. *Mĕšîaḥ yhwh* (1 Sam. 24:7a, 7b [Eng. 6a, 6b], 11 [Eng. 10]; 26:9, 11, 16, 23; 2 Sam. 1:14, 16; 19:22 [Eng. 21]; Lam. 4:20); *mĕšîaḥ ʾĕlōhîm* (2 Sam. 23:1).

30. *Mĕšîḥî*, "my anointed one" (1 Sam. 2:35; Ps. 132:17); *mĕšîḥekā*, "your anointed one" (Hab. 3:13; Ps. 84:10 [Eng. 9]; 89:39, 52 [Eng. 38, 51]; 132:10; 2 Chron. 6:42); *mĕšîḥô*, "his anointed one" (1 Sam. 2:10; 12:3, 5; 16:6; 2 Sam. 22:51 = Ps. 18:51; Ps. 2:2; 20:7 [Eng. 6]; 28:8; Isa. 45:1 [Cyrus]). Cf. the plural form *mĕšîḥay*, "my anointed ones" (1 Chron. 16:22 = Ps. 105:15).

měšîhekā, "your anointed one," refers to Israel as a whole. With remark-able boldness, the latter text identifies a foreigner, Cyrus the Persian, as měšîhô, "his anointed one." The prophet does not thereby envision the "eschatological messianic deliverer," but the historical figure chosen by Yahweh to serve as his agent of deliverance for exiled Israel.[31]

Remarkably, Dan. 9:25–26 and Isa. 61:1 represent the only instances outside Psalms in which the verb māšah and/or its cognate noun māšîah refer to someone whose role approximates that of the messiah as under-stood by the definition quoted earlier: "a figure who will play an author-itative role in the end time, usually the eschatological king." As in extra-biblical examples of anointing accounts, in the overwhelming majority of cases, the anointed one was a historical figure, either priestly or royal, without any hint of eschatological significance.

We turn our attention now to a consideration of the triad of titles/of-fices commonly ascribed to the messiah: prophet, priest, and king. Al-though it is almost axiomatic in Protestant tradition to interpret Jesus' messiahship in these terms,[32] the question must be posed whether or not the Israelites of the Old Testament period did so. This question can be answered only by examining the Old Testament texts themselves. Al-though our understanding of the messiah obviously must take into ac-count later interpretations of the Old Testament texts, and especially later revelation in the person of the messiah himself, when we are trying

31. This deliverance would prove to be temporary and to provide only an ethnically and geographically limited solution to the nation's problem. Cf. the previous verse (Isa. 44:28), which refers to Cyrus as Yahweh's "shepherd" who performs his every desire and calls for the rebuilding of Jerusalem and the temple. On this text, see Brevard S. Childs, *Isaiah*, OTL (Louisville: Westminster John Knox, 2001), 353–54.

32. The tradition is attested as early as the second century B.C. Note *Testament of Levi* 8:14–15: "From Judah a king will arise and shall found a new priesthood in ac-cord with the gentile model and for all nations. His presence is beloved, as a prophet of the Most High, a descendant of Abraham, our father" (H. C. Kee, trans., "Testa-ments of the Twelve Patriarchs," in *The Old Testament Pseudepigrapha*, vol. 1, *Apoca-lyptic Literature and Testaments*, ed. J. H. Charlesworth (Garden City, N.Y.: Doubleday, 1983), 791. John Calvin, in his *Institutes of the Christian Religion* (bk. 2, chap. 15), appears to have been the first major Christian theologian to interpret Christ's work in these terms. For a study of Calvin's interpretation, see John F. Jensen, *Calvin's Doctrine of the Work of Christ* (London: Clark, 1956). Jensen offers helpful background to Calvin's formulation, but he also observes that Calvin pays scant atten-tion to Christ's prophetic office. Not all would concur with Calvin's categorization of Jesus' offices. Some prefer to speak of the singular office of Christ (i.e., the Messiah), whose tasks are multidimensional: prophetic, priestly, kingly. G. C. Berkouwer (*The Work of Christ* [Grand Rapids: Eerdmans, 1965], 58–65), for example, speaks of both "threefold office" and of three aspects of one office. Millard J. Erickson (*Christian Theology*, 2d ed. [Grand Rapids: Baker, 1998], 780–87) prefers to speak of the Christ's revealing, ruling, and reconciling functions.

to recover the ancient Israelites' own perceptions, we are limited to the texts and traditions available to them.

The Messiah as Prophet

As already noted, many today would argue that the messiah held the office of eschatological prophet.[33] On the basis of key Qumran texts and scattered references in the intertestamental literature, scholars have argued that at the turn of the ages many Jews of Palestine anticipated the appearance of an anointed eschatological prophet whom heaven and earth would obey.[34] Evidence for this expectation may be drawn from the New Testament Gospels as well; Jesus seems to have gone out of his way to distance himself from such expectations. He did, indeed, include himself in the class of prophets when he explained his own rejection in Nazareth with a proverb, "A prophet is not without honor except in his home town and among his own relatives and in his own household,"[35] but this is hardly a claim to prophetic messiahship. In John's Gospel, at least two individuals surmise that Jesus must be a prophet,[36] and the Synoptic Gospels attest to a widespread perception of Jesus as "one of the prophets,"[37] or even "the prophet."[38] However, only in one instance in the Gospels does the reference to Jesus as a prophet have obvious messianic connotations. With respect to Jesus' triumphal entry into Jerusalem, Matthew notes uniquely that in response to the query concerning the identity of the one whom the crowds of Jerusalem were hailing as "the son of David . . . who comes in the name of the Lord," some answered dismissively, "This is the prophet Jesus, from Nazareth in Galilee" (Matt. 21:11). If there is an eschatological prophet in the Gospels, it is not Jesus but John the Baptist, who appears on the scene to herald the arrival of the messiah in fulfillment of Mal. 3:1 and 4:5.[39] In reality,

33. See, for example, Graeme Goldsworthy, *Preaching the Whole Bible as Christian Scripture* (Grand Rapids: Eerdmans, 2000), 230.

34. For a brief discussion, see Collins, *The Scepter and the Star*, 116–23; for greater detail, see Zimmermann, *Messianische Texte aus Qumran*, 312–417.

35. Mark 6:4; cf. Matt. 13:57; Luke 24:19 (the Emmaus disciples); John 4:44; cf. Jesus' oblique reference to himself as a prophet in Luke 13:33.

36. The Samaritan woman (4:19); the healed blind man (9:17).

37. Matt. 16:14; 21:46; Mark 6:15; Luke 7:16; 9:8. The Pharisees were skeptical of Jesus' prophetic status (Luke 7:39; John 7:52).

38. John 1:21 (in contradistinction to the messiah mentioned in v. 25); 6:14; 7:40 (in contradistinction to the messiah mentioned in v. 41).

39. John 1:19–28. In Luke 1:76, Zecharias refers to John the Baptist as "the prophet of the Most High" who will prepare the way before the Lord. Cf. Matt. 14:5; Mark 11:32; Luke 20:6.

Jesus perceived himself as one greater than a prophet, whose arrival would be announced by Yahweh's prophetic messenger.[40] Even so, the perception of Jesus as the eschatological prophet persists to this day.

But is this a valid perception? Apart from the rather flimsy evidence regarding prophecy as an office into which one could be inducted by anointing,[41] the Old Testament texts on which such hopes might have been based are few and far between. No prophet in the Old Testament is referred to as "the anointed one." The only text that links the verb *māšaḥ*, "to anoint," with a prophet is 1 Kings 19:16, where Elijah is commanded by Yahweh to anoint Elisha *lĕnābî'*, "to be a prophet," in his place, but here one finds no hint of any reference to an eschatological prophet.

More to our point is Isa. 61:1–3, in which an apparently messianic figure speaks in the first person of his anointing by the Spirit of God to proclaim good news to the afflicted. This text is intriguing, not only because it provides the only occurrence of the verb *māšaḥ*, "to anoint," in the prophets, but also because of the detail with which the mission of the anointed one is described. In translation the text reads as follows:

> The Spirit of Adonai Yahweh is upon me,
> because Yahweh has *anointed* me
> to bring good tidings to the afflicted;
> he has sent me
> to bind up the brokenhearted,
> to proclaim liberty to the captives,
>   and the opening of the prison to those who are bound;
> to proclaim the year of Yahweh's favor,
>   and the day of vengeance of our God;
> to comfort all who mourn;
> to provide for those who mourn in Zion
> to give them a garland instead of ashes,
>   the oil of gladness instead of mourning,
>   the mantle of praise instead of a faint spirit;
> that they may be called oaks of righteousness,
>   the planting of Yahweh that he may be glorified.

Although the passage does not use the noun *māšîaḥ*, it yields several interesting observations concerning the role and mission of the anointed one. First, as one anointed by Yahweh, this person is distinguished from Yahweh. Second, the person's self-consciousness of having been anointed by Yahweh recalls David's self-designation as "the anointed of the God of Jacob" (*mĕšîaḥ 'ĕlōhê ya'ăqōb* [2 Sam. 23:1]) and numerous

40. Matt. 11:9–10; Luke 7:26–27.
41. Van Groningen (*Messianic Revelation in the Old Testament*, 33) cites Ps. 105:15 (= 1 Chron. 16:22) and 1 Kings 19:16.

other references to Yahweh's anointed.[42] Third, the anointing is presented as the cause/occasion for the receipt of the Spirit of Yahweh.[43] This reminds the reader of 1 Sam. 16:13, according to which Samuel's anointing of David was followed immediately by the Spirit of Yahweh rushing upon him and remaining on him from that point on. Fourth, the anointing was purposeful (that he might bring good news to the afflicted) and associated with the official sending (*šālaḥ*) of the person as an agent of Yahweh.

On the surface, the verbal nature of his mission sounds prophetic, and this is how most critical scholars interpret the passage. They tend to identify the speaker here as a prophetic herald who announces a message of good news,[44] and in so doing associate this person with the servant figure of Isa. 40–55. I have no objection to the latter identification, but as John Oswalt has correctly noted, this person does not "simply hurl words at the poor." Rather, he inaugurates a reign of righteousness and justice, and he sets the captives free.[45] No prophet has this authority. And with the Spirit of Yahweh upon him, this anointed person is to be linked with the shoot/branch from the stem/roots of Jesse on whom the Spirit of Yahweh rests in Isa. 11:1–5.[46] Some interpret the linking of this passage with the servant and the messiah in Luke 4:17–21 as the early Christian church's "legitimate reader response" to Isa. 61.[47] But Jesus' appropriation of the role of the anointed one in this passage is based not merely on a new reading of the passage; it accords perfectly with a grammatical-historical interpretation of the text itself.

The only remaining texts involving prophets/prophecy that might be construed as messianic are found in Deuteronomy. In Deut. 18:15–22, Moses announces to the Israelites that Yahweh will raise up for Israel a prophet like himself from among their people. To him they must listen. At first glance, the use of the singular noun *nābî³* and the fact that the comparison is made with one man (Moses) seem to point to a future individual,[48] but within the broader context of chapters 17–18, which deal with the institutions of judgeship (17:8–13), kingship (17:14–20), and

42. 1 Sam. 2:10; 2:35; 16:6; 2 Sam. 19:22 [Eng. 21]; 22:21; 2 Chron. 6:42; Ps. 2:2, 18:50; 45:8 [Eng. 7]; 89:21 [Eng. 20].

43. Peter recognized the connection between anointing, Holy Spirit endowment, and empowerment when he said of Jesus of Nazareth, "how God anointed him with the Holy Spirit and with power, and how he went about doing good, and healing all who were oppressed by the devil; for God was with him" (Acts 10:38).

44. For the most recent summary of the debate, see Childs, *Isaiah*, 501–8.

45. John N. Oswalt, *The Book of Isaiah: Chapters 40–66*, NICOT (Grand Rapids: Eerdmans, 1998), 561–68.

46. So also Oswalt, *The Book of Isaiah*, 564.

47. Childs, *Isaiah*, 505.

48. Cf. Deut. 34:9–12.

priesthood (18:1–8), it is preferable to interpret this text primarily as a prediction of either the continued existence of the institution of prophecy or a succession of prophets, rather than as a prediction of an eschatological messianic prophet.[49] Peter seems to have interpreted the prophet like Moses in this collective sense in Acts 3:12–26, where he declares that Jesus the Messiah (v. 20), the servant raised up by God (v. 26), represents the fulfillment of the predictions of the prophets. By citing Deut. 18:15, he suggests that the prophetic lineage may be traced all the way back to Moses himself.

Throughout the New Testament we clearly see Jesus portrayed as a second Moses in a typological/analogical sense.[50] Within this context, New Testament scholars generally adduce Peter's citation as evidence for a messianic interpretation of Deut. 18:15, but this interpretation of Peter's citation is less certain than it appears. Despite scholars' virtually unanimous agreement that Jesus is presented here as "the prophet like Moses," the focus of attention in vv. 22–23 is on the prophetic institution, not the messiah. Ben Witherington is on the right track when he links vv. 20–21 and 26 to determine Luke's understanding of eschatology,[51] but he fails to see the significance of vv. 22–25 as a minor digression whose purpose is to clarify the last clause of v. 21, "about which God spoke by the mouth of his holy prophets from ancient times," an interpretation reinforced by v. 26. Peter highlights the seriousness of the prophetic message by (1) referring to prophets as "his [God's] holy prophets"; (2) tracing the origins of the institution back to Moses; (3) quoting Moses in calling on the people to give heed to the prophet who will come in everything he says; and (4) adding a warning from Lev. 23:29 that those who do not pay attention to the prophetic message will be destroyed. This sets the stage for v. 26, by which he declares that, beginning with Samuel,[52] all who followed in Moses' prophetic train pointed to this day. The focus in these verses seems not to be on a messianic prophet like Moses, but on the prophetic institution, at the heart of whose message will be the messiah. The prophets, in fact, are care-

49. So also Kaiser, *The Messiah in the Old Testament*, 58. Robert Polzin (*Moses and the Deuteronomist: A Literary Study of the Deuteronomistic History* [New York: Seabury, 1980], 61) suggests that "the prophet like Moses" may be the narrator of the Deuteronomic History. For a discussion of the ways in which this passage has been interpreted, see van Groningen, *Messianic Revelation in the Old Testament*, 251–53.

50. For a classic discussion of Moses in early Judaism, see J. Jeremias, "Μωυσῆς," *TDNT*, 4:848–64; for the New Testament treatment, see pp. 864–73.

51. Ben Witherington III, *The Acts of the Apostles: A Socio-Rhetorical Commentary* (Grand Rapids: Eerdmans, 1991), 184–88.

52. The first explicit announcement of the messiah actually came from the lips of Samuel's mother (1 Sam. 2:10), but messianic history begins formally with Samuel's anointing of David in 1 Sam. 16:1–13.

fully distinguished in this context from the messiah, who is referred to by a remarkable range of designations: his (God's) servant Jesus (v. 13), the Holy One (v. 14), the Righteous One (v. 14), the Prince of life (v. 15), his (God's) Messiah/Christ (v. 18), Jesus the appointed Messiah/Christ (v. 20), his (God's) servant (v. 26), and the promised seed of Abraham sent by God to bring blessing to the world (vv. 25b–26). Peter seems to suggest that the prophetic institution was raised up especially to proclaim the coming of the messiah. Remarkably, with this speech he appears to place himself in that train of prophets, and his hearers are admonished to listen to him, even as they should have listened to the prophets of old.

We should be equally cautious about finding a reference to a prophetic messiah in Stephen's citation of Deut. 18:15 in Acts 7:37. As is the case with Acts 3:22, New Testament scholars generally see in "a prophet like me" a reference to Christ.[53] But this interpretation deflects from the overall thrust of the speech, whose purpose is to trace the history of Israel's spiritual obstinacy. A major portion of Stephen's speech in Acts 7 is devoted to Moses, specifically reviewing his call to the ministry of deliverance (vv. 20–34), followed by a summary statement of the people's rejection of him despite his lofty standing with God and his status in the community (vv. 35–38), and ending with a prolonged indictment (vv. 39–43). The citation of Deut. 18:15 occurs within vv. 35–38, where the emphasis clearly is on Moses, the one sent by God to rule and deliver Israel (v. 35), the one who performed signs and wonders before them for forty years (v. 36), the paradigmatic prophet (v. 37), and the one who received the oracles from God and passed them on to the people.[54] We detract from Stephen's focus if we isolate the quotation in v. 37 and impose on it a messianic significance. Stephen's attention is not on "a prophet like me," let alone the messiah,[55] but on "me," that is, Moses, who predicts that he is not the last prophet whom God will raise up. If this passage establishes any link between Moses and Jesus, it is only analogical, inasmuch as the present rejection of Jesus fits Israel's long-standing pattern of rebellion against God, as supremely illustrated by their response to Moses, God's agent of deliverance and revelation.

53. See, for example, Witherington, *Acts of the Apostles*, 271; John B. Polhill, *Acts*, NAC 26 (Nashville: Broadman, 1992), 199–200.

54. Note the fivefold repetition of the demonstrative pronoun: τοῦτον τὸν Μωϋσῆν, "this Moses" (v. 35a); followed by τοῦτον, "this one (whom)" (v. 35b); οὗτος, "this one" (v. 36); οὗτός ἐστιν ὁ Μωϋσῆς ὁ, "this is the Moses who" (v. 37); and οὗτός ἐστιν ὁ, "this is the one who" (v. 38).

55. Ernst Haenchen (*The Acts of the Apostles: A Commentary* [Philadelphia: Westminster, 1971], 282) is correct in observing that "the speaker does not come to the theme of Jesus until verse 52."

Even if Peter and/or Stephen viewed Jesus as a messianic prophet "like Moses," are we thereby authorized to read their use of Deut. 18:15 back into the original context? Despite the rise of Mosaic messianism in the intertestamental period, two facts remain. First, the literary context of Deut. 18:15 provides no hint whatsoever that Moses' original hearers should have understood his prediction of a prophet like himself either eschatologically or messianically. Second, nowhere else in the Old Testament was this passage or the prophetic institution itself interpreted messianically. And Deut. 34:10–12 is no exception:

> Since then, no prophet has risen in Israel like Moses, whom Yahweh knew face to face, for all the signs and wonders that Yahweh sent him to perform in the land of Egypt against Pharaoh, all his servants, and all his land, and for all the mighty power and for all the great terror that Moses performed in the sight of all Israel.

Some scholars appeal to this epitaphic comment on Moses as evidence for a fundamental messianic hope pervading the entire Pentateuch and the anticipation of a messianic prophet still to come who will supersede Moses.[56] However, this interpretation depends upon a predisposition to look for messianic notions everywhere and is without foundation in the text itself. It is preferable to read the statement simply as an observation that at the time of the final composition of the Book of Deuteronomy, and probably the Pentateuch as a whole, no prophet had arisen in Israel who could match the power and influence of Moses. Strictly speaking, the narrator's intention is to offer retrospective honor to Moses, who, with respect to his intimacy with Yahweh and to the awe-inspiring signs and wonders that he performed, was without peer in Israel's history. The vision is not prospective but retrospective. It does not anticipate someone who eventually would appear on the scene and supersede Moses in greatness and power as much as it recognizes the unique status of Moses in the history of the prophetic institution to the time of the writing of this "death narrative."[57]

Of course, a collective interpretation of Deut. 18:15 does not rule out an individual fulfillment.[58] Nor does this prevent later readers from link-

---

56. Sailhamer ("The Messiah and the Hebrew Bible," 13) expresses a relatively common view when he declares, "In the Pentateuch, for example, the Messiah is a prophetic priest-king like Moses."

57. This form-critical designation we may apply to Deut. 32:48–34:12; cf. Gen. 48:1–49:33 (Jacob); Josh. 23:1–24:31 (Joshua); 1 Kings 1:1–2:11 (David).

58. One may argue that the author of 1 Samuel perceived Samuel as a second Moses, and this may be argued for other prophets as well. On Ezekiel as a second Moses, see Daniel I. Block, *The Book of Ezekiel: Chapters 25–48*, NICOT (Grand Rapids: Eerdmans, 1998), 498–501, 604–7, and passim.

ing this prophetic figure with the "messenger" whom Yahweh would send to clear the way before him when he returns to the temple (Mal. 3:1), or with Elijah the prophet, who will come before the great and terrible day of Yahweh breaks in (Mal. 3:23 [Eng. 4:5]). But this runs counter to the ending of Malachi, which sees Moses as a figure from the past (*"Remember* the Torah of Moses"), in contrast to Elijah, who represents the future. Nevertheless, while later usage of a text may reinforce our understanding of a passage in its original context, it is not determinative for its original meaning. In any case, in the Malachi passages, the messenger/prophet announces the coming of the messiah. He himself is not the messiah, though this did not stop the people in Jesus' day from blurring the distinctions and anticipating the arrival of an individual eschatological prophet (John 1:21–22; 6:14; 7:40–41).

This does not mean that the messiah could not exercise prophetic functions. Jesus was indeed an eschatological figure who frequently engaged in prophetic activities, but this does not make a messianic figure out of Moses or any other Old Testament prophet. If Jesus was a prophetic figure, this role derived not from any link with Moses or the rest of the professional prophets, but from his connection with David, who, as "the anointed of the God of Jacob" (2 Sam. 23:1), claimed prophetic inspiration (vv. 2–3a). Accordingly, Peter was well within the bounds of grammatical-historical exegesis when he linked David's prophetic activity with knowing "that God had sworn to him an oath to seat one of his descendants on his throne" (Acts 2:30), for this is precisely the subject of David's "oracle" in 2 Sam. 23:3b–7. But this does not mean that technically David held the office of prophet. No, the one who was anointed by the Spirit of God as king (not as prophet) also prophesied by that same Spirit.

According to John 1:1, as the "Word" of God, Jesus is indeed the supreme declaration of the mind of God, and according to Heb. 1:1–2, the climactic and eschatological agent of divine revelation. Significantly, the author of the latter, fascinating text does not write, "God, after he spoke long ago to the fathers by prophets in many portions and in many ways, has in these last days spoken to us by *the [supreme] Prophet.*" No, he has spoken to us by *a Son*" (NRSV for ἐν υἱῷ). A generic gulf exists between the prophetic institution and the messiah. And with this observation we return to the central point of this paper. With hindsight we do indeed see analogical connections between the ministry of Jesus and the work of the prophets. However, there is no evidence within the Old Testament itself that anyone in ancient Israel understood the office of prophet typologically, that is, as foreshadowing "a future figure who will play an authoritative role in the end time."

The Messiah as Priest

A second office that the messiah is often thought to fill is the office of priest. The tradition of a priestly messiah has a long history, being widespread in various branches of Judaism in the last century before the birth of Christ.[59] The search for the origins of this interpretation leads naturally to the use of the expression *hakkōhēn hammāšîaḥ*, "the anointed priest," for the Aaronic priesthood in Lev. 4:3, 5, 16; 6:15. But this raises the question of whether or not ancient Israelites ever viewed the high priest as a messianic figure, that is, as an eschatological high priest who would come and serve as priest among God's people. In responding to this question, I offer two observations, both of which may be controversial.

First, from a general perspective, there is no hint in the priestly legislation of the Torah that the ancient Israelites ever saw in the tabernacle service as a whole a foreshadowing of the cross. And if there is no obvious foreshadowing of the cross in the sacrifices in general, then we should not expect any messianic anticipation in the person or ministry of the high priest. However, with this observation I do not deny that the tabernacle and the sacrificial system pointed to a reality beyond the present and the mundane. On the contrary, according to Exod. 25:8–9, 40, on Mount Sinai Yahweh prescribed forms of worship that represented a replica (*tabnît*) of the heavenly realities that he revealed to Moses. The author of Hebrews recognized this clearly when he characterized the earthly replica/model/copy as a *hypodeigma* (Heb. 8:5; 9:23);[60] the heavenly as the type (*typos* [Heb. 8:5; cf. Exod. 25:40; Acts 7:44]), as opposed to the earthly antitype (*antitypos* [Heb. 9:24]); the heavenly as the true (*alēthinos* [Heb. 8:2; 9:24]), as opposed to the shadow (*skia* [Heb. 8:5; 10:1]); the heavenly as the heavenly (*epouranios* [Heb. 8:5; 9:23]), as opposed to the earthly (*kosmikos* [Heb. 9:1]), creatorial (*ktisis* [Heb. 9:11]), and handmade (*cheiropoiētos* [Heb. 9:11, 24]). But nowhere does the Pentateuch or any succeeding Old Testament text suggest that when the faithful in Israel worshiped at the tabernacle or later in the temple, they looked to the Aaronic high priest as a foreshadowing of a future messianic high priest. It would be more accurate to say that when the faithful brought their sacrifices, their gaze was fixed upward to the heavenly realities that Moses saw rather than forward to a distant earthly fulfillment.

59. For discussion of priestly messianism in ancient Judaism, see Collins, *The Scepter and the Star*, 74–101; Zimmermann, *Messianische Texte aus Qumran*, 23–45.

60. LXX Exod. 25:8–9 reads *paradeigma*.

Second, far from identifying the Aaronic priesthood with the messiah, the Old Testament in general distinguishes the priesthood from the messiah. Speaking on behalf of Yahweh in 1 Sam. 2:35, an unnamed prophet predicts the end of the Elide priesthood and its replacement with "a faithful priest" (kōhēn ne'ĕmān) who is promised "an enduring house" (bayit ne'ĕmān),[61] but who will "walk before my anointed always" (kol hayyāmîm). As noted earlier, the expression měšîḥî does not yet have the status of technical title, but if David is the person in Yahweh's mind, then the Zadokite household seems to be the anticipated "faithful priest."[62] The fact that the priest "walks before" (hithallēk lipnê) Yahweh's anointed highlights the superior status of the latter, though it contrasts with other texts in which the king clearly is accountable to the priestly officials, especially in relationship to the Torah (e.g., Deut. 17:18). Although the Deuteronomic History and the Chronicler recount cultic actions performed by Davidic kings,[63] the narratives never confuse or conflate priestly and royal offices. The Davidic monarchs did indeed serve as royal patrons of the cult, but the assumption of high priestly roles was considered an illegitimate usurpation.[64] Nor do matters change in the minds of prophets who look forward to the restored Davidic house after the judgment of exile. In Ezekiel's great temple vision of chapters 40–49, the activities envisioned for the nāśî are primarily cultic, but he does not act as an officiating officer. As a royal figure, he is the sponsor and patron of cultic activity.[65]

61. Compare Yahweh's promise of "eternal priesthood" (kĕhunnat 'ōlām) to Phinehas in Num. 25:12–13.

62. This is the prevailing scholarly opinion. See, for example, Robert Gordon, 1 and 2 Samuel, LBI (Grand Rapids: Zondervan, 1986), 88; Ralph W. Klein, 1 Samuel, WBC 10 (Waco: Word, 1983), 27–28; Robert D. Bergen, 1 and 2 Samuel, NAC 7 (Nashville: Broadman, 1996), 84; Joyce G. Baldwin, 1 and 2 Samuel: An Introduction and Commentary, TOTC (Downers Grove, Ill.: InterVarsity, 1988), 62. Kaiser's contention (The Messiah in the Old Testament, 75–76) that "his house" is the subject of "will walk," and that "the faithful priest" is to be identified with "his messiah," is forced.

63. David twice used the ephod for oracular purposes, but the action was supervised by Abiathar the priest (1 Sam. 23:6–14; 30:7–8); he wore the ephod as he danced before Yahweh while the ark was brought to Jerusalem (2 Sam. 6:12–15); at the prophet Gad's encouragement, David built an altar and presented sacrifices to Yahweh on the threshing floor of Araunah (2 Sam. 24:18–25; 1 Chron. 21:18–27); when Solomon assumed the throne of David, he offered a thousand burnt offerings at Gibeon (1 Kings 3:4).

64. Second Chronicles 26:16–23 recounts how King Uzziah usurped high priestly prerogatives, but for this he was stricken with a severe skin disease from which he suffered until his death.

65. For discussion of the role of the nāśî in Ezekiel 40–49, see Daniel I. Block, "Bringing Back David: Ezekiel's Messianic Hope," in The Lord's Anointed, ed. Satterthwaite, Hess, and Wenham, 183–88.

This distinction between the house of David and the lineage of Aaron/ Zadok is maintained also in postexilic prophecy. Haggai will name Zerubbabel the Davidide governor and Joshua the Zadokite high priest in the same breath (Hag. 1:1, 12, 14; 2:2, 4), but efforts to interpret this as a fusion of Davidic and Aaronic power or a reflection of a diarchic form of government in the Persian province of Judah and of increasing political power of the priesthood are based more on preconceived Wellhausenian notions of the history of the priesthood than on the evidence itself.[66] In Haggai, what is more impressive than apparently increasing civil authority of the priesthood is the involvement of Zerubbabel in all the prophecies. It is natural for prophecies concerning the reestablishment of temple worship in Jerusalem to involve the priesthood, but Haggai's inclusion of Zerubbabel in these prophecies is striking. Although Zerubbabel was a Davidide, he was not the king. But evidently, even as governor, Zerubbabel functioned as the patron/sponsor of the cult, just as his ancestors David and Josiah had. Haggai's final prophecy, in fact, assures Zerubbabel that he, not Joshua, is Yahweh's signet ring, and that he, not Joshua, is Yahweh's chosen ruler.

The picture does not change in Zechariah. Zechariah recognizes Joshua as the high priestly authority, and in the visionary account of 3:1–5, he recounts the process by which he was made ceremonially fit to function as high priest, and then reports an oracular promise (vv. 6– 10) that he will serve in the temple. But the temple and the reestablishment of the cult require a temple builder. Although this function is not mentioned here, it seems that this is the reason that the messenger of Yahweh introduces his servant, "the Branch." Both expressions, "servant" and "branch," are royal Davidic epithets. And since the building of temples was a royal responsibility in Israel, and in the ancient Near East in general, some have rightly seen in vv. 6–10 a reflection of a royal temple-foundation or temple-completion ritual.[67] In either case, the prophecy distinguishes the office of the Zadokite priesthood from the role of Davidic temple builder.

66. See further, Deborah W. Rooke, *Zadok's Heirs: The Role and Development of the High Priesthood in Ancient Israel*, OTM (Oxford: Oxford University Press, 2000), 127–34.

67. For the former, see Rooke, *Zadok's Heirs*, 142, following Baruch Halpern, "The Ritual Background of Zechariah's Temple Song," *CBQ* 40 (1978): 171–73. The stress on Zerubbabel as the royal figure in the ceremony is recognized also by D. Petersen, "Zerubbabel and Temple Reconstruction," *CBQ* 36 (1974): 366–72. For the latter, see Joyce G. Baldwin, *Haggai, Zechariah, Malachi*, TOTC (Downers Grove, Ill.: InterVarsity, 1972), 121–22, followed by P. L. Redditt, *Haggai, Zechariah, Malachi*, NCBC (Grand Rapids: Eerdmans, 1995), 69–70.

This distinction is not compromised in the coronation ritual described in 6:9–15. To be sure, Joshua the high priest is crowned with the ‘áṭārâ, but even as Zechariah the prophet crowns him, he declares,

> Thus says Yahweh Ṣebaoth, "Behold a man whose name is Branch. From where he is he shall branch out and build the Temple of Yahweh. Yes, he is the one who shall build the Temple of Yahweh. He shall bear royal majesty, and he shall sit and rule on his throne. And he will be a priest on his throne, and harmonious counsel will exist between them."

Most prefer to translate wěhāyâ kōhēn ‘al kis’ô as "There shall be a priest beside his throne," which highlights the subordination of the priesthood to the Davidic house.[68] However, on syntactical grounds,[69] it is preferable to translate this clause as "And he will be a priest on his throne" (NIV, NASB), which strengthens the distinction between Zadokite priesthood and Davidic messiah. Joshua the Zadokite, who is addressed, is thereby distinguished from the Branch, the subject of the declaration. And he (Joshua) is told that someone else will function as priest while sitting on a throne. By this interpretation, the reference is not to a priestly official who gains royal power, but to a royal figure who exercises priestly power. But this raises a question: If the Old Testament is consistent in its distinction between Aaronic/Zadokite priesthood and Davidic royalty, where does this priestly dimension of the latter's role originate? The answer to this question awaits the following discussion.[70]

The Messiah as a Royal Davidic Figure

If the Old Testament knows nothing of the messiah as the eschatological prophet or the eschatological Aaronic high priest, then who is he? Only one answer remains: he is no more and no less than a royal Davidic figure.

68. The LXX makes the relationship more explicit by reading "at his right hand" in place of "on his throne." For a mistaken appeal to this verse to support notions of a joint civil authority shared between the priesthood and the Davidic governor in the postexilic community, see Carol L. Meyers and Eric M. Meyers, Haggai, Zechariah 1–8: A New Translation with Introduction and Commentary, AB 25B (Garden City, N.Y.: Doubleday, 1987), 362–63.

69. The initial waw consecutive precludes a change in subject from the previous clause.

70. In this discussion, I have not overlooked the reference in 4:14 to šěnê běnê hayyiṣhār, usually translated "two anointed ones" and generally thought to refer to Joshua and Zerubbabel. But this text is irrelevant to the present discussion, as demonstrated in two independent studies. See Rooke, Zadok's Heirs, 136–37, and the more detailed analysis by Rose, Zemah and Zerubbabel, 188–207.

The roots of royal messianism in Israel are found in four pentateuchal texts:[71] (1) Yahweh's promise that "kings would come from Abraham" (Gen. 17:6, 16; 35:11); (2) Jacob's prediction that the scepter would not depart from Judah (Gen. 49:10); (3) Balaam's oracular word that a star and scepter would rise from Jacob/Israel (Num. 24:17); and (4) Moses' charge that in response to a desire for a king, the Israelites should put on their throne one whom Yahweh would choose (Deut. 17:14–20). But for the historical foundations of royal messianism, we must turn to the narratives concerning Israel's transition from a tribally based administration to the monarchy in 1 Samuel. The prayer of Hannah (1 Sam. 2:1–10), uttered at the tabernacle in the presence of Eli the high priest on the occasion of her dedication of Samuel, concludes on a remarkably prophetic note:

> Yahweh! His adversaries shall be shattered.
> The Most High! He will thunder in the heavens.
> Yahweh will judge the ends of the earth;
>   he will give strength to his king,
> and exalt the horn of his anointed.

For Hannah, as for modern readers, the final statement is a riddle: Who is this king? And who is Yahweh's anointed?[72] We do not learn the final answer until 2 Sam. 5:1–3, which recounts how representatives from all the tribes of Israel came to Hebron and anointed David "as king" (*lĕmelek*) over Israel. As the basis for their action they cited an earlier oracular pronouncement: "Yahweh said to you, 'You are the one who shall shepherd my people Israel, and you are the one who shall serve as leader over them.'"[73] By their act of anointing David they acknowledge him as Yahweh's chosen king.

71. It also could be argued that the ultimate roots of royal messianism are found in Gen. 1–2, in which Adam is portrayed as a royal viceroy placed in the garden of God to tend it for him. The use of the verbs *ʿābad* and *šāmar* (later associated with priestly service in the tabernacle/temple) in 2:15 hints at the sacral dimension of Adam's royal role. On Adam as a royal gardener, see Manfred Hutter, "Adam als Gärtner und König (Gen. 2.8, 15)," *BZ* 30 (1986): 258–62. See also Richard S. Hess, "Splitting the Adam: The Usage of *ʾĀdām* in Genesis I–V," in *Studies in the Pentateuch*, ed. J. A. Emerton, VTSup 41 (Leiden: Brill, 1990), 1–16.

72. Hannah's note is reinforced in 1 Sam. 2:35 by the unnamed prophet of Eli's doom, who announces that Eli's replacement, a faithful priest, will walk before Yahweh's anointed "all the days."

73. Note the emphatic and parallelistic nature of the citation:

> *ʾattâ tirʿeh ʾet ʿammî yiśrāʾēl*
> *wĕʾattâ tihyeh lĕnāgîd ʿal yiśrāʾēl*

On the status of the *nāgîd* in the Hebrew Bible, see Mettinger, *King and Messiah*, 151–84.

But the line from Hannah's oracle to this citation is anything but straight. Indeed, the primary issue driving the intervening narrative is the identity of "Yahweh's anointed." During this period, the Israelites had to deal with two claimants to the title, first Saul and then David. Although Saul never identifies himself as the anointed one, the other three principal characters in the story—Yahweh, Samuel, and David— spoke freely of the ritual of Saul's induction into kingship as an anointing,[74] and repeatedly and openly acknowledged Saul as "Yahweh's anointed."[75] In so doing they obviously expressed a higher opinion of Saul's kingship than was held by the narrator of these accounts. In his mind there was only one true messiah. The narrator never speaks of the ritual of Saul's induction as an anointing, and he never applies the title "anointed one" to him.[76] On the contrary, he deliberately composes the respective accounts of the anointing of Saul and David so as to raise questions about the legitimacy of Saul's ascent to kingship and to highlight David's emergence as Israel's legitimate king. In the original historical context, the Israelites probably looked upon David as Saul's replacement, and modern commentators tend to do the same.[77] But the narrator apparently never viewed David as a replacement for Saul. For the narrator, the kingship of Saul was an illegitimate experiment from the beginning, improperly motivated and ill-conceived. In fact, the entire narrative of Saul's rise and reign is composed in ironical and farcical terms to serve as a foil against which to present David as Yahweh's anointed.[78] This is particularly evident in the contrasts be-

74. The verb *māšaḥ* occurs three times. Yahweh tells Samuel to "anoint" Saul as *nāgîd* over Israel (9:16); Samuel refers to Saul as one anointed by Yahweh as *nāgîd* over Israel (10:1); Samuel recognizes that he was sent by Yahweh to anoint Saul as king over Israel (15:1).

75. By Samuel: 1 Sam. 12:3, 5; by David: 24:7a, 7b, 11 [Eng. 6a, 6b, 10]; 26:9, 11, 16, 23; 2 Sam. 1:14, 16.

76. This observation renders unlikely the LXX's replacement of the MT's *wayyamlikû šām ʾet-šāʾûl lipnê yhwh* with *wayyimšaḥ šĕmûʾēl šām ʾet-šāʾûl lĕmelek* (καὶ ἔχρισεν Σαμουηλ ἐκεῖ τὸν Σαουλ εἰς βασιλέα) in 1 Sam. 11:15.

77. Walter Brueggemann (*First and Second Samuel*, Interpretation [Louisville: John Knox, 1990], 119) speaks of "David's eventual displacement of Saul"; Robert Gordon (*1 and 2 Samuel*, 149) notes the shift in focus in chapter 16 to "the man who . . . will replace him [Saul] on the throne."

78. This case is made convincingly by my student Kenneth Turner in a seminar paper, "Not Saul but David" (December 2000). In addition to the arguments made by Turner, we must ask whether Saul's kingship can really be taken seriously when, in response to the people's request for a king "like the nations," Yahweh gives them a Benjamite despite the ancient tradition of the scepter being reserved for Judah (Gen. 49:9–10). What renders this response doubly ironical is the fact that in the final chapters of the Book of Judges, the Benjamites had demonstrated that they not only were "like the nations" in general, but were like Sodom, the worst of the nations in particular. See the commentary on Judges 19–21 in Daniel I. Block, *Judges, Ruth*, NAC 6 (Nashville: Broadman & Holman, 1999), 515–86.

tween the descriptions of the caricatured anointing of Saul and the formal anointing of David.[79] For the narrator, only David was the man after Yahweh's heart, that is, Yahweh's ideal choice (1 Sam. 13:14). He was the first of the series of kings who would come from Abraham, the lion of Judah predicted by Jacob, the star and scepter foreseen by Balaam, the king whom Moses said Yahweh would choose, and the anointed one of whom Hannah spoke. Not only were David's enemies left with no option but to acknowledge him as Yahweh's anointed;[80] in his last oracular pronouncement, David also claimed the title "the anointed of the God of Jacob" (2 Sam. 23:1). Hereafter, Old Testament historians would mention other historical royal figures who were anointed,[81] but none of these was ever recognized as "the messiah" in a technical sense.

The conclusion that David was the anointed historical figure par excellence and that the eschatological messiah is to be found in his descendants is reinforced throughout the rest of the Old Testament. In the historical narratives we read of Nathan's oracle promising David and his descendants eternal title to the throne of Israel and of David's response recognizing the eternal (*lĕ'ôlām*) and universal (*zō't tôrat hā'ā-*

79. First, the story of Saul's anointing begins with a genealogy, giving the appearance of nobility, but the twofold reference to Benjamin signals a problem (1 Sam. 9:1); David arises out of obscurity from the family of Jesse, identified simply as a Bethlehemite (16:1). Second, the narrator characterizes Saul as one with obvious leadership potential (9:2), but as the youngest of eight sons, David is dismissed even by his own father (16:6–11). Third, the anointing of Saul interrupts his search for donkeys; David's anointing interrupts his tending sheep. Fourth, the anointing of Saul occurs in Ramah and climaxes his search for Samuel the seer (9:6–10:1); the anointing of David occurs in Bethlehem and climaxes the seer's search for him (16:1–13). Fifth, whereas for rhetorical effect the narrator has Samuel speak of Saul as one anointed to be king (*lĕmelek*) over Israel (15:1, 17), when he cites the divine command to anoint Saul, the goal of the anointing is merely *lĕnāgîd* rather than *lĕmelek* (9:16; cf. 10:1). Sixth, the narrator refers to the vessel used to anoint Saul generically as *pak*, "juglet" (10:1), but he explicitly identifies the instrument used to anoint David as *qeren haššemen*, "the horn of oil" (16:13). Seventh, the narrator describes Samuel's action with respect to Saul with the generic verb *yāṣaq*, "to pour" (10:1), but when he describes the anointing of David, he uses the technical expression *māšaḥ*, "to anoint" (16:12–13). Eighth, the narrator notes that whereas the Spirit of Yahweh came upon Saul temporarily after he had been anointed, merely inspiring prophetic activity (10:6–13) as one of three signs of his divine election, the Spirit of Yahweh came upon David at the time of his anointing and remained upon him permanently (16:13).

80. Any doubts concerning David as the divinely chosen anointed one evaporated with the death of Saul. Second Samuel 19:23 [Eng. 22] has Abishai proposing that Shimei be executed because he had cursed "Yahweh's anointed."

81. Absalom (2 Sam. 19:11 [Eng. 10]), Solomon (1 Kings 1:34, 39, 45; 5:15 [Eng. 1]; 1 Chron. 29:22), Jehu (1 Kings 19:16; 2 Kings 9:3, 6, 12; 2 Chron. 22:7), Jehoash (2 Kings 11:12; 2 Chron. 23:11), and Jehoahaz (2 Kings 23:30).

dām) implications of the oracle.[82] While critical scholarship consistently has stumbled over this text, especially 2 Sam. 7:19, I contend that David's response holds the key to both the eternalization and the universalization of the messianic hope in Psalms and the Prophets.

In Psalms, the messiah is never associated with anyone other than David, who, along with his descendants, is referred to as God's son (2:6–8),[83] Yahweh's firstborn (89:27–28 [Eng. 26–27]),[84] Yahweh's

82. 2 Sam. 7; 1 Chron. 17. I translate *zōʾt tôrat hāʾādām* in 2 Sam. 7:19 as "This is the revelation/instruction concerning humankind," a slight modification of Walter C. Kaiser's more technical "This is the charter for humanity." See Kaiser, *The Messiah in the Old Testament*, 78–83, and more fully, "The Blessing of David: The Charter for Humanity," in *The Law and the Prophets: Old Testament Studies Prepared in Honor of Oswald Thomas Allis*, ed. J. Skilton (Philadelphia: Presbyterian and Reformed, 1974), 310–18.

83. Psalm 2:6–8 and 89:27–28 [Eng. 26–27] are both based on 2 Sam. 7:14–15 (= 1 Chron. 17:13–14; cf. 22:10). For recent discussion of the importance of these texts in Paul's messianism, especially as expressed in Rom. 1:3–4, see Christopher G. Whitsett, "Son of God, Seed of David: Paul's Messianic Exegesis in Romans 2:3–4 [*sic*, read 1:3–4]," *JBL* 119 (2000): 661–81. אֲנִי אֶהְיֶה־לּוֹ לְאָב וְהוּא יִהְיֶה־לִּי לְבֵן, "I will become his father and he will become my son," in 2 Sam. 7:14 has long been acknowledged as an adaptation of an adoption formula. See S. Paul, "Adoption Formulae: A Study in Cuneiform and Biblical Legal Clauses," *Maarav* 2 (1978–80): 173–85, esp. 178. Although the formula is rooted in family law, in the second millennium B.C. it was used metaphorically to describe the relationship between a Hittite suzerain and a vassal king. To cite but one example, note how Shattiwaza of Mittanni described his relations with his overlord, Suppiluliuma I of Hatti:

> [The Great King] took me by the hand and rejoiced over me. . . . The Great King and Hero spoke as follows: "If I conquer Shuttarna and [the troops of] the land of Mittanni, I will not reject you but will adopt you as my son. I will stand by you and place you on the throne of your father.

The translation is by Gary Beckman, *Hittite Diplomatic Texts*, SBLWAW 7 (Atlanta: Scholars Press, 1996), 45 (no. 6B §3). For discussion, see Moshe Weinfeld, "The Covenant of Grant in the Old Testament and in the Ancient Near East," *JAOS* 90 (1970): 189–95; idem, *Deuteronomy and the Deuteronomic School* (Oxford: Clarendon, 1971), 77–81. Gary N. Knoppers ("Ancient Near Eastern Royal Grants and the Davidic Covenant Parallel?" *JAOS* 116 [1996]: 682) calls for a distinction between the adoption imagery employed in 2 Sam. 7 and the imagery of status and security found in Ps. 89.

84. Similar notions are attested in Egyptian sources. Especially striking is the resemblance of Ps. 89:27–28 [Eng. 26–27] to the words of a hymn addressed by a king to Re the sun god and composed for the conclusion of a ritual for the defeat of the dragon Apophis, his cosmic adversary:

> O my Father, Lord of the gods,
>   Great One (most ancient) of the great nineness!
> First primeval god of gods, who created humankind,
>   every thing that came to be became after he came to be.
> I am your son, your truly beloved,
>   the one with a divine heart, who went forth from your secret [place].

This is my English translation from the German of the hymn published by Jan Assmann, *Ägyptische Hymnen und Gebete* (Zürich and Munich: Artemis, 1975), 118. Psalm

anointed,[85] Yahweh's king (2:6; 18:51 [Eng. 50]), Yahweh's chosen one (89:20 [Eng. 21]), and Yahweh's servant.[86] He is the only one whom Yahweh is said to have anointed[87] and installed in Zion (2:2), and with whom he made an eternal covenant.[88]

The exclusively Davidic character of the messiah applies to the prophetic portrayal as well. In Isaiah, he is "Wonderful Counselor-Mighty El-Father of Eternity-Prince of Peace"[89] who sits on the throne of David (9:5-6 [Eng. 6-7]), and the "shoot" who springs from the stem of Jesse (11:1); in Jeremiah, the "righteous branch" raised up for David and named "Yahweh Our Righteousness" (23:5-6); in Ezekiel, the "sprig" from the descendants of David (17:22), and the shepherd and king set over Israel, Yahweh's servant David (34:23-24; 37:22-25); in Daniel, "the anointed one" (9:25-26);[90] in Hosea, David, Israel's king (3:5); in Micah, the ruler from Bethlehem who will rise and shepherd Yahweh's

---

89:7 speaks of the elevation of David to the status of *bĕkôr*, that is, the highest rank among the kings of earth. On *bĕkôr* as a title of sociological primacy, that is *primus inter fratres*, "first among brothers," rather than a title of chronological priority, see Daniel I. Block, "Marriage and Family in Ancient Israel: A Survey of Laws and Customs," in *Marriage and Family in the Ancient World* (Downers Grove, Ill.: InterVarsity, forthcoming).

85. Ps. 2:2; 18:51 [Eng. 50]; 45:8 [Eng. 9]; 89:21, 52 [Eng. 20, 51]; 132:17.

86. Ps. 89:21 [Eng. 20]; 132:10.

87. Ps. 45:7 [Eng. 8]; 89:20c-21 [Eng. 19c-20].

88. Ps. 18:51 [Eng. 50]; 132:10, 17.

89. Isa. 9:5 [Eng. 6]. The singular "His name [not 'names'] shall be called" suggests one long and complex theophoric name. John H. Walton (*The IVP Bible Background Commentary: Old Testament*, with Victor H. Matthews and Mark W. Chavalas [Downers Grove, Ill.: InterVarsity, 2000], 597) compares the name to the lengthy name given by Tiglath-Pileser III to the gates of Calah: "Gates of Justice, Which Give the Correct Judgment for the Ruler of the Four Quarters, Which Offer the Yield of the Mountains and the Seas, Which Admit the Produce of Mankind before the King Their Master."

90. Most modern scholars identify an "anointed ruler/anointed one" in Dan. 9:25-26 as Onias III, the high priest whose murder in 171 B.C. is reported in 2 Macc. 4:33-38. See John J. Collins, *Daniel*, Hermeneia (Minneapolis: Fortress, 1993), 355; John E. Goldingay, *Daniel*, WBC 30 (Dallas: Word, 1989), 262; Rex Mason, "The Messiah in the Postexilic Old Testament Literature," in *King and Messiah*, ed. Day, 358. However, this interpretation is doubtful because (1) it depends upon the unlikely dating of the composition of the book in the second century B.C.; (2) the association of the person's arrival with the rebuilding of Jerusalem and of the term itself with *nāgîd* in v. 26 points most naturally to a Davidic figure (see Joseph A. Fitzmyer, *The Dead Sea Scrolls and Christian Origins* [Grand Rapids: Eerdmans, 2000], 80); (3) the conjoining of *nāgîd* and *māšîaḥ* occurs elsewhere only with reference to an anointed king (1 Sam. 9:16; 10:1; 1 Chron. 29:22); and (4) as noted above, the Old Testament consistently distinguishes the Aaronic/Zadokite priesthood from Davidic royalty. John Oswalt ("משׁח," 1126) correctly notes that this is the only unambiguous reference to the eschatological messiah in the entire Old Testament. For additional defenses of the traditional interpretation, see Kaiser, *The Messiah in the Old Testament*, 204; J. Doukhan, "The Seventy Weeks of Daniel 9," *AUSS* 17 (1979): 1-22.

flock and be great to the ends of the earth (5:2–5); in Zechariah, "the branch" (3:8; 6:12), the king from Zion whose dominion will be to the ends of the earth (9:9–10), and Yahweh's shepherd, rejected by the sheep (12:10) and struck by Yahweh (13:7–8).

But there is one aspect of the messiah's role that calls for special comment: that of priest. Having asserted earlier that the Old Testament consistently distinguishes the Aaronic/Zadokite priesthood from the Davidic messiah, I did not thereby deny a priestly dimension to the messiah's role. On the contrary, this is what we should expect, given the fundamentally sacral nature of kingship in Israel and the surrounding world, and given the perspective of Israel's own prophets. With reference to the messiah's sacral status, Jer. 30:21 is especially instructive:

> Their leader [*addîr*] shall be one of their own,
>   and their ruler [*mōšēl*] shall come from their midst;
> I will bring him near, and he shall approach me,
>   for who would otherwise dare to approach me, declares
>   Yahweh.[91]

In view of this Old Testament perspective, it is not surprising that the New Testament Book of Hebrews highlights the messiah's priestly role. The author of this intriguing letter is in perfect step with the Old Testament when he argues that the priesthood of the messiah (*ho Christos*) is superior to that of Aaron (5:1–7:28). In so doing he appeals to Ps. 110, a psalm in which, by oracular pronouncement, Yahweh installs (a member of) the Davidic house in office at his right hand (v. 1) and then promises him victory over all his enemies (vv. 2–3; cf. 5–7). In v. 4 the psalm takes a surprising turn, shifting from a present oracle to a past oath by which Yahweh had sworn irrevocably that the royal figure, who sits in Zion at his right hand, should also serve as priest forever. Lest the king or his subjects see in this oath a challenge to the Aaronic priesthood or a blurring of offices, the oath quickly adds *ʿal dibrātî malkî-ṣedeq*, "after the order of Melchizedek."[92] This statement is based on the tradition preserved in Gen. 14:18, according to which Abraham encountered in Salem (= Jerusalem) a royal figure identified enigmatically as *malkî-ṣedeq melek šālēm . . . kōhēn lēʾēl ʿelyôn*, "Melchizedek, king of Salem, priest of El Elyon." Melchizedek represents the pre-Israelite form of

91. I am grateful to my colleague Peter Gentry for reminding me of this text. For the messianic interpretation of the verse, see John A. Thompson, *The Book of Jeremiah*, NICOT (Grand Rapids: Eerdmans, 1980), 562.

92. Rooke's rendering of the phrase, "on account of Melchizedek" or "for the sake of Melchizedek" (*Zadok's Heirs*, 100–101), is not convincing and in any case does not affect my argument.

monarchy, in which royal and priestly offices were combined and held by the same person.[93] But in Ps. 110 the focus is not on the king's sacerdotal duties. Deborah Rooke correctly observes that the distinctive features of this priesthood are its bestowal by divine oath ("Yahweh has sworn and will not change his mind") and its eternity ("You are a priest forever [lĕ'ôlām]").[94] Perhaps this was why in the Old Testament no Davidide ever claimed this divine oath as a basis for attempting to rein in Aaronic/Zadokite authority or exerting himself over the official priesthood in Jerusalem.[95] Rather than attaching royal prerogatives to the priesthood, Ps. 110 attaches priestly prerogatives to the monarchy, but it does so without compromising the Aaronide-Davidide distinction or subsuming the Aaronic priesthood in the Davidic house. Instead, the psalm appeals to the kind of kingship that existed in Jerusalem in the time of Abraham, the father of Israel.

Some may object to my understanding of the Old Testament messiah in exclusively Davidic terms by drawing attention to the Servant Songs[96] in Isaiah, particularly the fourth song (Isa. 52:13–53:12), whose Davidic

---

93. For a survey of sacral kingship in Canaan and the ancient Near East, and the Israelite response, see H. Cazelles, "Sacral Kingship," *ABD* 5:863–66. For further discussion of this text as reflective of Canaanite influence on Israel's royal ideology, see John Day, "The Canaanite Inheritance of the Israelite Monarchy," in *King and Messiah*, ed. Day, 73–80.

94. Deborah W. Rooke, "Kingship as Priesthood: The Relationship between the High Priesthood and the Monarchy," in *King and Messiah*, ed. Day, 197–98. She observes, "The point of such an interpretation is this: if priesthood is usually defined on a functional basis so that it is those who are actually doing the job who are the priests, and not simply those who are eligible to do the job, then the king's occasional participation in cultic ceremonial is no real basis on which to call him a priest, because he is not doing the kind of job which a priest would normally be expected to do in order to earn the designation 'priest.' However, the oath has been sworn to him that he *is* a priest, and a priest *for ever*, so that though he is not a priest in the sense of one who carries out the regular functions of the sanctuary attendant, because of his vocation and his relationship to Yahweh he is nonetheless an *ex officio* priest, a mediator between his God and his people, and will remain such as long as he lives; no-one can deprive him of his mediating priestly status. Indeed it could also be taken as a kind of warning that for the king there is no evading the responsibility of mediation, no choice not to be a priest or carry out priestly duties, who were permitted by their lineage but who were perhaps unable or unwilling to serve as priests."

95. This contrasts with the Hasmonean rulers, specifically John Hyrcanus, who laid claim to the Melchizedekian precedent by adopting the title "High Priest of God Most High" (Josephus, *Jewish Antiquities* 16.163; *b. Rosh Hashanah* 18b; *Assumption of Moses* 6:1). Although the Hasmoneans were Aaronides, they were formally disqualified from the high priesthood because they were not of Zadokite descent. More seriously, they were disqualified from the kingship because they were not of Davidic descent. But this did not stop them or their followers from perceiving them in idealized and even messianic terms. See especially the eulogy given to Simon in 1 Macc. 14:4–15. But not all viewed the Hasmonean rulers favorably. For a scathing evaluation of their usurpation of the Davidic throne, see *Psalms of Solomon* 17:5–8.

96. So called and isolated by Bernhard Duhm, *Das Buch Jesaja*, HKAT (Göttingen: Vandenhoeck & Ruprecht, 1892).

nature they question. But as I have been wrestling with this matter in recent months, it has struck me that this may be the ace in the hole. The importance of Isaiah 53 as a messianic text is reflected in the frequency with which allusions to this song appear in the New Testament.[97] But in what sense is this song a royal Davidic text? This question may be answered from several angles.

First, the designation of the subject of this song as the servant of Yahweh (52:13) points in the direction of David. Admittedly, a variety of groups and individuals in the Old Testament were referred to as Yahweh's servants:[98] Israel/Jacob as a nation,[99] the patriarchs,[100] Moses,[101] Joshua,[102] Caleb,[103] prophets,[104] Davidic kings and governors,[105] an official of the court,[106] even foreigners,[107] and "the Branch."[108] Among those on this list, one of the most obvious candidates for the status of messianic servant is Moses, who is referred to as Yahweh's ʿebed more than forty times. Even more impressive is the fact that eighteen of the twenty-four occurrences of the phrase ʿebed Yahweh,[109] and all four occurrences of the related phrase ʿebed ʾĕlōhîm, "servant of God," apply to Moses.[110] It is not surprising, therefore, that some have argued that the messianic servant in the Servant Songs of Isaiah is

97. According to NA²⁷, the New Testament contains forty-eight citations or allusions to Isa. 52:13–53:12, a figure exceeded only by Dan. 7, which is alluded to or cited fifty-nine times. Allusions to the fourth Servant Song occur in Matthew, Mark, Luke, John, Acts, Romans, 1 Corinthians, Ephesians, Philippians, Hebrews, 1 Peter, 1 John, and Revelation.

98. Many of these (excluding instances in which a person addressing God refers to himself as "your servant" [e.g., 2 Sam. 7:26]) are conveniently tabulated by Rose, *Zemah and Zerubbabel*, 210–11. See also *HALOT* 2:775.

99. Isa. 41:8; 44:1, 2, 21; 45:4; 48:20; Jer. 30:10; 46:27, 28; Ezek. 28:25; 37:25; Ps. 136:22.

100. As a group: Exod. 32:13; Deut. 9:27; as individuals: Abraham: Gen. 26:24; Ps. 105:6, 42; 1 Chron. 16:13; Isaac: Gen. 24:24; Jacob: Ezek. 28:25; 37:25.

101. Exod. 14:31; Num. 12:7, 8; Deut. 34:5; Josh. 1:1, 2, 7, 13; 8:31, 33; 9:24; 11:12, 15; 12:6a, 6b; 13:8; 14:7; 18:7; 22:2, 4, 5; 24:29; 1 Kings 8:53, 56; 2 Kings 18:12; 21:8; 1 Chron. 6:34 [Eng. 49]; 2 Chron. 1:3; 24:6, 9; Neh. 1:7, 8; 9:14; 10:30 [Eng. 29]; Ps. 105:26; Mal. 3:22 [Eng. 4:4]; cf. Dan. 9:11.

102. Josh. 24:29; Judg. 2:8.

103. Num. 14:24.

104. As a group: 2 Kings 9:7; 17:13, 23; 21:10; 24:2; Ezra 9:11; Jer. 7:25; 25:4; 26:5; 29:19; 35:15; 44:4; Ezek. 38:17; Dan. 9:6, 10; Amos 3:7; Zech. 1:6; as individuals: Ahijah: 1 Kings 14:18; 15:29; Elijah: 1 Kings 18:36; 2 Kings 9:36; 10:10; Jonah: 2 Kings 14:25; Isaiah: Isa. 20:3.

105. David: 2 Sam. 3:18 and twenty-eight other times; Hezekiah: 2 Chron. 32:16; Zerubbabel: Hag. 2:23.

106. Eliakim: Isa. 22:20.

107. Nebuchadnezzar: Jer. 25:9; 27:6; 43:10; Job: Job 1:8; 2:3; 42:7, 8.

108. Zech. 3:8.

109. Deut. 34:5; Josh. 1:1, 13, 15; 8:31, 33; 11:12; 12:6; 13:8; 14:7; 18:7; 22:2, 4, 5; 2 Kings 18:12; 2 Chron. 1:3; 24:6.

110. 1 Chron. 6:34 [Eng. 49]; 2 Chron. 24:9; Neh. 10:30 [Eng. 29]; Dan. 9:11.

Moses.[111] Combining this evidence with the prominence of second exodus motifs in Isa. 40–55, Gordon Hugenberger argues that the servant of Yahweh in the Servant Songs is indeed a second Moses.[112]

A detailed critique of Hugenberger's position is impossible here, but preliminarily this interpretation may be questioned on several counts. First, nowhere does the Pentateuch or the rest of the Old Testament portray Moses as an eschatological messianic figure. Second, although Moses is frequently referred to as the servant of Yahweh, and he obviously enjoyed a very special relationship with God,[113] when applied to him, 'ebed yhwh functions as an honorific rather than an official title.[114] Third, Mosaic features in Isa. 40–55 are less obvious than Hugenberger suggests. While I do not deny the presence of new exodus imagery in Isa. 40–55,[115] the focus is entirely on Yahweh's direct deliverance of Israel, and the emphasis is on gathering Israel from the far reaches of the earth, which certainly is different from the original exodus.[116] Fourth, the Mosaic interpretation overplays the role of Moses (he is

111. See most recently Gordon Hugenberger, "The Servant of the Lord in the 'Servant Songs' of Isaiah: A Second Moses Figure," in *The Lord's Anointed*, ed. Satterthwaite, Hess, and Wenham, 105–39.

112. Ibid., 122–28.

113. As Helmer Ringgren has observed ("עָבַד *'ābad*," *TDOT* 10:394).

114. As one whom Yahweh knew face to face, Moses enjoyed a unique relationship with Yahweh, and as his agent he performed signs and wonders in the land of Egypt and generally demonstrated awesome power before the Israelites (Deut. 34:10–12). Moses served as Yahweh's specially commissioned (Ps. 105:26) agent of deliverance for his people (Exod. 1–18), the mediator of his covenant God (Exod. 19–24), the prophet par excellence and mouthpiece for his revelation (Exod. 25–31; Lev. 1–Num. 6; etc.), who left Israel the Torah, a permanent written record of the revealed will of God. Inasmuch as Moses was the sponsor of the tabernacle cult, he also fulfilled a role normally played by kings. However, the Old Testament never presents the messiah as a second Moses.

115. Bernhard W. Anderson ("Exodus Typology in Second Isaiah," in *Israel's Prophetic Heritage*, ed. B. W. Anderson and W. Harrelson [New York: Harper, 1962], 339–60) cites 40:3–5; 41:17–20; 42:14–16; 43:1–3, 14–21; 48:20–21; 49:8–12; 51:9–10; 52:11–12; 55:12–13. To these Hugenberger ("Servant of the Lord," 123) adds 42:13; 44:27; 54:3, 13, and references to the original exodus in 41:4, 9; 44:2, 7–8; 46:3–4; 48:8; 52:4.

116. Many of the allusions to the exodus may be more apparent than real, and the recognition of these motifs often derives more from a predetermination to find them than from the bare facts of the text. Given the terrain that the Israelites would need to traverse on their return from Babylon and Assyria, the references to passing through desert wasteland and crossing rivers make perfect sense without knowledge of the trek from Egypt. Also, the parallels between the first exodus and the regathering of Israel from the nations are far from exact, especially the nature of the crises that these divine actions resolved. As Isaiah himself recognized in 52:4, Israel went down to Egypt of their own free will and in peaceful circumstances to sojourn there (so also Oswalt, *The Book of Isaiah*, 362). According to the Joseph narratives of Genesis, they were invited to Egypt by the prime minister and assigned the best location to live in by pharaoh's command (Gen. 47:11). However, the exiles were dragged off first to Assyria and then to Babylon as captives against their will and scattered to the four winds. Furthermore, from a theological perspective, the nature and function of the two "ex-

out of the picture entirely) and underplays Yahweh's commitment to his eternal covenants.[117] Fifth, as I have demonstrated in my work on Ezekiel's vision of the promised restoration of Israel,[118] apart from any link with Israel's unique traditions concerning their exodus from Egypt, the prophetic picture of restoration parallels in many respects extrabiblical texts that describe the return of divine images to their temples and the correlative restoration of the population and the return of peace and prosperity to the land. In many of the contexts cited as second exodus texts in Isaiah, the emphasis actually is on the personal presence of Yahweh (not Moses) and the manifestation of his glory.[119] Sixth, few of the special features that characterize David's relationship with Yahweh are ever applied to Moses.[120]

---

iles" were radically different. The Egyptian sojourn was voluntary and providentially positive in its purpose: to preserve the family of Jacob while famine ravaged the land of Canaan (Gen. 45:1–11; 50:19–21), and to provide favorable circumstances (in the choice region of Goshen) for this family to multiply and become a vast people (Exod. 1:1–7), and a nation separate from the Canaanites among whom the patriarchs lived (cf. the threat to Israel's separate ethnic identity described in Gen. 34, esp. vv. 15–16). The subsequent enslavement of Israel by the Egyptians also must be seen as a positively providential act, intended to isolate the Israelites from the Egyptian population and to create in them a sense of need for deliverance. In the providential plan of God, Egypt served as the incubator in which this seed consisting of one family could sprout and grow into a great nation (Exod. 1:1–7). In contrast, the exile of the Israelites to Mesopotamia was involuntary and providentially negative: the Assyrians and Babylonians leveled the land and carried off the remnant of the population as agents of divine punishment for Israel's persistent idolatry and covenantal infidelity. Mesopotamia functioned as a smelter whose flames were to purge the nation of its moral and spiritual dross (Ezek. 22:17–22). Several texts do indeed refer to Egypt as an "iron furnace" (*kûr habbarzel* [Deut. 4:20; 1 Kings 8:51; Jer. 11:4]), but Egypt is never portrayed as a place of purification.

117. The judgments of 722 and 586 B.C. had transpired precisely as Yahweh had predicted in the covenant curses recorded in Lev. 26 and Deut. 28 (cf. Dan. 9:12–14), but the epilogues to those curses declared that the banishment of Israel could not be the last word. The issue in bringing Israel back from the nations where Yahweh would scatter them was not to repeat the original exodus, as if this were some sort of rebirth of the nation, but to demonstrate Yahweh's fidelity to his original word and to Israel his covenant partner.

118. Daniel I. Block, *The Gods of the Nations: Studies in Ancient Near Eastern National Theology*, rev. ed. (Grand Rapids: Baker, 2000), 113–47; idem, "Divine Abandonment: Ezekiel's Adaptation of an Ancient Near Eastern Motif," in *Perspectives on Ezekiel: Theology and Anthropology*, ed. Margaret S. Odell and John T. Strong, SBLSymS 9 (Atlanta: Scholars Press, 2000), 15–42.

119. Isa. 40:1–11; 41:1–4, 17–20; 43:14–17; 44:6–8, 24–28; 46:3–4; 48:8–11; 51:9–13; 52:11–12; 55:6–13.

120. Yahweh makes no covenant with him; he promises him no eternal dynasty or descendants or throne; he grants him no kingdom; only once is he referred to as Yahweh's chosen one (Ps. 106:23), but there his role is intercessory rather than royal; he is never referred to as the son of God, or *māšîaḥ*, "the anointed one," or even "shepherd" of Israel or Yahweh's flock. Numbers 27:16–17 applies the term *rō'eh* to his successor, but it is avoided for Moses. If anything, Moses failed in this role inasmuch as he was unable to bring the flock to pasture, that is, to the safety of the promised land. Also, he never bears

While support for identifying Moses as the messianic servant is tenuous, the evidence for David is overwhelming. First, no one else, not even Moses, is referred to as Yahweh's servant as frequently as David. Second, on some forty occasions the name "David" and *ʿebed* appear in appositional relationship,[121] which compares with only sixteen such associations with Moses.[122] Third, the designation of David as the servant of Yahweh is often associated with terms that relate expressly to (1) the Davidic covenant: *běrît*, "covenant";[123] *ḥesed*, "covenant faithfulness";[124] *ṭôb*, "good, covenant benefactions";[125] *dbr*, *ʾmr*, "promise";[126] *nišbaʿ*, "to swear, oath";[127] (2) the specific Davidic privilege: eternal *bayit*, *bānîm*, *zeraʿ*, "house/dynasty, sons, seed";[128] eternal *kissēʾ*, "throne";[129] eternal *mamlākâ*, "kingdom/kingship";[130] (3) David's status: the one specially chosen (*bāḥar*) by Yahweh;[131] *rōʿeh*, "shepherd," of Yahweh's flock;[132] *hammāšîaḥ*, "the anointed";[133] (4) and David's close association with Jerusalem/Zion.[134]

any of the other epithets applied to the messianic figure: "Branch" or "Yahweh Our Righteousness," let alone a grand throne name like "Wonderful Counselor-Mighty El-Father of Eternity-Prince of Peace." Furthermore, the prophetic books (according to the Protestant canon) refer to Moses as Yahweh's servant only twice (Dan. 9:11; Mal. 3:22 [Eng. 4:4]), but in both instances the view is retrospective to the Torah of Moses and the covenant stipulations given by Yahweh at Sinai.

121. 2 Sam. 3:18; 7:5, 8, 26 (// 1 Chron. 17:4, 7, 24); 1 Kings 3:6; 8:24, 25, 26 (// 2 Chron. 6:15, 16, 17); 8:66; 11:13, 32, 34, 36, 38; 14:8; 2 Kings 8:19; 19:34 (// Isa. 37:35); 2 Kings 20:6; Jer. 33:21, 22, 26; Ezek. 34:23, 24; 37:24, 25; Ps. 78:70; 89:4, 21; 132:10; 144:10; 2 Chron. 6:42. Cf. also the headings to Ps. 18; 36.

122. Exod. 14:31; Num. 12:7, 8; Josh. 1:1, 2, 7; 9:24; 11:15; 1 Kings 8:53, 56; 2 Kings 21:8; Neh. 1:7, 8; 9:14; Mal. 4:4; Ps. 105:26.

123. 1 Kings 8:24 = 2 Chron. 6:15; Jer. 33:21; Ps. 89:4 [Eng. 3] (cf. v. 3), 22 [Eng. 21] (cf. vv. 28, 34).

124. 2 Sam. 7:8 (cf. v. 15) = 1 Chron. 17:7 (cf. v. 13); 1 Kings 3:6; 8:24; 2 Chron. 6:42; Ps. 18:1 [Eng. psalm title] (cf. v. 20); 36:1 [Eng. psalm title] (cf. vv. 5, 10); Ps. 89:21 (cf. vv. 1, 2, 14, 24, 28, 33, 49).

125. 2 Sam. 7:26 (cf. v. 28) = 1 Chron. 17:24 (cf. v. 26); 1 Kings 8:66. On *ṭôb* and its cognates as designations for covenantal benefactions in Israel and environs, see I. Höver-Johag, "בֹּוט *ṭôb*," *TDOT* 5:301–2, 311–12.

126. 1 Kings 8:24, 25, 26 = 2 Chron. 6:15, 16, 17; 2 Kings 8:19.

127. Ps. 89:4 [Eng. 3], 21 [Eng. 20] (cf. vv. 34, 50 [Eng. 35, 49]); 132:10.

128. 2 Sam. 7:8 (cf. vv. 11–16) = 1 Chron. 17:7 (cf. vv. 11–14); 1 Kings 11:38; Jer. 33:21, 22, 26; Ps. 18:1 [Eng. 2] (cf. v. 51 [Eng. 50]); 89:4 [Eng. 3], 21 [Eng. 20] (cf. v. 28 [Eng. 27]).

129. 2 Sam. 7:8 (cf. v. 16) = 1 Chron. 17:7 (cf. v. 15); Ps. 89:4 [Eng. 3], 21 [Eng. 20] (cf. v. 28 [Eng. 29], 35 [Eng. 36]); 132:10 (cf. vv. 11, 12); Jer. 33:21.

130. 2 Sam. 7:8 (cf. v. 16) = 1 Chron. 17:7 (cf. v. 15); 1 Kings 11:34.

131. 1 Kings 11:13, 32, 34; Ps. 78:70; 89:4 [Eng. 3], 21 [Eng. 20] (cf. v. 20 [Eng. 19]). Cf. the association of "my servant David" with the choice of Jerusalem as the place to establish Yahweh's name (1 Kings 11:13, 36; Ps. 132:10 [cf. v. 13]).

132. 2 Sam. 7:8 = 1 Chron. 17:7; Ezek. 34:23, 24; 37:24, 25; Ps. 78:70 (cf. vv. 71–72).

133. Ps. 18:1 (cf. v. 20); 89:21 [Eng. 20] (cf. v. 39 [Eng. 38]); 132:10; 2 Chron. 6:42.

134. 1 Kings 11:32, 36; 19:34 = Isa. 37:35; 2 Kings 20:6; Ps. 132:10 (cf. v. 13).

It goes without saying that the Old Testament often uses the term ʿebed for slaves and as a nontechnical self-designation, expressing a person's obsequiousness and humility before a perceived superior,[135] especially in prayers addressed to God.[136] However, 2 Kings 16:7, which intriguingly conjoins the vassal terms ʿebed and bēn, may provide the key to the riddle of the messianic servant. In this nontheological context, Ahaz of Judah pleads with his overlord, Tiglath-pileser of Assyria, "I am your servant and your son; come up and deliver me from the hand of the king of Aram."[137] Given this correlation of "servant" and "son," we do well to ask which Old Testament character was identified both as the servant of Yahweh and as Yahweh's son. There is only one answer: David.[138]

Two texts are especially important for their presentation of David as both the son of God and the servant of Yahweh: 2 Sam. 7:8, 14 = 1 Chron. 17:7, 13; and Ps. 89:21 [Eng. 20], 27–28 [Eng. 26–27]. In both passages the terms ʿebed and bēn describe the special vassal relationship between David and Yahweh. Accordingly, David was specially chosen to rule Yahweh's people on his behalf, and Yahweh assumed responsibility to protect David and ensure the eternality of the dynasty.[139]

To identify the messianic servant with Moses not only forces the evidence of Isaiah, but also overlooks the consistent witness of the rest of prophetic Scripture. Wherever the messiah is both characterized as a servant and associated with a specific name, that name is always "David" or a person with a Davidic connection. Especially significant is Ezekiel's portrayal of the servant in 34:23–31 and 37:21–28, according to which in the future Yahweh will install his servant David as shepherd/king over his people Israel.[140] Ezekiel's

135. Often the superior is addressed as ʾǎdōnay: Jacob before Esau (Gen. 32:5, 19 [Eng. 4, 18]); Nathan before David (2 Sam. 9:11). In several instances the expression "your servant" occurs in connection with pleas for divine favor/grace (ḥēn) (Gen. 18:3; 19:19; Num. 11:11).

136. This is especially evident in the prayers of Moses (Exod. 4:10; Deut. 3:24; Num. 11:11), David (1 Sam. 23:10, 11a, 11b; 2 Sam. 7:19, 20, 21, 25, 26, 27a, 27b, 28, 29a, 29b; 24:10; 1 Chron. 17:17, 18a, 18b, 19, 23, 24, 25a, 25b, 26, 27; 21:8), and Solomon (1 Kings 8:28, 29, 30, 52; 2 Chron. 6:19a, 19b, 20, 21); and it occurs fifty-seven times in Psalms, fourteen of which occur in Ps. 119. For discussion and references, see H. Ringgren, "עָבַד," TDOT 10:393–94.

137. H. Ringgren ("עָבַד," TDOT 10:387–90) also cites 2 Kings 17:3 (Hoshea and Shalmaneser); 2 Kings 24:1 (Jehoiakim and Nebuchadnezzar); 2 Chron. 12:8 (Rehoboam and his princes on the one hand, and Pharaoh Shishak on the other); Ezra 9:9 (the returned exiles and the Persian king).

138. With the exception of a late idealizing reference to Hezekiah (1 Chron. 32:16), David is the only king of Israel ever referred to as Yahweh's servant.

139. But note also Ps. 2.

140. Remarkably, in Ezekiel the servant is not the agent of Israel's regathering and return to the land. These both are direct actions of Yahweh, after which the servant is installed to function as a symbol of the new realities, that is, the fulfillment of Yahweh's eternal promises to Abraham, to Israel, and to the Davidic dynasty. For fuller discussion of these texts, see Block, "Bringing Back David," 172–83.

picture of the messiah accords fully with other prophets who also identify the messianic figure as Davidic: Jer. 23:5 speaks of raising up for David "a righteous Branch" (*ṣemaḥ ṣaddîq* [cf. 33:15]); Amos 9:11 of restoring (*hēqîm*) the fallen hut of David; Isa. 9:5–6 [Eng. 6–7] of a child upon the throne of David; and Isa. 11:1 refers to "a shoot from the stump of Jesse." Finally, note Zech. 3:8, according to which a *malʾak*, quoting Yahweh, declares, "I will bring in my servant *ṣemaḥ* [Branch]." This *ṣemaḥ* is rightfully understood as a Davidic figure,[141] an interpretation confirmed by Zech. 6:12, where the "Branch" is identified as the eschatological person who will build the temple of Yahweh, bear royal honor, and sit and rule on the throne.

The Messiah as a Suffering Servant

If my conclusions regarding the servant of Yahweh in Old Testament prophecy are correct, I still need to account for the origins of the notion of the messiah as a "suffering servant of Yahweh" in Isa. 53. The notion of a suffering messiah appears in only two prophetic books, Isaiah and Zechariah. But only the former identifies the messiah in terms of "the servant of Yahweh," and that in the Servant Songs. A consecutive reading of these songs yields an evolving portrait of the servant. In the first (42:1–4 [9?]), the person is gentle but strong, establishing justice in the earth and bringing his Torah to all. In the second (49:1–6), we learn of the servant's salvific role for Israel and luminary role for the nations, but we also learn that his work will be accompanied by great frustration. He

141. Although this "Branch" has usually been identified with Zerubbabel, and this declaration viewed as an announcement of the imminent elevation of the governor to kingship, Wolter H. Rose (*Zemah and Zerubbabel*) recently has argued that the term, which should be interpreted as "vegetation, greenery, growth," refers to a future figure who may be called messianic by his definition: "a future royal figure sent by God who will bring salvation to God's people and the world and establish a kingdom characterized by features like peace and justice." His definition of the messianic expectation is stated on pp. 23, 249.

Zechariah's use of *ṣemaḥ* seems to have been borrowed from Jer. 23:5–6, in which the earlier prophet declares, "Look, days are coming when I shall raise up for David a righteous *ṣemaḥ*, and he will reign as king. He will act wisely and do justice and righteousness in the land. In his day Judah will be saved, and Israel will dwell securely. This is the name by which he will be called, 'Yahweh our Righteousness.'" Cf. 33:15. Ezekiel, Jeremiah's contemporary, referred to the future messianic figure as *rak*, "sprig, shoot" (17:22). In Isa. 11:1, the earlier prophet had referred to the future messiah as "a shoot" (*hōṭēr*) that will spring from the "stem" (*gēzaʿ*) of Jesse, and a "branch" (*nēṣer*) from his roots that will bring fruit. Although these botanical references to the messiah figure prominently in the texts from Qumran (see Collins, *The Scepter and the Star*, 49–73; Zimmermann, *Messianische Texte aus Qumran*, 49–127, passim), the only hint of the motif in the New Testament occurs in Luke 1:78, where the use of *anatolē*, "sunrise," apparently derives from the LXX, which uses this term to render *ṣemaḥ* in Jer. 23:5; Zech. 3:8; 6:12 (Zimmermann, *Messianische Texte aus Qumran*, 51).

expresses a sense that his efforts have been in vain, but he is secure, knowing that God will vindicate him. The picture darkens in the third song (50:4–9 [11?]), as the servant suffers physical abuse and torture from his hearers. With a clear sense of divine mission and unflinching obedience to Yahweh, he gives himself over to those who lash and humiliate him. In the fourth song (52:13–53:12), the light goes out for the servant. Quietly and without protest he takes upon himself the sins of the people and suffers execution at their hands.

Since the rise of higher criticism, the identity of this servant has been hotly debated, and current scholarship is characterized by a frustrating lack of consensus.[142] Even a summary presentation of the views held is impossible here, so I will get directly to the point and declare, on the basis of the foregoing discussion, that the most likely candidate behind any messianic servant figure in the prophets is David. This includes the suffering servant of Isaiah.[143]

Though Hugenberger ultimately rejects the evidence, he has provided a helpful summary of the support for the Davidic interpretation of Isaiah 53. (1) The expression "my servant" is commonly used of royal figures in Isaiah (37:35) and elsewhere. (2) The declaration that Yahweh has put his Spirit on his servant accords with a royal identity and finds explicit support in 11:1–3.[144] (3) The role of the servant as one who brings forth justice and establishes it to the ends of the earth (42:1–4; 51:4) accords with royal functions. (4) The reference to the response of kings (52:14–15) and the promise of victory (52:12–13) supports a royal interpretation. (5) The botanical imagery (53:2) recalls 11:1 and other horticultural Davidic messianic references. To these we might add (6) the reference to his "superhuman anointing" in 52:14,[145] and (7) the notice of a rich burial, which suits a royal person (53:9).

---

142. For an excellent summary and bibliography of the various positions held by scholars, see Hugenberger, "The Servant of the Lord," 106–19.

143. Hugenberger's identification of the *suffering* servant with Moses rests upon a superficial comparison of their roles. Admittedly, Moses volunteered his life as a substitute for his people (Exod. 32:30–35), but he did not submit himself to their rejection and violence. In any case, Yahweh rejected his offer, and many Israelites did indeed die for their own sins.

144. Cf. also Isa. 61:1–3 and 1 Sam. 16:13.

145. Although *mišḥat* is traditionally and generally translated "disfigurement" (e.g., James Barr, *Comparative Philology and the Text of the Old Testament* [Oxford: Oxford University Press, 1968], 284–85, with *mēʾiš*, "inhumanly deformed"), the etymology is problematic. *HALOT* is indecisive, suggesting a derivation from *mšḥ* III on p. 644, and *šḥt*, "to be ruined," on p. 1472. However, with support from 1QIsᵃ, it is preferable to derive the word from *mšḥ*, "to anoint." So also D. Barthélemy, *Critique textuelle de l'Ancien Testament*, OBO 50.2 (Göttingen: Vandenhoeck & Ruprecht, 1986), 384–87; and Peter Gentry (in a review of Oswalt, *The Book of Isaiah*, in *BRT* 8 [1998]: 151–52), who translates the verse as follows: "Just as many were astounded at you, so his appearance was a superhuman anointing; his form more than humanity."

However, two additional considerations argue for a Davidic interpretation of Isa. 53. The first derives from the Old Testament itself. In Zech.
11:8 and 12:10, the postexilic prophet Zechariah joins his prophetic pre-
decessor in portraying him as one whom the people reject (11:8; 12:10),
and as one who is struck in accordance with the will of Yahweh for the
ultimate good of the people (13:7–9). Beyond the motif of suffering, it is
scarcely accidental that these texts share a common pastoral metaphor,
specifically presenting the messiah as Yahweh's shepherd. On the one
hand, ancient Near Easterners commonly perceived kings as shepherds
installed by the deity.[146] On the other hand, and more importantly, the
Old Testament presents David in particular as the divinely appointed
shepherd charged to govern Israel, Yahweh's flock. When the tribes of
Israel anointed David in Hebron, they recognized this formally with
their declaration "Yahweh said to you, 'You are the one who shall shepherd my people Israel, and you are the one who shall serve as leader over
them'" (2 Sam. 5:1–3). This accords with Yahweh's later affirmation "I
took you from the pasture, from following the sheep, that you should be
ruler over my people Israel" (2 Sam. 7:8).[147] With his portrayal of the suffering shepherd, Zechariah appears intentionally to have been building
on the royal dimension of Isa. 53.

Although Isaiah and Zechariah share the image of a suffering messiah, Isaiah's portrayal of the messiah as a substitute sacrifice for the
people is quite exceptional in the Old Testament[148] and has long been a
source of puzzlement. What are the biblical antecedents for this motif?[149] The guilt offering (ʾāšām) provides the most likely answer on three
counts. First, Isa. 53:10 specifically declares the servant to be an accept-
able ʾāšām to Yahweh. Second, in the Mosaic regulation the ʾāšām was
the only type of regular offering that required a ram (Lev. 5:14–26 [Eng.

---

146. For brief discussion and bibliography, see J. A. Soggin, "רעה rʿh to tend," *TLOT*
3:1248.

147. = 1 Chron. 17:7. See also Ezek. 34:23, 24; 37:24, 25; Ps. 78:70 (cf. vv. 71–72).

148. The New Testament appropriates Ps. 22:2, 12–19 [Eng. 1, 11–18] for the passion
of Christ, but there is no hint in the psalm of the victim serving as a substitutionary sin
offering for the people. Contrary to the views of some, the servant's role in Isa. 53 is not
priestly; he functions as the victim of the sacrifice, not as the officiating priest.

149. With hindsight, I suggest a link with the substitute ram in Gen. 22 and the Passover lamb in Exod. 12–13, except that in neither of these cases does the substitution involve sin or a sin offering. A link with the substitutionary sacrifice of the Day of
Atonement (Lev. 16) may also be proposed, but this ritual called for a bull to be sacrificed
as a sin offering for Aaron (v. 11), and a goat for the people (v. 9). To be sure, a ram was
involved, but it was offered as a burnt offering (v. 3). Failing this connection, we may appeal to the standard sin offering as prescribed in Lev. 4–5, but this regulation also called
for a bull (4:1–26), or a goat (4:27–31), or a female lamb or goat (4:32–5:6), or two turtle-
doves or young pigeons (5:7–10), or an ephah of flour (5:11–13).

5:14–6:7]), that is, a male sheep. Third, the fact that ʾayil, the Hebrew word for "ram," was often used of rulers[150] facilitates the adaptation of the Hebrew ʾāšām ritual to a royal substitutionary ritual.

The second argument derives from outside the Old Testament. John Walton has recently drawn attention to a potentially significant ancient Mesopotamian analog to the experience of the servant in Isa. 53, namely, the ritual of the substitute king.[151] According to the Assyrian ritual, in response to an omen (such as an eclipse of the sun or moon) that threatened the life of the king, diviners would choose a man from the population (in some texts one of high standing, in others a common man, or even a half-wit) to serve as a substitute king and take the curse of the omens upon himself. He would be dressed in the king's robes and given the insignias of royalty (crown, weapon, scepter), as well as a queen, who would share his fate. Playing the role of the king, the substitute would not only sit on the throne, but also present offerings before the altar and offer incense on the incense altar. During this time (which varied, apparently depending upon the length of the omen threat), the true king would perform various purifying rituals. Meanwhile, the substitute would take upon himself the evils that threatened the king by reciting omen litanies, having them transcribed, and keeping them in a fold in the hem of his robe. The ritual reached its climax with the execution of the substitute king for the sake of the true king and his prince, thereby achieving their redemption. The king or his agents would prepare a tomb for the man and give him a royal funeral. They would burn the royal garments and accoutrements of office, perform elaborate apotropaic rituals, and recite penitential psalms and litanies to ensure that the evils would descend to the netherworld with the substitute king and never return. This ritual was thought to effect the purification of the king and his land and to ward off the omens. Presumably, the substitution allowed the gods to do what they intended—act against someone— not by fooling them, but by providing them with a victim on whom to achieve their aims.[152]

150. Exod. 15:15; 2 Kings 24:15; Jer. 25:34; Ezek. 17:13; 30:13; 31:11, 14; 32:21; 39:18. For a discussion of this usage, see Patrick D. Miller, "Animal Names as Designations in Ugarit and Hebrew," *UF* 2 (1970): 181–82.

151. Briefly noted in *Bible Background Commentary*, 633, but more fully developed in a paper read at the annual meeting of the Society of Biblical Literature, Nashville, November 2000: "The Imagery of the Substitute King Ritual in Isaiah's Fourth Servant Song."

152. For the texts, see S. Parpola, *Letters from Assyrian and Babylonian Scholars*, SAA 10 (Helsinki: Helsinki University Press, 1993), nos. 1, 2, 3, 4, 12, 25, 189, 219, 220, 221, 314, 350, 351, 352. For full discussion of the ritual, see Jean Bottéro, "The Substitute King and His Fate," in *Mesopotamia: Writing, Reasoning, and the Gods*, trans. Z. Bahrani and M. Van De Mieroop (Chicago: University of Chicago Press, 1992), 138–55.

Of course, it is impossible to establish a direct connection between Isa. 53 and this Mesopotamian ritual, but the fact that the ritual of the substitute king is documented from the nineteenth century B.C. to the time of Alexander the Great attests to its persistence. Chronologically, the strongest evidence derives from Neo-Assyrian times, specifically the reigns of Esarhaddon (680–669 B.C.) and Ashurbanipal (668–627 B.C.), which increases the likelihood of Isaianic familiarity with the custom.[153] Not only did the Neo-Assyrians play an important role in Judean politics during the ministry of Isaiah (2 Kings 18–19 = Isa. 36–37), but also Isaiah's prophecies demonstrate awareness of Mesopotamian religion and custom elsewhere in the book.[154]

The thematic affinities between the fourth Servant Song and the Mesopotamian ritual are obvious. The substitutionary role of the victim, that is, one person commandeered to take on himself the curse/omen of another/others and dying in his/their place, provides the most obvious link. But there are several additional, more subtle connections. First, just as the ritual elevates the substitute to kingship, so the song begins with a notice of the exaltation of the victim (52:13). Second, Isaiah's servant king "sprinkling"[155] many nations (52:15) recalls the ablutions in the *bit sala'mê* ("house of sprinkling of water") of the Mesopotamian ritual. Third, Isaiah's reference to the burial of the servant as a wicked man, but with the rich (v. 9), makes perfect sense in the light of the Mesopotamian ritual. Fourth, the pleasure that Yahweh takes in crushing the servant (53:10) is reminiscent of Marduk's intentional striking of the substitute.[156]

While the links are impressive, obviously the prophet adapts the custom for his own unique theological, specifically messianic, purposes. Most notably, he parodies the ritual by reversing the roles. Whereas the substitute king ritual has a commoner taking on himself the curse that hangs over the king and dying in his place, the Servant Song has the

153. Assuming the fundamentally Isaianic origin of Isa. 40–66, with J. Alec Motyer, *The Prophecy of Isaiah* (Downers Grove, Ill.: InterVarsity, 1993); Oswalt, *The Book of Isaiah;* and Barry G. Webb, *The Message of Isaiah,* BST (Downers Grove, Ill.: InterVarsity, 1996), 33–37.

154. The heavenly revolt of Helel (14:12) recalls the "Myth of Anzu" (Benjamin R. Foster, *Before the Muses: An Anthology of Akkadian Literature* [Bethesda, Md.: CDL, 1993], 461–85); the oracle naming Bel and Nebo (46:1–13) attests to familiarity with Mesopotamian spoliation of the divine images of conquered cities. Cf. Block, *Gods of the Nations,* 113–34.

155. I follow D. Barthélemy (*Critique textuelle de l'Ancien Testament,* 384–87) and Peter Gentry (in his review of Oswalt, 152) in deriving *yazzeh* from *nzh,* "to sprinkle," against Oswalt (*The Book of Isaiah,* 374), who, following the LXX, accepts a root *nzh* II, "to startle," in Arabic.

156. For further discussion of the parallels, see Walton, "Substitute King Ritual," 3–4.

king (interpreting the servant as above) taking upon himself the sins of the common people and being slain in their place.

To this consideration I add a further observation. Although New Testament usage of an Old Testament text is not necessarily determinative for establishing the meaning of Old Testament texts in their original historical and literary contexts,[157] this interpretation of Isa. 53 sheds potentially interesting light on Jesus' self-identification as "the good shepherd" in John 10.[158] The editors of the twenty-seventh edition of *Novum Testamentum Graece* (Nestle-Aland) correctly recognize allusions to Ezek. 34:11–16, 23 and 37:24 in John 10, but apparently they see no link with Old Testament prophecy in v. 11, particularly 11b. Indeed, commentators in general seem to have missed a significant nuance of Jesus' statement "I am *the* good shepherd; *the* good shepherd lays down his life for the sheep."

157. The same is true of the usage of Isa. 53 at Qumran. In his paper in this volume, Richard S. Hess ("Messiahs Here and There") draws attention to the intriguing frag. 1 of 4Q491c, lines 7–11 of which have been translated as follows:

> [7] . . . I am counted among the gods and my dwelling is in the holy congregation; [my] des[ire] is not according to the flesh, [but] all that is precious to me is in (the) glory (of) [8][. . .] the holy [dwell]ing. [W]ho has been considered despicable on my account? And who is comparable to me in my glory? Who, like the sailors, will come back and tell? [9][. . .] Who bea[rs all] sorrows like me? And who [suffe]rs evil like me? There is no-one. I have been instructed, and there is no teaching comparable [10][to my teaching . . .] And who will attack me when [I] op[en my mouth]? And who can endure the flow of my lips? And who will confront me and retain comparison with my judgment? [11][. . . friend of the king, companion of the holy ones . . . incomparable, f]or among the gods is [my] posi[tion, and] my glory is with the sons of the king.

This translation is in Florentino García Martínez and Eibert J. C. Tigchelaar, eds., *The Dead Sea Scrolls Study Edition: Volume 2 (4Q274–11Q31)* (Leiden: Brill; Grand Rapids: Eerdmans, 2000), 980–81. Cf. Martínez, *The Dead Sea Scrolls Translated: The Qumran Texts in English*, trans. W. G. E. Watson, 2d ed. (Leiden: Brill; Grand Rapids: Eerdmans, 1996), 118 (*War Scroll* [4Q491], frag. 11, col. i, lines 14–18). Although the significance of this fragment is still open to discussion, it suggests that some in the Qumran community linked the suffering servant of Isa. 53 with an exalted, perhaps divine, personage. For a discussion of this text, see Israel Knohl, *The Messiah before Jesus: The Suffering Servant of the Dead Sea Scrolls*, trans. D. Maisel (Berkeley and Los Angeles: University of California Press, 2000), 15–20. Whether or not Knohl's identification of the author of this autobiographical text as Menahem, a respected scholar in Jerusalem at the turn of the era, proves correct, the application of Isa. 53 to an individual messianic figure anticipates the New Testament interpretation of Jesus Christ as the servant. Collins (*The Scepter and the Star*, 138–49) suggests that the reference to "teaching" points to a Mosaic-type teacher rather than to a Davidic figure.

158. The motif of Jesus as the suffering servant of Yahweh is present also in the Synoptic Gospels. See R. F. O'Toole's recent study, "How Does Luke Portray Jesus as Servant of Yahweh?" *Bib* 81 (2000): 328–46.

One could make too much of the use of the article in these statements, but it is remarkable that Jesus does not say, "I am *a* good shepherd; *a* good shepherd lays down his life for the sheep," as if he were defining the conduct of good shepherds and then classifying himself as
one belonging to this category. No, he identifies himself as *the* good
shepherd. But this raises several intriguing questions.

First, "Which good shepherd?" to which he answers, "The one who
gives his life for the sheep."

Second, "And who might this be?" This question is not answered, but
if one searches the Old Testament for direct references or allusions to a
shepherd who voluntarily gives his life for the sake of his sheep, the
search is in vain—until one comes to Isa. 53. The repeated reference to
the shepherd whom Yahweh sets over Israel as "my servant David" in
Old Testament narrative (2 Sam. 7:8 = 1 Chron. 17:7), prophetic texts
(Ezek. 34:23, 24; 37:24, 25), and Psalms (e.g., 78:70–72) supports the interpretation of the servant in Isa. 53 as a Davidic figure, one whom Yahweh has called to shepherd his flock.[159] However, the Servant Song describes an incredible if ironical act of self-sacrifice. In accordance with
the pleasure of Yahweh (Isa. 53:10), the shepherd voluntarily gives himself over to his sheep, takes upon himself their sins, and allows them to
kill him, knowing that by this act he renders himself a guilt offering,
thereby bearing their sins and justifying many. With this interpretation
of Isaiah 53, the significance of Jesus' self-identification as the shepherd
who gives his life for the sheep becomes apparent.

Conclusion

I must bring this long and often complex discussion of the messiah in
the Old Testament to a close. There can be no doubt that the New Testament writers interpreted Jesus' messianic role primarily in Davidic terms,
from Matthew's genealogy (Matt. 1:1–17); to Peter's confession "You are
the Messiah, the Son of the Living God" (Matt. 16:16); to Paul's identifi-

159. The lexical and thematic links between Isaiah's fourth Servant Song and Jer. 23:5–6
provide additional support for my Davidic interpretation of the former text. (1) Both contexts
involve the sheep metaphor (Isa. 53:6–7; Jer. 23:1–4). (2) Both texts use the verb *hiśkîl*, "to suc-
ceed, prosper," to declare the figure's effectiveness (Isa. 52:13a; Jer. 23:5c). (3) Both texts
highlight the "righteous" character of the figure. Isaiah 53:11 names him "the Righteous One"
(*ṣaddîq*). Jer. 23:5–6 identifies him as a "righteous Branch" (*ṣemaḥ ṣaddîq*) raised up for David, whose name will be called "Yahweh Our Righteousness" (*yhwh ṣidqēnû*). (4) Both texts
emphasize the figure's justifying action on behalf of the sheep. According to Isa. 53:11, "my
servant will justify [*yaṣdîq*] many." According to Jer. 23:5–6, the "righteous Branch" executes
justice and righteousness (*ṣĕdāqâ*), and is named "Yahweh *Our* Righteousness," presumably
because he effects righteousness in and for us.

cation of the Messiah Jesus as God's Son, "who was born of a descendant of David according to the flesh, who was declared to be the Son of God with power by the resurrection from the dead" (Rom. 1:3–4); to the author of Hebrews' anticipation of the return of the Messiah, who "having been offered once to bear the sins of many, shall appear a second time" (Heb. 9:28); to the vision of John, who paints a glorious scene of the redeemed gathered around the heavenly throne, worshiping and singing the praises of "the Lion from the tribe of Judah," "the Root of David," that is, "the Lamb," who was slain, thereby purchasing for God with his blood people from every tribe and tongue and people and nation, and constituting them a kingdom of priests to reign over God's earth (Rev. 5:5–10). If the New Testament portrayal of the life and ministry of Jesus contains Mosaic or prophetic or Aaronic features (which it does), these features should be interpreted as retrospective and analogical adaptations of Old Testament motifs rather than as fulfillments of Old Testament expectations. But these analogical links are not accidental. From the eternal and timeless perspective of the divine author of Scripture, modes of revelation to Israel were chosen that would facilitate the interpretation of the life and mission of the messianic Son of God in the historical future. However, this is different from saying that the Old Testament believers saw in Moses or Aaron or the prophets foreshadowings of the future (in terms of time-space realities) messiah.

Although complex, the Old Testament picture of the messiah gains in clarity and focus with time. But the messianic hope is a single line that begins in broadest terms with God's promise of victory over the serpent through "the seed of the woman" (Gen. 3:15),[160] then is narrowed successively to the seed of Abraham (Gen. 22:18), the tribe of Judah (Gen. 49:10), the stem of Jesse (Isa. 11:1), the house/dynasty of David (2 Sam. 7), and finally the suffering and slain servant of Yahweh (Isa. 53). This is the shepherd and guardian of our souls, who bore our sins in his body on the cross that we might die to sin and live to righteousness, and be healed by his wounds (1 Pet. 2:21–25). This is the great shepherd of the sheep, through whose blood the eternal covenant is sealed and whom the God of peace raised from the dead. May we, who are called to this grace, be divinely equipped in every good thing to do the will of God, and may he work in us that which is pleasing in his sight, through Jesus the Messiah, to whom be the glory forever and ever. Amen (Heb. 13:20–21).[161]

160. Apparently, at first Eve thought that this promise was fulfilled in Cain (Gen. 4:1).

161. I am grateful to my assistant Kenneth Turner for his careful reading of a draft of this paper, and to my colleague Peter Gentry for his support and particularly for his comments concerning both textual and interpretive matters addressed in this paper. Of course, any defects in the essay are my own responsibility.

TWO

If He Looks Like a Prophet and Talks Like a Prophet, Then He Must Be . . .

A Response to Daniel I. Block

J. Daniel Hays

In the Book of Ecclesiastes, Qohelet says that "there is nothing new under the sun." Dan Block's paper is a reminder that Qohelet's field is metaphysics and not the study of Old Testament messianism. Indeed, Block has given us several new ideas to ponder—ideas that challenge our thinking regarding the concept of messiah. Block has questioned the traditional understanding of the messiah as prophet, priest, and king. He argues that the prophetic and priestly aspects are not present in Old Testament messianic passages, and that the royal image—that of David—dominates the messianic picture. Furthermore, Block even proposes that this royal Davidic image is to be identified with the suffering servant of Isaiah's Servant Songs. Truly, he has given us a lot to think about.

I commend Dan Block for his excellent paper. He is not afraid "to boldly go where no one has gone before" if that is where his texts lead him. He has staked out a fairly radical position, but then, as is typical of Block, he also has buttressed his case with solid exegesis. This is the kind of paper that sharpens our thinking. I thoroughly enjoyed it.

In the spirit of healthy (and friendly) dialogue, however, I would like to interact with several of Block's arguments, raise a few questions, and suggest a counterargument or two.

Determining Messianic Texts: Methodology

First, I make a few comments regarding methodology and definitions. What constitutes a messianic text? What are the criteria for determining whether or not a text is contributing to the messianic picture? Block defines his goal as answering the question "What kind of person did the Israelites of the Old Testament expect the messiah to be?" Although this type of language is common, it should be noted that the phrase "Israelites of the Old Testament" is rather vague and perhaps misleading. To whom is he referring? Preexilic Israel? Postexilic Israel? The Israelites who lived through the events of the Old Testament, or the Israelites who were involved in the final formulation and structure of the canon? If we examine those who witnessed the events, then we find Israel frequently indifferent to the messianic prophecy. After the "ancient Israelites" of the northern kingdom turned away completely from Yahweh, did they have any messianic understanding at all? Throughout the Old Testament, the so-called people of God often are not seeking after Yahweh, and they are usually not much concerned with his eschatological program. In addition, the history of Old Testament Israel and Judah is littered with false prophets and false gods. Clearly, this is not the testimony to messianism that we are looking for. If, on the other hand, we are searching for the understanding of "ancient Israel" during the final stages of the canonical development of the Old Testament, then the data from Qumran and the understanding of first-century A.D. Judaism (as reflected in the New Testament and in Jewish writings of this era) would provide some of our most relevant material. It is important in our study of Old Testament messianism that we not lapse back into some type of history-of-religions approach, merely tracing the religious thought of the people without any concern for the actual voice of God on the matter. Block does distinguish his methodology from the history-of-religions approach, but in so doing he rephrases his question from "What did the *Israelites* of the Old Testament think?" to "How did the *writers* (and original readers) of the Old Testament perceive the messiah?" Thus, he attempts to anchor his approach in authorial intent. I like his second question better than his first, but it is a very different question, and it opens up a complex issue. Why should we assume that the original readers understood the text in the same way that the writer intended it? The message of Jeremiah is a good case in point. Also, if we focus on the writer, does the word "writer" refer to both the human and the divine authors? And is the divine author communicating only to the immediate audience? Can the Hebrews in Jerusalem during the Babylonian siege grasp the meaning of Jeremiah's new covenant better than the community at Qumran or the Christians in the first century? Likewise, if the New Testament interprets an Old Testament text as messianic, should we include this in our reconstruction of the messianic picture? Block perhaps is a little inconsistent on this issue. Sometimes he seems to be pushing for an "Old Testament only" concept of messianism, one in which it is not valid to use New Testament or even intertestamental interpretation of Old Testament texts. Yet at other times he drifts over into the New Testament, using New Testament citations, for example, in attempting to prove the messianic centrality of Isa. 53 or in connecting Jesus to the good shepherd of Ezek. 34. This is a critical issue, because if we can bring early Christian interpretation or Jewish intertestamental interpretation of messianic texts into the discussion—and I believe we should—then several of Block's central arguments lose much of their convincing appeal.

The Term "Messiah"

I appreciated Block's discussion of the Hebrew term *māšîaḥ* ("messiah"). His data are a good reminder that biblical concepts usually are too broad and complex to be reduced to simple word studies or to investigations based on usage of one word only. For example, merely analyzing the usages of *ekklēsia* cannot adequately cover the biblical concept of church. Silva addresses this problem in his book *Biblical Words and Their Meaning*. Words and concepts, Silva writes, are separate entities. "Word-bound" approaches to what really are concept studies can lead us astray.[1] I suggest that the concept of messianism in the Old Testament cannot adequately be described merely by looking at the verses that use the word "anointed" or "anointed one," and that the use of this

1. Moisés Silva, *Biblical Words and Their Meaning: An Introduction to Lexical Semantics*, rev. ed. (Grand Rapids: Zondervan, 1994), 26–28. Duvall and Hays call this "Word Study Fallacy #6—The Word Concept Fallacy." See J. Scott Duvall and J. Daniel Hays, *Grasping God's Word: A Hands-On Approach to Reading, Interpreting, and Applying the Bible* (Grand Rapids: Zondervan, 2001).

word is not the determining factor in whether or not a text is messianic. The image of the messiah and the idea of messianism comprise a broad concept that far outreaches the few instances where the term "anointed" is used. It is the concept that we are seeking to define, not merely one particular Hebrew word.

Christ as Prophet

Block argues that the concept of messiah as eschatological prophet is not present in the Old Testament and would not have been understood in this manner by Old Testament audiences. However, he does then acknowledge that this view was prevalent among the Jews of Palestine both before and during the time of Christ. He then makes the puzzling statement that "Jesus seems to have gone out of his way to distance himself from such expectations." However, as I hope to show below, the writers of the New Testament appear to anchor the picture of Christ quite firmly in this very image, that of eschatological prophet.

Block himself cites quite a few instances where the term "prophet" is used of Jesus in the New Testament, but he argues that these texts do not have messianic connotations. I tend to disagree, noting that many encounters of Jesus with the Jews in the Gospels where the term "prophet" is used are permeated with messianic connotations. Consider John 6:14–15, for example. Jesus has just fed the crowd of five thousand. The text reads, "After the people saw the miraculous sign that Jesus did, they began to say, 'Surely this is the prophet who is to come into the world.' Jesus, knowing that they intended to come and make him king by force, withdrew again into the hills by himself." The reference to the "prophet who is to come" certainly is a reference to Deut. 18, and the immediate connection to "king" in the very next verse definitely implies a messianic understanding.[2] Texts such as this, along with the evidence from Qumran, appear to indicate that many people in first-century Palestinian Judaism, at least, connected the image of "the prophet" with the image of king in their messianic concept.

Perhaps more to the point, however, is examining what the author of the Gospel was trying to say in this episode. Beasley-Murray, for exam-

---

2. Another good example is Luke 13:31–34. In this text, Jesus refers to himself as a prophet who will suffer a prophet's fate. See Ben Witherington III, *Jesus the Seer: The Progress of Prophecy* (Peabody, Mass.: Hendrickson, 1999), 333. There is a strong case for connecting this reference back to the Servant Songs of Isaiah. If this connection is correct, then, of course, this text also refers to Jesus as a messianic prophet. See further discussion of this text below.

ple, sees considerable significance in this citation in regard to John's meaning for the feeding of the multitude in John 6:1–17. He writes, "The statement as to the nearness of the Passover (v. 4), the identification of Jesus as the prophet who should come (cf. Deut. 18:15), and the discussion on the bread from heaven within the discourse (vv. 31–33) combine to indicate that the feeding miracle is understood as falling within the fulfillment of the hope of the second Exodus."[3] Thus, if Beasley-Murray is correct, it is John, and not just the people, who is connecting Jesus with "the prophet who is to come," referring to Deut. 18.[4]

Indeed, one of the critical scriptural texts on this issue is Deut. 18:18–19, which reads, "I will raise up for them a prophet like you from among their own people; I will put my words in his mouth, and he will tell them everything I command him. Anyone who does not listen to my words that the prophet speaks in my name, I myself will call to account." Admittedly, taken by itself in the context of Deuteronomy, the messianic connection of this passage perhaps is not at all clear. However, the Book of Acts will make a very strong and clear connection between this text and Jesus as the Messiah, and this identification, in my opinion, strikes a serious blow at Block's position. Not only did the Jews of the first-century A.D. interpret Deut. 18 as messianic, but also the early church did likewise, proclaiming Jesus as the fulfillment of that messianic prophecy.

Deuteronomy 18:18–19 is cited twice in Acts, once by Peter in Acts 3:22–23 and once by Stephen in Acts 7:37. Peter's use of the text in Acts 3 is particularly revealing. Block argues that Peter cites this text merely to demonstrate that Jesus the Messiah represents the fulfillment of the predictions of the prophets. A close analysis of the text, however, points to the strong probability that Peter is doing much more than that with his citation of Deut. 18. Johnson, for example, writes,

> This citation serves the double function of establishing with absolute clarity the connection between the resurrected Jesus and the "prophet like Moses" whom God promised to "raise up," and of serving as a programmatic prophecy for the next section of the narrative: depending on their response to this "raised prophet" who challenges them

3. George Beasley-Murray, *John*, WBC 36 (Waco: Word, 1987), 88. Carson adds, "Against some contemporary commentators, it is important to note that John does not argue that the people are wrong in this judgment, but only in their estimate of its significance" (D. A. Carson, *The Gospel according to John*, PNTC [Leicester, England: InterVarsity; Grand Rapids: Eerdmans, 1991], 271).

4. For detailed discussion of the connection between Moses and Jesus in the Gospel of John, see T. F. Glasson, *Moses in the Fourth Gospel*, SBT 40 (Naperville, Ill.: Allenson, 1963); Wayne A. Meeks, *The Prophet-King: Moses Traditions and the Johannine Christology*, NovTSup 14 (Leiden: Brill, 1967).

through the deeds and words of the apostles will the fate of the people be decided.[5]

Johnson stresses the importance of Jesus' prophetic role not only in this text, but also throughout the theology of Luke. Witherington concurs, spending numerous pages tracing the multitude of texts in Luke in which the prophetic role of Jesus is disclosed.[6]

Stephen also cites Deut. 18:15 in Acts 7:37. This citation strikes at two of Block's arguments. He has argued that the messianic picture did not include the prophet image, and he also has suggested that Moses was not a messianic figure. Johnson, however, regards the parallelism between Jesus and Moses as a critical aspect of the prophetic structure of the Book of Acts. "Jesus," Johnson writes, "is portrayed as the prophet like Moses."[7] Tannehill takes a similar view: "In case any should miss the connection between Moses and Jesus, Stephen cites the Scripture about the coming prophet like Moses (7:37) which had already been applied to Jesus in 3:22."[8] Furthermore, Johnson notes that Stephen's speech regarding Moses is structured so as to "correspond precisely with the story of Jesus as Luke himself tells it." Johnson underscores the importance of this observation, adding, "Luke uses the prophetic pattern established by his reading of the Moses story to structure his entire two-volume work."[9] I am particularly intrigued by Johnson's suggestion that this understanding of Moses as a messianic forerunner connects Luke and Acts and perhaps is the backdrop for understanding Luke 24:27: "And beginning with Moses and the prophets, he explained to them what was said in all the scriptures concerning himself."[10]

5. Luke Timothy Johnson, *The Acts of the Apostles*, SP 5 (Collegeville, Minn.: Liturgical Press, 1992), 74. Bruce draws a similar conclusion: "From the earliest days of the apostolic preaching, it appears, this text from Deuteronomy was invoked as a Mosaic prediction of Jesus" (F. F. Bruce, *The Book of the Acts*, rev. ed., NICNT [Grand Rapids: Eerdmans, 1988], 86–87). Others who interpret this text in a similar fashion, connecting Jesus with the prophet of Deut. 18, include Witherington, *Jesus the Seer*, 332; Ernst Haenchen, *The Acts of the Apostles* (Oxford: Blackwell, 1971), 209; Robert C. Tannehill, *The Narrative Unity of Luke-Acts: A Literary Interpretation*, vol. 2 (Minneapolis: Fortress, 1990), 57; and John Polhill, *Acts*, NAC 26 (Nashville: Broadman, 1992), 135–36.

6. Witherington, *Jesus the Seer*, 333–38.

7. Johnson, *The Acts of the Apostles*, 12–14.

8. Tannehill, *The Narrative Unity of Luke-Acts*, 91–92. Bruce (*The Book of the Acts*, 142) states that Stephen's speech presents Moses as a "forerunner" of the messiah. Nor is this understanding limited to New Testament scholars. In his commentary on Deuteronomy, Cragie notes that Deut. 18:15–22 finds its prophetic fulfillment in Jesus (and he cites Acts 3:22–23). Cragie also points to the similarities between Jesus and Moses, and concludes that there is a prophetic aspect in this similarity. See Peter C. Cragie, *The Book of Deuteronomy*, NICOT (Grand Rapids: Eerdmans, 1976), 263.

9. Johnson, *The Acts of the Apostles*, 13.

10. Ibid.

Block also cites Isa. 61:1–3. As mentioned above, I do not think that just because this text uses the word "anointed," it carries any more weight than other messianic texts. So I do not see Isa. 61 as any more pertinent than, say, the Servant Songs. However, I am puzzled by Block's argument that this text predicts a royal personage rather than a prophetic one. Note that one of the central features of this text is that the individual is called to make proclamation. Such a ministry of proclamation certainly is a prophetic one. Indeed, this text actually resembles a prophetic call, and yet it also seems to reach back and connect to the Servant Songs. As Childs points out, this passage actually presents a "servant-prophet," a blending of the two concepts.[11]

Block also argues that the Isa. 61 text refers to a Davidic king rather than a prophetic figure, because prophets do not have authority to free captives and prisoners and proclaim the year of liberation (61:1). However, are the prophets not spokespersons for Yahweh? Do they not speak with the authority of Yahweh as they proclaim his plan for the present and future? In his call, Jeremiah is given authority over nations and kingdoms—to uproot and tear down, to destroy and overthrow, to build and to plant (Jer. 1:10). Is the proclamation of liberty for the captives above and beyond Jeremiah's call? Furthermore, there is no indication in the David narratives of David's involvement in the release of any captives. So there does not seem to be any foreshadowing or typological elements in David's life that connect to this concept. There is, on the other hand, one, and only one, central liberator of the captives in the Old Testament, and it is not David, but Moses.[12]

However, I do agree with Block that Moses is not the main figure behind Isaiah's Servant Songs. On the other hand, I find his proposition that David is the servant, likewise, difficult to substantiate. For example, consider the second Servant Song, Isa. 49:1–6. Verse 1 states, "Before I was born, the Lord called me." Verse 5 adds a reference to being formed in the womb. This terminology is very similar to the terminology used in the call of Jeremiah. Thus, Childs concludes that Isa.

11. Brevard Childs, *Isaiah*, OTL (Louisville: Westminster John Knox, 2001), 504. It may be mere coincidence, but I find it interesting that it is precisely right after quoting this passage in the synagogue that Jesus states, "No prophet is accepted in his hometown" (Luke 4:24).

12. The exodus event casts a very long shadow all across the Old Testament because the exodus is the premier Old Testament paradigm of deliverance. As the Old Testament looks to deliverance in the future, the exodus often forms the referential point of beginning. Intertextual connections with the exodus are going to find their way into almost all Old Testament discussions of the deliverance motif.

49:1–6 is "about the office of a prophet" and that "the imagery of the call is prophetic and reminiscent of Jeremiah's call."[13]

Isaiah 49:2 goes on to state, "He made my mouth like a sharpened sword." This appears to be a reference to the prophetic vocation of proclamation of the word of Yahweh. As Oswalt observes,

> He will accomplish God's will not by military force but by a revelation of God's word. The power of God's word had been demonstrated again and again by the prophets. It was the power to break down and build up. As the preeminent prophet, the Messiah would hold that power in the fullest and purest manner.[14]

Note the similarity between this text and Jer. 1:9, where as part of Jeremiah's prophetic call, Yahweh states, "I have put my words in your mouth."[15] Also highly significant is the observation that this same phrase occurs in Deut. 18:17, which reads, "I will put my words in his mouth." Isaiah 49:2, therefore, is tightly connected to the terminology of prophetic call and also linked to Deut. 18. The image painted here is not one of a coming king, but of a servant who comes in a manner similar to the prophets.

Block also cites the fourth Servant Song, Isa. 52:13–53:12, as part of his argument, stating that "the designation of the subject of this song as the servant of Yahweh . . . points in the direction of David." This also is a claim that puzzles me. Indeed, there are aspects of the fourth Servant Song that seem specifically to differentiate between the servant and Davidic imagery. In 53:2, the prophet writes, "He had no beauty or majesty to attract us to him, nothing in his appearance that we should desire him." The point of this text is that the servant does not look like a king.[16] Note that the Hebrew terms in 53:2 that are translated "beauty" and "appearance" are both used specifically of David in 1 Sam. 16:12, 18. The text is stressing that the servant does not look like David. Oswalt, Westermann, and North all underscore the specific contrast between the servant and David that this verse presents.[17] One of the roles

13. Childs, *Isaiah*, 383. Drawing the same conclusion are John N. Oswalt, *The Book of Isaiah: Chapters 40–66*, NICOT (Grand Rapids: Eerdmans, 1998), 289; and Claus Westermann, *Isaiah 40–66*, OTL (Philadelphia: Westminster, 1969), 207.

14. Oswalt, *The Book of Isaiah*, 290.

15. Childs (*Isaiah*, 383) also notes this connection.

16. Oswalt (*The Book of Isaiah*, 382) notes that usually "deliverers are dominating, forceful, attractive people, who by their personal magnetism draw people to themselves and convince people to do what they want them to do." The individual described in the fourth Servant Song is quite different from this.

17. Oswalt, *The Book of Isaiah*, 382; Westermann, *Isaiah 40–66*, 261; Christopher R. North, *The Second Isaiah: Introduction, Translation, and Commentary* (Oxford: Clarendon, 1964), 237.

of this Servant Song appears to be to balance the royal aspects of the messianic picture with an image of an unkingly, lowly, unimposing, suffering servant.

Block also cites John Walton's description of a substitute king as a background for understanding and identifying the suffering servant in Isaiah. I found this discussion fascinating, and I was intrigued by the possibility that this custom may provide some helpful background for understanding the suffering servant motif in Isaiah. What I fail to grasp is how this custom supports a royal identification of the servant. After all, in the Mesopotamian ritual, it is not the king that dies, but rather, a commoner. To argue that this custom supports a royal identification of the suffering servant seems to stretch the evidence quite a bit.

I'm also not convinced that John 10 somehow connects David to Isa. 53, but perhaps I have misunderstood the complexity of Block's argument. I agree with him in seeing a direct connection between Jesus' claim to be the good shepherd and the prophecy of a coming Davidic shepherd in Ezek. 34. I also would add to that a direct connection to the shepherd in Jer. 23:16, which also is tied to David, although "shepherds" in Jeremiah is plural. Jesus claims to be the shepherd who lays down his life, implying that he will suffer. Therefore, Block argues, Jesus is combining the shepherd motif with the suffering motif of Isa. 53. This is possible but not at all clear. However, Block loses me on the next step. He argues that because Jesus combines the shepherd motif of Ezekiel with the suffering motif of Isaiah, the suffering servant in Isaiah must refer to David. I think that this perhaps is reading backward, and I am cautious of a methodology that states that just because two images are blended together, those two images must be identical in reference.

In contrast to the fuzzy connection in John 10 between David and the suffering servant, the connection in Luke 13:31–34 seems to be a little clearer. Jesus states that he must move on toward Jerusalem because "no prophet can die outside Jerusalem." He then laments Jerusalem's habit of killing the prophets. Witherington notes that in this text Jesus calls himself a prophet who will suffer a prophet's fate—death in Jerusalem.[18] Surely, this is as clear an allusion to the suffering servant as that in John 10. This connection, however, focuses on Jesus as prophet and contains no mention of David.

It perhaps is possible to establish a connection between Isaiah's suffering servant and David via the lament psalms. To me, this is the avenue with the most potential for supporting Block's thesis. Childs makes this suggestion and cites Ps. 22:6–7 as an example. But Childs quickly notes that the prophetic office also is described with the suffering id-

18. Witherington, *Jesus the Seer*, 333.

iom, especially within the Book of Jeremiah. Commenting on Isa. 53, Childs writes, "Much like Jeremiah, the description of prophetic suffering depicts a calling, even an office, into which a servant of God has been summoned."[19]

So, before I move on, let me summarize what I have argued concerning the prophetic office dimension of the messianic promise. The Book of Acts makes a very clear statement that Jesus is the coming prophet of Deut. 18. Isaiah 49:1-2 connects the servant with the prophetic call and with the prophetic ministry of proclaiming the word of Yahweh. Isaiah 52:13-53:12 presents a servant who is unsightly and unroyal in appearance. As the other prophets suffered, so he too will suffer, and even more so. Isaiah 61:1-3 also presents the "anointed one" in a ministry of prophetic proclamation. The royal connotations in these texts are extremely vague, if present at all.

Christ as Priest

Block's challenge to the traditional view of Christ as a great high priest is more complicated than his challenge to the prophetic image. Likewise, my response is more complicated because I agree with Block to some extent. So my comments will be a mixture of rebuttal and affirmation.

Block's statement that there is no obvious foreshadowing of the cross in the sacrifices is quite thought provoking. I wonder what John the Baptist meant in John 1:29 when he proclaimed, "Behold the lamb of God!" Although this verse is controversial and numerous interpretive options have been suggested, at least a few scholars (Ridderbos, Barrett, Morris) have suggested that John is making an explicit reference to some type of fulfillment of the sacrificial system as a whole.[20] This would imply that John the Baptist, at least, saw some foreshadowing of Jesus in the sacrificial system. However, this observation does not really affect Block's actual argument.

I agree in general with Block's distinction between the priesthood of Aaron/Zadok and the priestly activities of the king. However, I suspect that the line was not as clear as Block proposes. He notes that in keeping with the custom of the ancient Near East, the Davidic monarchs served as patrons of the cult, but, he argues, they never assumed high priestly

19. Childs, *Isaiah*, 414.

20. Herman N. Ridderbos, *The Gospel according to John: A Theological Commentary*, trans. John Vriend (Grand Rapids: Eerdmans, 1997), 73; C. K. Barrett, *The Gospel according to St. John*, 2d ed. (Philadelphia: Westminster, 1978), 177; Leon Morris, *The Gospel according to John*, NICNT (Grand Rapids: Eerdmans, 1971), 147–48.

roles. However, many monarchs of the ancient Near East did participate in the cult to a degree that certainly exceeded the term "patron."
Oppenheim, for example, points out that the Assyrian kings often functioned as high priests.[21] Indeed, this high priestly role of the kings is
mentioned frequently in the Assyrian annals.[22] So the distinction between royal and priestly functions, at least in ancient Mesopotamia, was
not at all clear. Thus, Block's statement that the biblical narratives never
confuse or conflate priestly and royal offices perhaps is overstated.
David is frequently involved in priestlike activities, and some of these
also seem to go beyond mere royal patronage. For example, in commenting on Ps. 110, Kraus writes,

> Of the priestly activity of David and of his descendants we hear in 2 Sam.
> 6:14, 18; 24:17; 1 Kings 8:14, 56. The king wears priestly vestments
> (2 Sam. 6:14), blesses the people, intercedes for the cultic assembly in
> prayer, and presides over the rites. Yes, he even presents the offering
> (1 Sam. 13:9; 2 Sam. 6:13, 17), draws near to God like the high priest (Jer.
> 30:21), and also, in the conceptions of Ezekiel concerning the "prince," he
> stands in the midst of the worship (Ezek. 44:3; 14:16ff; 22ff; 46:2ff).[23]

In Ps. 110, David clearly is connected to the priesthood, although it is
the priesthood of Melchizedek rather than the priesthood of Aaron or
Zadok.[24] Block states, "Melchizedek represents the pre-Israelite form of
monarchy, in which royal and priestly offices were combined and held
by the same person." Yet it perhaps is not entirely convincing to argue
that David's priestly activities are completely different from those of the
Aaronic priesthood and mirror instead the old priest-king pattern of pa-
triarchal Israel. Instead, it appears that David blurs the image of priest
and king together, as did many kings in the region. Thus, when a Davidic messianic figure begins to emerge in Scripture, it is no surprise
that he is pictured as both priest and king.

In addition, to say that David's type of priesthood is different from
the Aaronic/Zadokite priesthood does not eliminate the basic image of
one who is both priest and king. Perhaps, as Block suggests, the image

21. A. Leo Oppenheim, *Ancient Mesopotamia: Portrait of a Dead Civilization*, rev. ed.
(Chicago: University of Chicago Press, 1977), 99.

22. Daniel David Luckenbill, ed., *Ancient Records of Assyria and Babylonia*, 2 vols.
(Chicago: University of Chicago Press, 1926–27). Note the references to the priestly activ-
ities of Adad-nirari II (I:357), Assurnasirpal (I:532), Shalmaneser (I:616), and Sargon
(II:117).

23. Hans-Joachim Kraus, *Psalms 60–150*, trans. Hilton C. Oswald (Minneapolis: Augsburg, 1989), 351.

24. See Eugene Merrill, "Royal Priesthood: An Old Testament Motif," *BSac* 150 (January–March 1993): 50–61.

of king is stronger than the image of priest, but that fact does not erase the priestly image nor does it subsume the priestly image completely under the narrow category of monarchy. Melchizedek is identified as a king in Gen. 14:18, but he also is identified as a priest in the same verse. His priestly activity is not presupposed by his office of kingship; it is specifically mentioned. His role in blessing Abraham and receiving a tenth of Abraham's recovered possessions clearly reflects his role as priest, and not as king. Likewise, in David's life, the two elements are both there. He is a king who often acts like a priest, not just a mere patron of the cult.

Block argues that it is doubtful whether the ancient Israelites ever viewed the high priest as a messianic figure. At first glance, I would tend to concur with Block—one certainly does not get any sense of messianism reading through Leviticus. On the other hand, in intertestamental Judaism, one of the central eschatological figures was a high priest, and we have to assume that they developed this image from their Scriptures. Phinehas the priest is seen as an eschatological leader in Sirach and in Jubilees. The Qumran texts reveal numerous references to a future high priest. Indeed, this future high priest is a central eschatological figure in much of the Qumran literature.[25] So certainly, at least by the time of the Qumran texts there were some "ancient Israelites" who viewed the high priest as messianic. Of course, this does not establish that this was a valid view or that this was the view that the biblical authors intended. But it does establish that some "ancient Israelites," at least those during the time of the Qumran texts, connected the priesthood with the eschatological messianic figure.

Finally, I do not think that Block has addressed adequately the theme of Christ as high priest in the Book of Hebrews. Block argues that Hebrews uses the sacrifice and priesthood image in regard to Christ in a type/antitype sense rather than a prophecy/fulfillment sense. Thus, the tabernacle looks toward heavenly realities "upward" rather than prophetic realities on earth "forward," and, Block suggests, the author of Hebrews is doing the same with the priesthood of Christ. However, is the image of Christ in heaven to be totally differentiated from the image of Christ on earth? The priesthood of Jesus Christ is a central theme of Hebrews, and Old Testament texts, particularly from Psalms and from the Pentateuch, are cited throughout. The Davidic connection definitely is present, bringing the imagery down to earth, and Jesus likewise is connected to the Melchizedekian priesthood via David and Ps. 110. Furthermore, the picture of Jesus as priest throughout the book clearly is not as a royal patron of the cult, but as the traditional Israelite high

25. Marinus de Jonge, "Messiah," *ABD* 4:781–83.

priest. In fact, Jesus is referred to as "the high priest" (*archiereus*) fifteen times.

Conclusions

Early in his paper, Block makes a statement that I affirm. He states that the messianic view cannot be limited to one single view. This certainly is true. Indeed, the picture of the messiah that emerges in the Old Testament is multifaceted and multihued. However, in contrast to this statement affirming a complex, multihued picture of the messiah, Block then attempts to subsume all of the Old Testament messianic images under the royal Davidic image, thus ignoring the multifaceted and multihued concept.

The Old Testament writers who produced the messianic image did not write modern word studies, nor did they produce crystal-clear photographs. Rather, they painted complex, multifaceted images of the one who was to come. Their word images resemble expressionist paintings: the main image is clear, but the boundaries are blurry and a bit surreal. Three of the main images—and probably there are more than three— present the coming one as prophet, priest, and king. Sometimes these images are presented separately, and sometimes they are combined or merged together—a priest-king like David, a prophet-priest-deliverer like Moses.

In conclusion, I obviously have some reservations about Block's central thesis, and I would suggest to the contrary that the Old Testament does portray the coming messianic figure as prophet, priest, and king. However, I thank Dan Block for a fine, thought-provoking paper. To me, the strength of the paper is the identification of the royal Davidic theme as the dominant messianic theme in the Old Testament. Block clearly has established this, and I find his arguments helpful. His paper also serves to challenge our traditional thinking. He has sent us back to the text with questions and doubts in search of biblical answers. I like Dan Block's model of scholarship: he is not afraid to challenge tradition if he believes that he has scriptural evidence. This is healthy for Evangelicalism and it should be encouraged.

THREE

New Lenses to Establish Messiah's Identity?

A Response to Daniel I. Block

M. Daniel Carroll R.

I must confess that when I was asked to respond to Dan Block's paper, I was initially a bit apprehensive. The second paragraph of his essay lists a numbered series of relevant questions for consideration for a fuller reflection on messiah in the Old Testament. Mercifully, Dr. Block narrows his focus to one particular aim: "The purpose of this paper is to explore the Old Testament portrayal of the messiah, with the hope of coming to a realistic understanding of how the ancient Israelites viewed this intriguing figure." Toward this end, he subdivides his presentation into five principal parts: a discussion of the term "the anointed one," and the messiah as prophet, priest, a royal Davidic figure, and the suffering servant.

Block's paper, "My Servant David," can serve as a helpful resource. In my mind, it makes at least three positive contributions. To begin with, in the first major section ("The Messiah as the Anointed One"), Block provides a number of interesting lexical details through his word study on the verb *māšaḥ* and the noun *māšîaḥ*. From this overview Block concludes that the designation "the anointed one" did not necessarily—indeed, did not very commonly—carry eschatological connotations. Second, I very much appreciate the attention given to particular texts, not only in the sense of listing the verses that might buttress his argument, but also in terms of expositing in some detail relevant passages (Deut. 18:15–22 and Isa. 53 and 61 are cases in point). Third, Block provides many of his readers with what is, more than likely, new information that can illumine key passages for Christian faith. In this vein, I am thinking explicitly of his reporting of John Walton's work on the Mesopotamian "ritual of the substitute king" and its possible significance for Isa. 53.[1]

Obviously, there is too much information in Block's essay and too little space here to respond to each major point in any detail. Instead, I will limit my comments to three issues, each of which in one way or another concerns hermeneutical considerations of how to read and interpret Old Testament texts. Thus, ultimately, my observations center on matters of method. The first two of my three points deal with Block's section "The Messiah as Prophet" and the textual data found there; the final one puts forth a different perspective on how one might appreciate and even assimilate messianic passages in a new light and actually tries to point in a direction of reflection beyond what Block propounds in his paper.[2]

Considerations for Reading Texts

1. *One should not limit what might be relevant to a few expressly predictive passages or strict lexical data to define what "ancient Israelites" believed about messiah.* In his discussion of "The Messiah as Prophet," Block is suspicious of the notion that Jesus might have been understood as some sort of eschatological prophet. In his words,

> On the basis of key Qumran texts and scattered references in the intertestamental literature, scholars have argued that at the turn of the ages many Jews of Palestine anticipated the appearance of an anointed eschatological prophet whom heaven and earth would obey. Evidence for this expectation may be drawn from the New Testament Gospels as well; Jesus seems to have gone out of his way to distance himself from such expectations.

1. John Walton, "The Imagery of the Substitute King Ritual in Isaiah's Fourth Song," a paper read at the annual meeting of the Society of Biblical Literature in Nashville, November 2000. This information also is mentioned in John Walton, Victor H. Matthews, and Mark Chavalas, *The IVP Bible Background Commentary: Old Testament* (Downers Grove, Ill.: InterVarsity, 2000), 633.

2. Since this is simply a response, I make no attempt to provide exhaustive documentation in the footnotes. The notes are designed to be suggestive and to help direct the interested reader to some relevant sources.

He goes on to say,

> If there is an eschatological prophet in the Gospels, it is not Jesus but
> John the Baptist, who appears on the scene to herald the arrival of the
> messiah in fulfillment of Mal. 3:1 and 4:5. In reality, Jesus perceived him-
> self as one greater than a prophet, whose arrival was announced by Yah-
> weh's prophetic messenger.

Block also argues that no prophet in the Old Testament is called "the
anointed one," and then he turns to two passages (Isa. 61:1–3; Deut.
18:15–22) and offers interpretations that would discount any prediction
of a messianic prophet. He closes his discussion with these words:

> A generic gulf exists between the prophetic institution and the messiah.
> And with this observation we return to the central point of this paper.
> With hindsight we do indeed see analogical connections between the min-
> istry of Jesus and the work of the prophets. However, there is no evidence
> within the Old Testament itself that anyone in ancient Israel understood
> the office of prophet typologically, that is, as foreshadowing "a future fig-
> ure who will play an authoritative role in the end time."

I sense several problematic issues in this way of trying to comprehend
"how the ancient Israelites viewed this intriguing figure." First, by Block's
own admission, the notion of anointing (whether in relation to the verb or
the noun, "the anointed one") does not carry heavy eschatological weight
in the Old Testament. Consequently, to postulate that legitimate messianic
hopes should be based on such a lexical connection is not a strong argument. In fact, it is clear from intertestamental literature that Jewish messianic texts often do not even utilize the term *māšîaḥ*. The term "messiah,"
therefore, should be conceived more broadly—that is, conceptually as a
coming eschatological figure. In intertestamental Judaism there were several messianic paradigms, which served to present a very complex collage
of expectations. One of these figures was that of a prophet, but under this
rubric there were several combinations of portraits.[3]

Second, recent studies by several New Testament scholars, such as
Richard Horsley, Robert Webb, John Meier, N. T. Wright, and Scot
McKnight (even though within different historical reconstructions),

3. Note, for example, Howard M. Teeple, *The Mosaic Eschatological Prophet*, JBLMS
10 (Philadelphia: Society of Biblical Literature, 1957); John J. Collins, *The Scepter and the
Star: The Messiahs of the Dead Sea Scrolls and Other Ancient Literature*, Anchor Bible Reference Library (New York: Doubleday, 1995); Mark Adam Elliott, *The Survivors of Israel:
A Reconsideration of the Theology of Pre-Christian Judaism* (Grand Rapids: Eerdmans,
2000), 433–514. Note Collins's caution about limiting the discussion of messiah to the Hebrew term *māšîaḥ* (*The Scepter and the Star*, 11–12).

have brought to light the popular expectations for prophets sent from God in the time of Jesus.[4] Each of these scholars develops his own taxonomy for these individuals, but all highlight their existence and widespread impact. The evidence from other sources and from the New Testament itself points to the fact that there was some level of expectation of the inauguration of the eschatological age of national blessing at that time through the work, at least in part, of an/the eschatological prophet. It also seems clear that on the basis of his words and actions, Jesus was viewed by many of his listeners as fulfilling this role. The data becomes more telling against Block's thesis if it can be shown that Jesus did in fact understand and present himself as that prophet, and research today (as the cited scholars attest) does point precisely in that direction.

What is more, it is apparent that one of the intentional rhetorical-theological strategies of the Gospel writers was to present Jesus as the eschatological prophet. The New Testament writers, even as others within the Jewish tradition had done, developed this concept through connections with Deut. 18:15. In their view, this Pentateuchal passage pointed forward to a future person who would be like (and even greater than) Moses. This makes Block's attempt to explain away any possibility that this is claimed to have been fulfilled in Jesus in Acts 3:22–26 and 7:35–38 somewhat forced. Recent studies have demonstrated that Jesus is that eschatological prophet, for example, not only in these two pericopes in Acts, but also within the broader sweep of Luke-Acts.[5]

These assertions by themselves do not necessarily affect Block's central contention that later views concerning messiah and the messianic age do not reflect what "ancient Israelites" in the days of the classical prophets believed. Even if his understanding of how Jesus and other messiah figures were perceived is shown to be in need of revision (and I think

4. Richard A. Horsley with John S. Hanson, *Bandits, Prophets, and Messiahs: Popular Movements at the Time of Jesus* (New York: HarperCollins, 1985); Robert L. Webb, *John the Baptizer and Prophet: A Socio-Historical Study*, JSNTSup 62 (Sheffield: JSOT Press, 1991); John P. Meier, *A Marginal Jew: Rethinking the Historical Jesus*, 3 vols. (New York: Doubleday, 1991–2001); N. T. Wright, *Jesus and the Victory of God*, vol. 2 of *Christian Origins and the Question of God* (Minneapolis: Fortress, 1996); Scot McKnight, *A New Vision for Israel: The Teachings of Jesus in National Context* (Grand Rapids: Eerdmans, 1999); idem, "Jesus and Prophetic Actions," *BBR* 10, no. 2 (2000): 197–232.

5. David L. Tiede, *Prophecy and History in Luke-Acts* (Philadelphia: Fortress, 1980); Darrell L. Bock, *Proclamation from Prophecy and Pattern: Lucan Old Testament Christology*, JSOTSup 12 (Sheffield: JSOT Press, 1987); David P. Moessner, *The Lord of the Banquet: The Literary and Theological Significance of the Lukan Travel Narrative* (Minneapolis: Fortress, 1989); I. Howard Marshall, *Luke: Historian and Theologian*, rev. ed. (Grand Rapids: Zondervan, 1989), 125–28. For Acts 3:22ff. and 7:9–16, 37, 56, see especially Bock, *Proclamation from Prophecy and Pattern*, 191–94 and 215–25, respectively. Moessner argues that this motif is foundational to understanding the central section of Luke (9:51–19:44).

it is), this point might not alter Block's conviction that these beliefs were subsequent elaborations of those earlier ideas, which today can be gleaned clearly from a specific set of Old Testament passages. Block declares, "Even if Peter and/or Stephen viewed Jesus as a messianic prophet 'like Moses,' are we thereby authorized to read their use of Deut. 18:15 back into the original context?"[6] His answer, of course, would be no.

I disagree, however, with this sort of notion of the nature of how the Old Testament was understood in that more distant past. This leads me to a third, and more important, observation. Perhaps it is now no longer enough to remain within the parameters of more or less classical exegetical approaches in order to establish the textual evidence for a prophetic messiah—that is, by investigating if there are any actual predictions of such a person in the Old Testament in passages that we think can be legitimately taken as such and interpreted as we think they should be. What we find is that whatever *we* might deem to be proper readings of the Old Testament, the Jews of the intertestamental period and the first century believed that they were finding references and descriptions of figures related to the eschatological age that might not come so readily to our minds. For example, Scot McKnight's recent contribution to the *Bulletin for Biblical Research* points out that the actions of some of those first-century prophets were presented as preeminently Mosaic.[7] In other words, the expectations and the fund of texts for the profile of a prophet apparently were a bit different from what we might glean from a word study or from specific predictions. This recognition might nudge us to look at Deut. 18:15–22 again. Perhaps Block is correct in pronouncing that a prediction of a messianic prophet is not to be found in these verses (although, of course, this is a matter of debate). Nevertheless, the passage did establish a standard for the future, "final prophet." These lines allow that individual to be Mosaic, even if they are not a direct prediction of his coming. The final prophet becomes one more—the last—in the line of a succession of prophets "like me." Other elements (such as liberation from the empire, the exodus imagery, the time in the desert, the signs, etc.) fill out the Mosaic flavor of that future, eschatological prophet.

My hermeneutical point is this: any effort to get at what "ancient Israelites" believed about messiah must consider a broad range of evidence beyond our choice of predictive passages and lexical studies and our kind of interpretive practices. The fact that later Judaism was reading its Bible in a different way than some of us do might be an indicator that "ancient Is-

6. Block's admission about Peter and Stephen might reflect an awareness that his exegesis of the two Acts passages and his attempt to minimize the issue of the eschatological prophet are rather tenuous.

7. McKnight, "Jesus and Prophetic Actions."

raelites" did likewise.[8] Let us consider the possibility that intertestamental and first-century Judaism might have had some sort of interpretive connections to their forebears. This is one of Michael Fishbane's contentions, for example, in his postulation of what he labels "inner biblical exegesis."[9] To mention Fishbane at this point is not to endorse all of his thesis or his views of particular texts. The purpose here is to underscore that there might very well be much more going on within and between Old Testament texts in terms of interpretive practices of the "ancient Israelites" than we hitherto have imagined. Of course there were developments in the conceptualization over time concerning the messiah, but there also at the same time would have been some continuity with earlier views and interpretations. That is, there were levels of continuity, both methodologically and conceptually. Can we be as confident as Block is, then, in saying that we can know with settled certainty what "ancient Israelites" believed and how they read their Scripture, on the basis of our exegetical approaches?

Those of us who work in the field of Old Testament studies have learned a similar lesson in the last few years in regard to the nature of the religion of Israel. New archaeological data concerning the religion of Palestine have enriched and broadened a conception of that cult and set of beliefs that in an earlier era had been defined primarily by certain biblical materials. Today we are beginning to grasp how difficult it is to define the religious world of the "ancient Israelites." The emerging picture of religious practice and convictions is becoming increasingly complex, and various scholars have offered diverse reconstructions.[10] To answer the question "What did 'ancient Israelites' actually believe?" is more difficult than what might have been imagined just a few years ago. I assume that this would apply to reading strategies too. This first major caveat on Block's paper leads me to another hermeneutical point.

8. I am not claiming that Jewish hermeneutical practices remained unchanged and consistent over time. This in and of itself, however, should make one more cautious about being adamant about ancient hermeneutical practices. Nor am I trying to suggest that careful exegesis of Old Testament texts is no longer necessary; this sort of work is indispensable. My point is that we should be more circumspect (and better informed) about the results and implications of this study.

9. Michael Fishbane, *Biblical Interpretation in Ancient Israel* (Oxford: Clarendon, 1985).

10. The last few years have witnessed an explosion of publications in the field. Some helpful recent resources include Othmar Keel and Christoph Uehlinger, *Gods, Goddesses, and Images of God in Ancient Israel* (Minneapolis: Fortress, 1998); Patrick D. Miller, *The Religion of Ancient Israel*, Library of Ancient Israel (London: SPCK; Louisville: Westminster John Knox, 2000); Philip J. King and Lawrence E. Stager, *Life in Biblical Israel*, Library of Ancient Israel (Louisville: Westminster John Knox, 2001), 319–81; Ephraim Stern, *Archaeology of the Land of the Bible*, vol. 2, *The Assyrian, Babylonian, and Persian Periods (732–332 B.C.E.)* (New York: Doubleday, 2001).

2. *One should not restrict theological constructs by prioritizing some data to the exclusion of other information.* As one moves through Block's paper, it appears that part of his strategy is to demonstrate systematically that at the end of the day, messiah should not be regarded as a prophet, a priest, or one like Moses, but instead as a Davidic, royal figure. Once again, I believe that Block unnecessarily oversimplifies things.

Two observations are apropos. First, I do not see that the text requires the elimination of any "tones" and "brush strokes" in its description of the messiah and the eschatological age. Part of the richness of the Old Testament is that messiah can appear in so many different garbs, each providing a piece of the total picture, with none able to capture fully the breadth of his person and work. A particular passage might prioritize one or more of these descriptives, but these and others can be, and are, held in tension simultaneously.

Second, part of the nature of "intertextual" exegesis (if I might place some of what is going on in the text with the reappropriation of other biblical themes, passages, and vocabulary under this rubric) is precisely to develop comparisons and contrasts. That is a major component of how the text works, and this phenomenon should be expected and explored. It is precisely in this kind of details that key theological points are made and highlighted for the trained eye. Multidimensional theology, as it were, is the stuff of much of prophetic theology. The power of the total picture seems to reside in its composite nature, in the association of a plurality of notions and symbols.

Isaiah 61:1-3 can serve as a stellar example. I believe that Block is right to underline the Davidic identity of this figure. He duly notes the anointing (associated primarily with the royal office), the connection of the Spirit with the kingly hope of 11:1-5, and the authority to inaugurate a reign of justice and peace that no prophet could claim.[11] I fear, however, that to limit it to this one category is to ignore other key aspects of the portrait of this person.[12] A careful look at the textual data

11. Hugh Williamson links the anointing to that of Cyrus (Isa. 45:1) in *Variations on a Theme: King, Messiah, and Servant in the Book of Isaiah* (Carlisle: Paternoster, 1998), 176–78. This person, in his mind, would complete what Cyrus had left unfulfilled. If Williamson is correct, his observation could give an interesting, additional twist to the notion that this person is a royal figure.

12. The same is true, I believe, of Block's critique of those who underscore the Mosaic elements of the Servant Songs, whose interpretation he also would limit to a Davidic figure (35–41). Block directs his comments particularly at Gordon P. Hugenberger, "The Servant of the Lord in the 'Servant Songs' of Isaiah: A Second Moses Figure," in *The Lord's Anointed: Interpretation of Old Testament Messianic Texts*, ed. P. E. Satterthwaite, R. S. Hess, and G. J. Wenham (Carlisle: Paternoster; Grand Rapids: Baker, 1995), 105–40. An important recent work that also supports the view that the Servant is a Mosaic fig-

shows that the person is described as a prophetic figure as well: the phrase "Yahweh has sent me" echoes the experiences of other prophets (note, e.g., Exod. 3:14–15; Jer. 1:7; 19:14; Ezek. 2:3–4; 3:5–6; Hag. 1:12), one of Isaiah's contemporaries also claims to be empowered by the Spirit to do his task (Mic. 3:8), and the commission in Isa. 61 has to do preeminently with speaking (seven infinitives that clearly pick up terminology of several announcement passages in chapters 40–55). In addition, several scholars have shown how this passage appears to describe very self-consciously this commission with chapters 6 and 40 in mind.[13] Scholars also recognize that this passage has links to the Servant Songs.[14] In sum, what we have in this passage is what Williamson has called a "composite figure," one who incorporates royal, prophetic, and servant features.

We need to avoid becoming blind and deaf (to use Isaiah-like metaphors) to elements of the belief system of Israel. If my first major point tried to communicate that we can avoid missing the import of texts by incorporating input from other sources and not oversimplifying our concept of the "ancient Israelite," here a complementary and related caution is being put forth. We must become more careful readers of the text and put on new lenses appreciative of and more sensitive to its literary-theological techniques and rich tapestries.

3. *Discussions might consider exploring new perspectives for analyzing the identity and mission of messiah, both in biblical times and today.* My final point actually spins out of the previous one, but here I desire to bring a new element into the discussion. This last part of my response does not deal directly with Block's paper; rather, I want to suggest that his presentation of the servant messiah in Isaiah has missed something important.

---

ure is Klaus Baltzer, *Deutero-Isaiah: A Commentary on Isaiah 40–55*, trans. Margaret Kohl, ed. Peter Machinist (Minneapolis: Fortress, 2001).

13. For example, Grace I. Emmerson, *Isaiah 56–66*, OTG (Sheffield: Sheffield Academic Press, 1992), 75–76; Christopher R. Seitz, "How Is the Prophet Isaiah Present in the Latter Half of the Book? The Logic of Chapters 40–66 within the Book of Isaiah," *JBL* 115, no. 2 (1996): 219–40; Williamson, *Variations on a Theme*, 178–83. Some interpreters, of course, try to identify this figure with a specific person, such as Trito-Isaiah (e.g., Claus Westermann, *Isaiah 40–66*, OTL [Philadelphia: Westminster, 1969], 364–67), or with a community in a corporate sense (e.g., Elizabeth Achtemeier, *The Community and Message of Isaiah 56–66* [Minneapolis: Augsburg, 1982], 86–94). The various sources cited here and the commentaries offer surveys of the various interpretive options. The precise identity of the person, however, is not relevant at this point; the purpose of my observation is simply to highlight the multidimensional description and the links with the other passages that would underscore prophetic features.

14. In addition to sources cited in the previous note, see Brevard S. Childs, *Isaiah*, OTL (Louisville: Westminster John Knox, 2001), 500–506.

Part of the (hoped-for) genius of a conference such as this is that one of its goals is to offer an Evangelical forum for dialogue on interpretations of Scripture with partners from the United States and abroad. That is, these conferences want to take seriously both the ancient and modern contexts of the Bible. Different latitudes can give rise to new perspectives on texts and theological debates. My background is Latin America, and the experience of life "south of the border" definitely has marked how theology is done there and how I personally process the theological task. Out of that backdrop I propose insights that relate the identity of messiah to the mission of the people of God. I am convinced that no discussion of who *he* is can be separated from who *we* are and what *we* are about. Let me explain.

As many know, liberation theology consciously drew on Marxist thought (although most are not aware of the variety of Marxisms that actually exist and how liberationists made use of them).[15] Although I am not a Marxist or a liberation theologian—I would categorize myself as a "concerned, contextualized Evangelical"—I suggest that one helpful category that we can utilize in discussions on messiah is that of utopia.[16] It seems to me that several components of that concept can contribute to our reflection. Any hope of a future different from life in the present still must somehow be tangibly grounded in the present; eschatology cannot be irrelevant or disembodied. At the same time, the future utopia also is a call to action in the here and now; it cannot be associated with a passive and resigned acceptance of the status quo in the interim until a more just and glorious future arrives, but rather must motivate us to promote change as we are able.

This orientation might open up some new vistas into the messiah texts, and specifically into the Servant Songs of Isaiah. Permit me to work this out in a brief fashion. Even if we hold to the conviction that in the final analysis the servant is to be identified with an individual, the text also makes lexical and thematic connections between the Servant

15. See M. Daniel Carroll R., *Contexts for Amos: Prophetic Poetics in Latin American Perspective*, JSOTSup 132 (Sheffield: Sheffield Academic Press, 1992), 109–20 (note especially the discussion and notes on pages 112–13); idem, "Liberation Theology: Latin America," in *The Oxford Illustrated History of the Bible*, ed. John Rogerson (Oxford: Oxford University Press, 2001), 316–27.

16. See Gustavo Gutiérrez, *A Theology of Liberation: History, Politics and Salvation*, trans. and ed. Sister C. Inda and J. Eagleson (Maryknoll, N.Y.: Orbis, 1973), 213–50; Ignacio Ellacuría, "Utopía y profetismo," in *Mysterium Liberationis: Conceptos fundamentales de la teología de la liberación*, ed. Jon Sobrino and Ignacio Ellacuría, 2 vols. (San Salvador: UCA, 1993), 1:393–442. An Old Testament scholar who is very concerned about social issues and has written about the power of the texts that speak of future hope is Walter Brueggemann. Of his many writings, I mention here only his seminal *Prophetic Imagination*, 2d ed. (Minneapolis: Fortress, 2001).

Song passages and other texts that say that Israel as a people is the servant of Yahweh.[17] Too often the debate has forced interpreters to decide between either a corporate identity of some sort or a specific individual. Yet the fact that the tension exists indicates that the textual data can support each side to some extent. The best option perhaps is that the "messianic" servant is distinguished from the nation, even as he embodies the divine ideals for Israel. He is what Israel should have been and becomes an exemplar after which it can model its own life and mission. In a recent publication, Williamson emphasizes what he calls the "democratization" of the Davidic role and identity of the servant king by looking at Isa. 55:3–5 and other passages (note especially Isa. 41–42; 49:1–6; 51). The task of bringing justice to the nations is Israel's responsibility, too, through its interconnections with this obedient servant of Yahweh.[18]

The servant, then, in an ultimate manner truly is an individual, but not one who is disconnected from the people. Discussions on his identity, then, do well to recognize this overlap and should not neatly line up arguments eliminating Israel from the identity of the servant. To do so is to miss that the overlap is purposeful; I would say that the overlap is *missiological.* It is interesting to note in the Servant Songs how often the nation's emotions and responses are recorded (of course, Isa. 53 is a wonderful example of this). For me, this is no accident. These descriptions are both an indictment and a call to ancient Israel and to the people of God today. We are identified with the servant (an exegetical fact), and in the present we should live out and work toward the future he brings (the lesson from liberation theology).

17. Literary readings make this abundantly clear, and recent commentators are increasingly more sensitive to these textual connections (such as between 41:8–10 and 42:1–9, the first Servant Song). Examples include Childs, *Isaiah,* and Baltzer, *Deutero-Isaiah.* Although each offers a different interpretation, both of these works see connections and a dynamic literary-theological movement as one progresses through this part of Isaiah. This intricate interweaving of the textual data becomes more evident once one moves beyond just the various servant passages. Note, for example, Sawyer's observations regarding the "daughter of Zion" texts that link with the servant material, even as contrasts are also highlighted (John F. A. Sawyer, "Daughter of Zion and Servant of the Lord in Isaiah: A Comparison," *JSOT* 44 [1989]: 89–107). Interestingly, within these Zion passages there is also the movement between collective and more individualistic interpretations.

18. Williamson, *Variations on a Theme,* 116–29. Note also, for example, Edgar W. Conrad, *Reading Isaiah,* OBT (Minneapolis: Fortress, 1991), 143–52; Childs, *Isaiah,* 431–38; Baltzer, *Deutero-Isaiah,* 465–74. Several scholars have noted as well the movement from the single servant figure of Isa. 40–55 to the "servants" of Isa. 55–66. See, for example, W. A. M. Beuken, "The Main Theme of Trito-Isaiah: 'The Servants of Yahweh,'" *JSOT* 47 (1990): 67–87; Williamson, *Variations on a Theme,* 192–202 (for other sources, see 192 n. 38).

On the one hand, this claim returns to my earlier observations about the multivalent nature of the descriptions of messiah. On the other hand, I am now taking this step a bit further by saying that the identity of the messiah has ethical implications that should draw the people of God to reflect his character and pursue his justice. The eschatological age—our "utopia," as it were—that messiah establishes is to be evident within our lives and communities, especially since we know that it is in part already here. The messiah lives among and within us through his Spirit, and the age to come has been inaugurated in the life and ministry of Jesus. Reading should change our lives, because we are, in a very profound theological and missiological sense, part of the identity of the messiah, even as his identity is foundational to ours. In the future, the New Testament tells us, we will be conformed to his image. Mine is perhaps a plea to complicate the reading of the Servant Songs, but I do believe that this exercise will help us mine the text for all its worth.

Conclusion

In conclusion, let me say that I count it a privilege to be able to have read this paper from an Old Testament colleague whom I respect professionally and whom I have had the good fortune to get to know personally better over the last several years. My comments are essentially methodological and are designed to stimulate further discussion on how we read texts, in this case the messianic passages of the Old Testament. May our work together stimulate us to a sounder faith and a more faithful life before the Messiah.

Part 2

THE MESSIAH IN THE DEAD SEA SCROLLS

FOUR

The Messiah
in the Dead Sea Scrolls

CRAIG A. EVANS

After cataloging a whole series of factors that led to the Jewish revolt, Josephus asserts that more than anything else, what incited his compatriots was an "ambiguous oracle" in their sacred Scriptures, whereby it was understood that one from their own country would arise and rule the world (*Jewish War* 6.312). This is a significant admission on the part of Josephus, who throughout his works studiously avoids the topic of messianism. In various places Josephus describes Jewish beliefs to his readers, often presenting the differing views of the various sects, but never does he discuss messianism. In fact, the only occurrences in his writings of χριστός ("christ," or "messiah") are in reference to Jesus of Nazareth and his following,[1] not to a tenet of Jewish faith. If Josephus were taken at face value, one would have no reason to think that messianism played a role in Israel's attempt to throw off the Roman yoke or, for that matter, that it was an important doctrine at all.

---

1. See *Jewish Antiquities*, 18.63–64, the so-called Testimonium Flavianum, in which a brief overview of Jesus' ministry and death is provided, and 20.200–203, which mentions the execution of James the brother of Jesus, "the one called 'Christ.'"

But the tendentiousness of the wily survivor of Israel's first disastrous revolt against Rome is widely recognized. Of course, the historian and apologist himself lets slip an important clue as to the importance and influence of Jewish messianism in mentioning the "ambiguous oracle." The scrolls of Qumran, interpreted in the light of other texts from late antiquity, not only confirm the currency of messianism, but also show that the messianism indirectly attested by Josephus rests upon the same scriptural foundation. This specific point will be taken up shortly.

We will find that the Dead Sea Scrolls confirm, clarify, and in one or two instances surprise. Although the scrolls do not live up to many of the sensational and sometimes irresponsible claims made in the popular press, it is nonetheless difficult to overemphasize their importance for our understanding the messianic hopes and expectations of the approximate time of Jesus and his contemporaries. Some of the most important of these features will be explored in this paper.

A General Assessment of the Raw Data

At the outset, it is necessary to define and clarify a few things. By "messiah"[2] I mean the traditionally understood eschatological agent, anointed by God for the redemption of Israel. He normally is understood as Davidic,[3] although there are variations on this theme. The raw data of the scrolls themselves at first blush could suggest that this figure was of relatively minor importance at Qumran. Of the approximately 870 scrolls, some 650 are nonbiblical.[4] Of these only six, or at most

2. The word "messiah" comes from the Greek *messias* (cf. John 1:41; 4:25), which is itself a transliteration of the Hebrew *māšîaḥ* (2 Sam. 22:51; 23:1), meaning one who is "anointed" (with oil). *Māšîaḥ* occurs some 38 times in the Old Testament. The Greek equivalent is *christos* (cf. LXX 2 Sam. 22:51; 23:1), which occurs some 529 times in the New Testament (about half in Paul; more than half, if one includes the Pastorals). The nominal form is derived from the verbs *māšaḥ* (Hebrew) and *chriein* (Greek), which mean "to anoint" or "to smear (with oil)." When the nominal form is definite (Hebrew *hammāšîaḥ*; Aramaic *māšîḥāʾ*), it usually is translated "the messiah." The Greek definite form, *ho christos*, usually is translated "the Christ."

3. See the summary in G. Vermes, *Jesus the Jew* (London: Collins, 1973), 130–34. In this paper I will not discuss anointed prophets or heralds.

4. For a convenient catalogue of the scrolls and related materials, see S. A. Reed, *The Dead Sea Scrolls Catalogue: Documents, Photographs and Museum Inventory Numbers*, ed. M. J. Lundberg, SBLRBS 32 (Atlanta: Scholars Press, 1994). For texts, with English translation and principal bibliography, see F. García Martínez and E. J. C. Tigchelaar, eds., *The Dead Sea Scrolls Study Edition*, 2 vols. (Leiden: Brill, 1997–98). The precise number of scrolls is unknown and changes from time to time owing to critical regroupings of scroll fragments. At the present time, the best estimate is that there are some 870 to 880 scrolls in all.

eight, scrolls actually refer to an "anointed" personage who is to be understood as the eschatological messiah.[5] These scrolls are the *Damascus Document* (CD), the *Rule of the Community* (1QS), the *Rule of the Congregation* (1QSa = 1Q28a), the *Pesher on Genesis*[a] (4Q252), possibly *Non-Canonical Psalms*[b] (4Q381),[6] possibly *Paraphrase of Kings* (4Q382),[7] *Narrative*[a] (4Q458), and the *Messianic Apocalypse* (4Q521).[8] Six scrolls refer to the "prince" or the "prince of the congregation."[9] They are the *Damascus Document*, the *Rule of Blessings* (1QSb = 1Q28b), the *War Scroll* (1QM), the *Pesher on Isaiah*[a] (4Q161), the *Rule of War* (4Q285), and the *Apocryphon of Moses* (4Q376).[10] Four scrolls refer to the "branch of David."[11] They are the *Pesher on Isaiah*[a] (4Q161), *Florilegium* (4Q174), the *Pesher on Genesis*[a] (4Q252), and the *Rule of War* (4Q285).[12] Two scrolls already mentioned refer to the "prince" as the "scepter" (*Damascus Document, Pesher on Isaiah*[a]), alluding to Num. 24:17: "A star has gone forth from Jacob, and a scepter has arisen from Israel."[13] Two other scrolls refer to the "scepter" of Num. 24 and probably should be understood in a messianic sense (*War Scroll, Testimonia*),[14] while two other scrolls refer to "scepter" without an allusion to the Num. 24 or Gen. 49 passages (*Rule of Blessings, Messianic Apocalypse*). Here too the epithet probably should be understood in a messianic sense.[15] Finally, there are four scrolls that speak of a "son" who may be messianic (*Florilegium*, the *Son of God Scroll*, the *Prayer of Enosh*, and *Narrative*[a]).[16] Apart from the reference in *Florilegium*, which is a quotation of 2 Sam. 7:14a ("I will be a father to him, and he will be my son") and a comment

5. For "anointed" (or "messiah"), see 2 Sam. 2:4; 12:7; Ps. 2; 89.

6. 4Q381 15 7 could read, "I your messiah have gained understanding," but the text also could read, "I have gained understanding from your discourse."

7. 4Q382 16 2 could read, "[m]essiah of Isra[e]l," but most of the letters are uncertain, and some scholars read ". . . statutes . . . ."

8. The specific passages are CD 12:23–13:1; 14:19 (= 4Q266 10 i 12); 19:10–11; 20:1; 1QS 9:11; 1QSa 2:11–21; 4Q252 1 v 3–4; 4Q381 15 7 (?); 4Q382 16 2 (?); 4Q458 2 ii 6; 4Q521 2+4 ii 1.

9. For "prince," see Ezek. 44:3; 45:7, 16, 22; 46:2, 4; for "congregation," see Num. 27:16.

10. The specific passages are CD 7:20 (= 4Q266 3 iii 19–21); 1QSb 5:20; 1QM 3:15 (= 4Q496 10 iv 3–4); 5:1; 4Q161 2–6 ii 15; 4Q285 4 2–6; 5 4; 6 2; 4Q376 1 iii 1–3.

11. For "branch of David," see Jer. 23:5; 33:15; Zech. 6:12.

12. The specific passages are 4Q161 7–10 iii 22; 4Q174 1 i 11; 4Q252 1 v 3–4; 4Q285 5 3–4.

13. The specific passages are CD 7:20 (= 4Q266 3 iii 19–21); 4Q161 2–6 ii 15.

14. The specific passages are 1QM 11:6–7; 4Q175 12.

15. The specific passages are 1QSb 5:27–28; 4Q521 2 iii 6.

16. The specific passages are 4Q174 1 i 11; 4Q246 1:9; 2:1 (twice); 4Q254 4 2; 4Q369 1 ii 6; 4Q258 15 1.

that "this is the 'branch of David' who will arise with the interpreter of the law," the other son passages are disputed.[17]

Notice that several scrolls were mentioned more than once in this brief overview of the principal messianic terminology.[18] In all, thirteen scrolls contain messianic material: CD, 1QS, 1QSa, 1QSb, 1QM, 4Q161, 4Q174, 4Q175, 4Q252, 4Q285, 4Q376, 4Q458, and 4Q521. All thirteen[19] of these scrolls were produced by the "Community of the Renewed Cov-

17. The figure in 4Q246 variously called "the son of the great God," "the son of God," or "son of the Most High" has been interpreted as the messiah, as a Jewish king, or as the antichrist. The quotation of Zech. 4:14 ("two sons of oil") in 4Q254 seems to be in the context of an exegesis of Gen. 49:8–12, Jacob's blessing on Judah. If so, the "two sons of oil" may have been understood as the "anointed of Aaron and of Israel," that is, the anointed high priest and the anointed king-messiah. The "first-born son" of 4Q369 has been interpreted variously as the messiah or collectively as Israel. I suppose it might even refer to David in a historical sense. Finally, the "firstborn" of 4Q458 does not actually say "son," though that probably is implied. Whether the reference is to David, Israel, or to the messiah is impossible to determine because of the fragmentary condition of the text. In 4Q458 2 ii 6, there is reference to one "anointed with the oil of the kingdom." Even this reference could be to the historical David, not necessarily to the awaited messiah.

18. For a more comprehensive overview of messianic terminology, see M. G. Abegg and C. A. Evans, "Messianic Passages in the Dead Sea Scrolls," in *Qumran-Messianism: Studies on the Messianic Expectations in the Dead Sea Scrolls*, ed. J. H. Charlesworth, H. Lichtenberger, and G. S. Oegema (Tübingen: Mohr [Siebeck], 1998), 191–203. For a recent critical discussion of many of these texts, see F. García Martínez, "Messianische Erwartungen in den Qumranschriften," in *Der Messias*, ed. Ingo Baldermann et al., JBT 8 (Neukirchen-Vluyn: Neukirchener Verlag, 1993), 171–208; ET: "Messianic Hopes in the Qumran Writings," in *The People of the Dead Sea Scrolls*, by F. García Martínez and J. Trebolle Barrera, trans. W. G. E. Watson (Leiden: Brill, 1995), 159–89. For bibliography of Qumran messianism, see Charlesworth, Lichtenberger, and Oegema, eds., *Qumran-Messianism*, 204–14.

19. 4Q458 and 4Q521 may not be sectarian. G. Vermes ("Qumran Forum Miscellanea I," *JJS* 43 [1992]: 303–4) and D. Dimant ("The Qumran Manuscripts: Contents and Significance," in *Time to Prepare the Way in the Wilderness*, ed. D. Dimant and L. H. Schiffman, STDJ 16 [Leiden: Brill, 1995], 23–58, here 48) contend that 4Q521 is not sectarian. Dimant ("The Qumran Manuscripts," 46) also catalogs 4Q458 as lacking Qumran terminology. But certain themes and emphases do suggest that they also are products of the Qumran community. Forms of "piety," "pious," or "pious ones" (חסידים [cf. 4Q521 2+4 ii 5, 7]) are found in 4Q171 1–10 iv 1, a sectarian text. The "poor" (ענוים [cf. 4Q521 2+4 ii 12]), a favorite self-designation in Qumran literature, appears in 1QSb 5:22; 1QM 14:7; 1QH 6:3; 13:21; 23:14; 4Q161 7–10 iii 3, 15; 4Q163 18–19 1; 4Q171 1–10 ii 8, all sectarian literature. The prophetic passage that is alluded to in 4Q521 2+4 ii 8, 12 (i.e., Isa 61:1–2) also appears in 11QMelch and is alluded to in 1QS 9:23; 10:19 ("until 'the day of vengeance'") and 1QM 7:5 ("prepared for 'the day of vengeance'"). "Scepter" (שבט [cf. 4Q521 2 iii 6]) appears in CD 7:19–20; 1QM 11:6–7; 4Q161 2–6 ii 19. "Uncleanness" (טמאה [cf. 4Q458 2 i 5]) appears many times in the sectarian writings (e.g., CD 7:3; passim; 1QS 4:10; 1QSa 2:3; 1QpHab 8:13). To "swallow up" (בלע [cf. 4Q458 2 ii 4]) also appears frequently in the sectarian writings (e.g., 1QpHab 11:5, 7, 15; 17:8; 4Q163 1 3). To "be justified" (צדק [cf. 4Q458 2 ii 5]) also finds expression in the sectarian writings (e.g., 1QS 3:3; 1QH 5:23; 17:14). We cannot be dogmatic about this question, but it seems at the very least that 4Q458 and 4Q521 speak in ways quite congenial to the thinking of the Community of the Renewed Covenant.

enant," as the Qumran sectarians often are called today.[20] So the evidence at first glance seems to cut in two directions: not many scrolls are concerned with messianism (fewer than 2 percent of the nonbiblical scrolls), but those that are concerned with the topic have been produced by the sectarians. Judgments about Qumran's messianism will have to be mindful of these two observations. What we may say is that the Qumran sect was not a "messianic movement," but neither did the sect entertain ideas of final victory over its enemies without the leadership of a royal messiah.

Messianism and Eschatology in the Dead Sea Scrolls

Before launching into a discussion of the function of the messiah of the Dead Sea Scrolls, a few words on the eschatological setting envisioned by the Qumran sect will be helpful.[21] The Community of the Renewed Covenant believed that the end, or eschaton, was drawing near. According to CD 20:14, "From the day of gathering in of the unique teacher until the destruction of all the men of war who turned back with the man of lies there shall be forty years." This is understood to mean forty years after the death of the Teacher of Righteousness, which occurred perhaps in 60 B.C.,[22] shortly after Roman occupation of Jerusalem. Some of Qumran's Scripture commentaries, the *pesharim*, were written before this event, while others may have been written, or rewritten, after and in response to it. But the end did not come. Nevertheless, expectations of it coming soon continued to be held at Qumran, probably right up to the great war with Rome in A.D. 66–70.

20. This designation is reflected in a recent collection of papers: E. Ulrich and J. C. VanderKam, eds., *The Community of the Renewed Covenant: The Notre Dame Symposium on the Dead Sea Scrolls*, CJAS 10 (Notre Dame: University of Notre Dame Press, 1994). See especially S. Talmon's essay, "The Community of the Renewed Covenant: Between Judaism and Christianity," 3–24.

21. I depend here primarily on recent work by John Collins: see J. J. Collins, "Messianism in the Maccabean Period," in *Judaisms and Their Messiahs*, ed. J. Neusner et al. (Cambridge: Cambridge University Press, 1987), 97–109; idem, "Messiahs in Context: Method in the Study of Messianism in the Dead Sea Scrolls," in *Methods of Investigation of the Dead Sea Scrolls and the Khirbet Qumran Site: Present Realities and Future Prospects*, ed. M. O. Wise et al., Annals of the New York Academy of Sciences 722 (New York: New York Academy of Sciences, 1994), 213–27; idem, *Apocalypticism in the Dead Sea Scrolls*, LDSS (London: Routledge, 1997), 52–109; idem, "The Expectation of the End in the Dead Sea Scrolls," in *Eschatology, Messianism, and the Dead Sea Scrolls*, ed. C. A. Evans and P. W. Flint, DSSRL 1 (Grand Rapids: Eerdmans, 1997), 74–90.

22. His death may have been a few years earlier, before Rome's occupation of Jerusalem in 63 B.C.

Qumran's eschatology seems to have been primarily restorative; that is, it was focused on the restoration of Israel. The principal elements of Qumran's eschatological hopes seem to be a righteous, "anointed"[23] high priest serving in the temple according to proper interpretation of Scripture; a restored Davidic monarchy; a purified and holy remnant of Israel, at whose core would be the Community of the Renewed Covenant, who would be truly faithful to the covenant now fully restored;[24] and a period of divine blessing upon the land. The end of the world, a general resurrection, and some sort of heavenly, nonearthly existence (which often characterizes Christian eschatology) do not appear to be central ideas at Qumran. Indeed, the doctrine of the resurrection is itself only weakly attested. Émile Puech recently has argued that the men of Qumran believed in the resurrection, inspired by Dan. 12, and that this hope is attested in many places in the scrolls.[25] But apart from 4Q521 and possibly 4QPseudo-Ezekiel[b] (4Q386) and the "son of God" text (4Q246), there is little evidence in the Dead Sea Scrolls for belief in the resurrection, especially resurrection of the body. According to 4Q521, God will "heal the wounded, give life to the dead, and proclaim good news to the poor." Here we hear echoes of Isa. 26:19 ("Your dead shall live, their bodies shall rise. O dwellers in the dust, awake and sing for joy!") and 61:1–2 ("The Lord has anointed me to proclaim good news to the poor"). 4QPseudo-Ezekiel[b] quotes and paraphrases portions of Ezekiel's "dry bones" vision (Ezek. 37:3–14), but it is not clear that Qumran's version of this vision actually goes beyond canonical Ezekiel's vision of national restoration to that of individual resurrection. In his review, John Collins rightly questions Puech's conclusions.[26] 4Q246 also may refer to resurrection. After the warfare described in 2:1–3, the author writes, "Until the people of God arise and they all have rest from the sword" (2:4). The text goes on to speak of an "eternal kingdom," peace, justice, and God's eternal rule (2:5–10). It is not clear, however, that "arise" refers to resurrection. It may, but probably it refers to the ascendancy of the people of God over their enemies.

In my judgment, what the men of Qumran anticipated was a restored Israel, a return to the golden age as they imagined it to have been. They

23. See 4Q375 1 i 9; 4Q376 1 i 1. Each text speaks of "the anointed priest."

24. The "renewed covenant" of Qumran seems to be the same covenant that God established with Israel at Sinai, a covenant that apostate Israel abandoned. For further discussion, see C. A. Evans, "Covenant in the Qumran Literature," in *The Concept of the Covenant*, ed. J. C. R. de Roo and S. E. Porter (Leiden: Brill, forthcoming).

25. É. Puech, *La croyance des Esséniens en la vie future: immortalité, resurrection, vie éternelle? Histoire d'une croyance dans le Judaïsme ancien*, vol. 1, *La résurrection des morts et le contexte scripturaire*, EBib 21 (Paris: Gabalda, 1993).

26. J. J. Collins, *DSD* 1 (1994): 246–52.

anticipated that this age would be final and not subject to the vicissitudes that marked Israel's checkered history. This anticipation was based on several Scriptures that were understood in a prophetic sense. To these Scriptures we now turn.

Key Scriptural Prophecies

Three passages in particular played an important, generative role in the rise of messianism: (1) Gen. 49:10; (2) Num. 24:17; and (3) Isa. 10:34–11:5. All three are interpreted in a messianic sense in the Dead Sea Scrolls and in other early Jewish and Christian writings. Let us briefly review their interpretation in the scrolls and in related texts.

(1) Gen. 49:10. In the *Commentary on Genesis A* (4Q252 1 v 1–7), Gen. 49:10–11 is cited and is understood to refer to the "branch of David."

> [1]A ruler shall [no]t depart from the tribe of Judah when Israel has dominion. [2][And] the one who sits on the throne of David [shall never] be cut off, because the "ruler's staff" is the covenant of the kingdom, [3][and the thous]ands of Israel are "the feet," until the righteous messiah, the branch of David, has come *(Gen. 49:10)*. [4]For to him and to his seed the covenant of the kingdom of his people has been given for the eternal generations.[27]

The passage also may be alluded to in 4QpIsa[a] 7–10 iii 25, again in a messianic sense. The messianic potential appears to have been enhanced in the LXX. All four Targumim to the Pentateuch render the passage in an explicitly messianic sense ("king messiah" is mentioned in vv. 10, 11, and 12). Jacob's blessing (Gen. 49:8–12) is referred to in *Testament of Judah* 1:6 ("My father declared to me, 'You shall be king'"), and in *Testament of Judah* 22:3 the blessing seems to be understood in a messianic sense. The description of the warrior messiah in Rev. 19:11–16 may have this passage, as well as Isaiah 11, in mind (compare Rev. 19:13 with Gen. 49:11), and it may be alluded to in Heb. 7:14. Christian messianic interpretation of the passage becomes commonplace in the second century (cf. Justin Martyr, *First Apology* 32; 54; *Dialogue with Trypho* 52; 120; Clement of Alexandria, *Christ the Educator* 1.5, 6; Irenaeus, *Against Heresies* 4.10.2).

(2) Num. 24:17. The interpretation of Num. 24:17 is similar to that of Gen. 49:10. It is quoted in *Testimonia* (4Q175) 12–13, though without explicit messianic interpretation. It is reasonable to assume that the passage was understood in a messianic sense, however. The same prob-

---

27. Translations of the scrolls are based on M. O. Wise, M. G. Abegg Jr., and E. M. Cook, *The Dead Sea Scrolls: A New Translation* (San Francisco: HarperCollins, 1996).

ably is true in the case of 1QM 11:6–7. Our passage is quoted and interpreted in the *Damascus Document* (CD) 7:

> [18]The star is the interpreter of the law [19]who comes to Damascus, as it is written, "A star has left Jacob, a scepter has risen [20]from Israel" *(Num. 24:17a)*. The latter is the prince of the whole congregation; when he appears, "he will shatter [21]all the sons of Sheth" *(Num. 24:17b)*.

The "interpreter of the law," perhaps the eschatological priest, is understood as the "star" of the Num. 24:17 prophecy, while the "prince of the whole congregation" is understood to be the "scepter."

All four Pentateuch Targumim paraphrase the passage in explicitly messianic terms. The Hebrew text's "a star shall come forth out of Jacob, and a scepter shall rise out of Israel" becomes in the Aramaic "a king shall arise out of Jacob and be anointed the messiah out of Israel" *(Targum Onqelos;* cf. *Targum Neofiti, Targum Pseudo-Jonathan,* and *Fragmentary Targum)*. Messianic interpretation of Num. 24:17 is widely attested in traditions dating to the first century and earlier *(Testament of Judah* 24:1–6; CD 7:20; 1QSb 5:27–28; 1QM 11:4–9; 4Q175 1:9–13; possibly Philo, *Life of Moses* 1.290; *Rewards and Punishments* 95; *Orphica* 31 = Aristobulus fragment 4:5). It probably is to this passage that Josephus refers when he says that his compatriots were misled by an "ambiguous oracle" promising that "one from their country would become ruler of the world" *(Jewish War* 6.312–313; cf. 3.400–402). The "star" that "stood over the city" of Jerusalem would only have fueled such speculation *(Jewish War* 6.289). At issue was not the messianic orientation of the oracle; rather, the question was to whom the oracle applied. Of course, Josephus here is being disingenuous. It is very probable that he too understood the passage in the way his contemporaries did. Instead, Josephus deliberately distanced himself from popular Jewish interpretation and applied the oracle to Vespasian, his patron, "who was proclaimed emperor on Jewish soil." Early Christians also were aware of the passage's messianic potential, as seen in the "star" of Matt. 2:2 and the magi's assumption that it pointed to the birthplace of the "king of the Jews." Simon ben Kosiba's nickname, bar Kokhba ("son of the star"), apparently was inspired by this passage. According to rabbinic tradition, this man claimed to be the messiah, or at least was proclaimed as such by some of his following (cf. *y. Taʿan.* 4:5/8; *b. Sanh.* 93b; Justin Martyr, *First Apology* 31; *Dialogue with Trypho* 106; Irenaeus, *Against Heresies* 3.9.2). Only after his defeat (A.D. 135) did the sobriquet change to bar Kozeba ("son of the lie").

(3) Isa. 10:34–11:5. In the Hebrew text, the oracle of Isaiah 11 anticipates the coming forth of "a shoot from the stump of Jesse, even a branch

[that] shall grow out of his roots" (v. 1). The Isaiah Targum renders the
verse, "And a king shall come forth from the sons of Jesse, and the messiah shall be exalted from the sons of his sons" (cf. *Targum Isaiah* 11:6:
"In the days of the messiah of Israel . . ."). Much earlier, the LXX had enhanced the messianic potential of Isa 11:10: "And there shall be in that
day the root of Jesse, even he who arises to rule over nations." Paul quotes
this passage and applies it to "Christ" (Rom. 15:12; cf. Rev. 5:5; 22:16;
Clement of Alexandria, *Miscellanies* 5.6). Isaiah 11 is taken in a messianic
sense in 4QpIsa[a] 7–10 iii 22–29, and is echoed in 1QSb 5:21–26, a passage
describing the blessing that is to be pronounced upon the "prince of the
congregation." In *4 Ezra* 13:2–10, Isa. 11:4 is alluded to and applied to the
man who "flew with the clouds of heaven" (cf. Dan. 7:13). Messianic interpretation of Isa. 11 underlies 4Q285 5:1–6 and probably *Testament of
Levi* 18:7 as well, and seems to have been very influential in early Judaism.[28] Early Christian writers were especially fond of Isa. 11.[29]

This brief overview of the interpretation of Gen. 49:10, Num. 24:17,
and Isa. 10:34–11:5 in late antiquity documents the relatively unified and
cohesive messianic expectation held by many Jews, even when members
of rival and, at times, antagonistic groups. This is not to say that there was
no diversity or that all Jews embraced messianism. But sometimes the diversity of Jewish messianism is exaggerated in critical scholarship, leaving the impression that no two groups held common views. In fact, many
Jews in late antiquity longed for the coming of a king, anointed by the
Lord, in fulfillment of Scripture—expressed particularly in the three texts
that have been discussed. This longing and the belief that the "ambiguous
oracle" finally had been fulfilled were the very things that "more than all
else incited them to the war," as Josephus admits.

However, the fulfillment of these prophecies, as well as many others,
was understood not as the end of human history but as the beginning of Israel's restoration, when the covenant with God finally and fully would be
renewed. The era of Gentile oppression, evidently regarded in some circles
as "exile,"[30] finally would be over. Israel's long-awaited anointed king at last
would arise and serve faithfully alongside a righteous, anointed high priest.

28. See R. Bauckham, "The Messianic Interpretation of Isa. 10:34 in the Dead Sea
Scrolls, 2 Baruch and the Preaching of John the Baptist," *DSD* 2 (1995): 202–16.

29. For v. 1, cf. Matt. 2:23; Acts 13:23; Heb. 7:14; Rev. 5:5; 22:16; Justin Martyr, *First
Apology* 32; *Dialogue with Trypho* 87; Clement of Alexandria, *Christ the Educator* 1.7; Irenaeus, *Against Heresies* 3.9.3; *Sibylline Oracles* 6:8, 16; 7:38; 8:254; for v. 2, cf. Eph. 1:17;
1 Pet. 4:14; Irenaeus, *Against Heresies* 3.17.1; for v. 3, cf. John 7:24; Clement of Alexandria, *Christ the Educator* 1.7; for v. 4, cf. John 7:24; Eph. 6:17; 2 Thess. 2:8; Rev. 19:11;
Clement of Alexandria, *Christ the Educator* 1.7; Irenaeus, *Against Heresies* 4.33.1; for v. 5,
cf. Eph. 6:14.

30. On Jewish ideas of Israel as being in a state of exile, see J. M. Scott, ed., *Exile: Old
Testament, Jewish, and Christian Conceptions*, JSJSup 56 (Leiden: Brill, 1997).

How Qumran specifically understood the messiah will concern us in the balance of the paper. Three specific issues will be addressed: (1) the evident expectation of two messiahs, one royal and one priestly; (2) the royal messiah and his role in the great battle of liberation; and (3) the royal messiah and his relationship to the priestly messiah.

Two Messiahs at Qumran

In the wake of the discovery of the Dead Sea Scrolls, a great deal of attention focused on Qumran's expectation of the appearance of two messiahs. Several times the *Damascus Document* speaks of a time when the "anointed of Aaron and of Israel" will appear (e.g., CD 12:23–13:1). It is on this basis, though not exclusively, that scholars began to speak of a diarchic or binary messianism at Qumran.[31] However, recently some scholars have challenged this near consensus. For example, Michael Wise and James Tabor have argued that Qumran's messianism is monarchic.[32] But the diarchic view remains widely held, and in my opinion is correct.[33]

31. The standard older treatment is K. G. Kuhn, "The Two Messiahs of Aaron and Israel," *NTS* 1 (1954–55): 168–80; repr. in K. Stendahl, ed., *The Scrolls and the New Testament* (New York: Harper, 1957; repr., New York: Crossroad, 1992), 54–64, 256–59. The *Damascus Document* epithet "messiah of Aaron and of Israel" (משיח אהרן וישראל) refers to two anointed figures, as in 1QS 9:15 (משיחי אהרן וישראל), not to one figure. S. Talmon and M. G. Abegg point to two examples in the Hebrew Bible in which a singular noun form, in construct with two nouns, is functionally plural: "the heads of Oreb and Zeeb" (Judg. 7:25, where "head" is singular) and "the kings of Sodom and Gomorrah" (Gen. 14:10, where "king" is singular). Examples in the Dead Sea Scrolls include CD 5:3–4; 1QS 6:6; 1QSa 2:18–19; 10:10; 1QM 3:13–14 ("the names of Israel and Aaron"); 4Q251; 11QT^a 43:8–9. It is important that all of these examples are from the sectarian literature. See M. G. Abegg Jr., "The Hebrew of the Dead Sea Scrolls," in *The Dead Sea Scrolls after Fifty Years: A Comprehensive Assessment*, ed. P. W. Flint and J. C. VanderKam, 2 vols. (Leiden: Brill, 1998), 1:334–35.

32. M. O. Wise and J. D. Tabor, "The Messiah at Qumran," *BAR* 18, no. 6 (1992): 60–65, esp. 60.

33. See F. M. Cross, "Notes on the Doctrine of the Two Messiahs at Qumran and the Extra-Canonical *Daniel Apocalypse (4Q246)*," in *Current Research and Technological Developments on the Dead Sea Scrolls: Conference on the Texts from the Judean Desert, Jerusalem, 30 April 1995*, ed. D. W. Parry and S. D. Ricks, STDJ 20 (Leiden: Brill, 1996), 1–13. On p. 2, Cross says, "A consistent doctrine of only two messiahs—one of Aaron and one of Israel—is evident throughout the sectarian Qumran literature." Collins agrees: diarchic messianism is "usually taken to be the norm at Qumran and to be the most distinctive feature of Qumran messianism" (*The Scepter and the Star*, 75). Qumran's diarchic messianism has been defended in a recent study by W. M. Schniedewind, "Structural Aspects of Qumran Messianism in the *Damascus Document*," in *The Provo International Conference on the Dead Sea Scrolls: Technological Innovations, New Texts, and Reformulated Issues*, ed. D. W. Parry and E. Ulrich, STDJ 30 (Leiden: Brill, 1998), 523–36.

The idea of two anointed personages is based on the Hebrew Scriptures themselves, as seen so clearly in Zechariah and Haggai,[34] but also attested in Jer. 33:15–18, where God makes this promise to a frightened and beleaguered Judah:

> In those days and at that time, I will cause to sprout for David a righteous Branch; and he shall execute justice and righteousness in the land. In those days Judah will be saved and Jerusalem will live in safety. And this is the name by which it will be called: "The Lord is our righteousness." For thus says the Lord: David shall never lack a man to sit on the throne of Israel, *and the levitical priests shall never lack a man in my presence* to offer burnt offerings, to make grain offerings, and to make sacrifices for all time. (italics added)

William Schniedewind draws attention to the way 4QFlorilegium adds a second personage, a priestly one, to the Davidic covenant, as expressed in 2 Sam. 7:13–14.[35] Note 4QFlor frags. 1–3, col. 1, lines 10–12: "He is 'the branch of David' who will arise *with the interpreter of the law*, who shall arise in Zion in the last days" (italics added).[36]

The diarchic nature of Qumran's messianism clearly is presupposed in two of the sect's most important and most authoritative writings: the *Damascus Document* and the *Rule of the Community*. Since these texts explain the sect's origin, reason for being, and requirements for membership, what they say about messianism should be accorded normative status, even if it is mentioned only in passing. No further corroboration should be required, though other scrolls offer additional evidence, such as the passage from 4QFlorilegium cited in the preceding paragraph.

34. J. C. VanderKam ("Jubilees and the Priestly Messiah of Qumran," *RevQ* 13 [1988]: 365) has expressed some doubt about the influence of either Zechariah or Haggai on Qumran's diarchic messianism. However, he expressed this doubt before the publication of 4Q254, in which a portion of Zech. 4:14 appears. See now C. A. Evans, "'The Two Sons of Oil': Early Evidence of Messianic Interpretation of Zechariah 4:14 in 4Q254 4 2," in *The Provo International Conference*, ed. Parry and Ulrich, 566–75. On the possibility that diarchic messianism may explain in part Jesus' actions in Jerusalem, see C. A. Evans, "Diarchic Messianism in the Dead Sea Scrolls and the Messianism of Jesus of Nazareth," in *The Dead Sea Scrolls Fifty Years after Their Discovery: Proceedings of the Jerusalem Congress, July 20–25, 1997*, ed. L. H. Schiffmann, E. Tov, and J. C. VanderKam (Jerusalem: Israel Exploration Society and the Israel Antiquities Authority, 2000), 558–67.

35. Schniedewind, "Structural Aspects of Qumran Messianism," 528.

36. The priestly identification of the "interpreter of the law" is suggested by 4Q177 2:2–5: [2]"[in the book of the prophet Zechariah, 'Here is a stone I have placed before Joshua the priest. Upon this one stone are seven eyes. I am] making an inscription on it, says the Lord' *(Zech. 3:9)*. As it [3][says . . .] concerning them it is written, I will heal [4][. . .] the men of Belial and all the rabble [5][. . .] them the interpreter of the law." The appeal to the model of Joshua the priest in Zechariah is very interesting, given Zechariah's diarchic orientation.

The Royal Messiah and Battle

We expect the royal messiah to play a leading role in the anticipated great war for Israel's liberation, but the priests also assist in the great eschatological battle, as seen in the *War Scroll*. This scroll describes in great detail the duties of the priests in organizing Israel for holy war, a war that was expected to perdure for forty years. Part of these preparations involved engraving various names and slogans on shields and other implements. According to 1QM 5:1, "On the sh[ie]ld of the prince of the whole congregation they shall write his name, the names 'Israel,' 'Levi,' and 'Aaron,' and the names of the twelve tribes of Israel according to their order of birth." The name of the "prince of the whole congregation" joins the names of Israel, Levi (the patriarch of the priestly tribe), and Aaron (the Levite through whom the high priest descends), as well as the names of the other patriarchs. This is highly distinguished company. These names emphasize that all of renewed Israel will be represented by the prince.[37]

Priestly duties also are spelled out in the great *Temple Scroll* (11QT^a). According to col. 58, Israel's king

> [18]must not go to battle prior to coming to the high priest to inquire of him about the judgment of the Urim [19]and Thummim. The king will go out to battle and return guided by the priest—the king and all the Israelites [20]with him. He must not go out by his own decision prior to inquiring of the judgment of the Urim [21]and Thummim. Then he shall succeed in all his ways because he went out by the judgment that . . .

The high profile of the priests in the *War Scroll* reflects the role that Scripture gives to the high priest in times of war. We see this in Deut. 20:1–4, where it is the priest who speaks to Israel on the eve of war (see 1QM 10 for the priestly exhortation). In Josh. 6, the priests play a prominent role in bringing down Jericho's walls—blowing trumpets, carrying the ark of the covenant, and participating in the march (see 1QM 8–9 for the priestly trumpeting). The *War Scroll* has greatly expanded and embellished the scriptural teaching pertaining to the priests' duties in wartime.

Although the royal messiah is not depicted in the *War Scroll*—at least in that part of it that is extant—his involvement in the great struggle between the "sons of light" and the "sons of darkness" very probably is pre-

---

37. It is analogous to Jesus' appointment of the Twelve (Mark 3:14), as well as his promise that the Twelve will sit on twelve thrones judging the twelve tribes of Israel (Matt. 19:28 = Luke 22:28–30). The number twelve signifies the restoration of the "whole congregation" of Israel.

supposed. 1QM 11:1–2 alludes to David's defeat of Goliath, while 11:2–3 alludes to David's victory over the Philistines. Allusions to David's great military victories suggest that his anointed successor also will enjoy great victories over Israel's contemporary oppressors. 1QM 11:4–7 quotes Num. 24:17 and says, "He rules from Jacob." Who is this who "rules"? It probably is the royal messiah. In 1QM 11:11, the author reminds God of his promise to "display the might of your hand against the Kittim," that is, against the Romans.

The royal messiah may only be implied in the *War Scroll* (and may actually have made an appearance in the original, full text), but he makes unmistakable appearances in other texts. The two most important are the *Pesher on Isaiah*[a] (4Q161) and the *Rule of War* (4Q285), both of which are based on Isa. 10:34–11:5, and the latter of which may have been part of another version of the *War Scroll*. The first pesher on Isaiah (4Q161 7–10 iii 5–20) reads,

5["Right now, the Lord God of Hosts is pruning the treetops with a hook. The tallest of all are hewn down,] 6[the mightiest are laid low. The forest] thickets [will be cut down] with iron tools, the trees of Lebanon, for all their majesty, 7[will fall." *(Isa. 10:34)* This refers to the] Kittim, who will fall at the hand of Israel and the humble 8[of Judah, who will . . .] the Gentiles, and the mighty will be shattered, and [their coura]ge will dissolve. 9[. . . The "tallest" of all will be cut down" refers to the warriors of the Kit[tim,] 10[who . . . as for the verse that say]s, "The forest thickets will be cut down with iron tools," they are 11[. . .] for war against the Kittim. "The trees of Lebanon, for [all their majesty, 12will fall": they are the] Kittim, who will be put into the power of the nobles of [Israel . . .] 13[. . .] when he flees befo[re Is]rael . . . 14[*vacat*] 15["A rod will grow from] Jesse's stock, a sprout [will bloom] from his [roots;] upon him wi[ll rest] the spirit of 16[the Lord: a spirit of] wisdom and insight, a spirit of good coun[sel and strength], a spirit of true know[ledge] 17[and reverence for] the Lord, he will delight in reverence for] the Lord. [He will not judge only] by what [his eyes] see, 18[he will not decide only by what his ears hear;] but he will rule [the weak by justice, and give decisions] 19[in integrity to the humble of the land. He will punish the land with the mace of his words, by his lips' breath alone] 20[he will slay the wicked. 'Justice' will be the girdle around] his waist, 'Tr[uth' the girdle around his hips"] *(Isa. 11:1–5)*.

The second passage (4Q285 frags. 4–5) reads,

4:2[. . . the p]rince of the Congregation to the [Mediterranean] Sea [. . .] 3[. . . And they shall flee] from Israel at that time [. . .] 4[. . . And the high priest] shall stand before them and they shall arrange themselves against them [in battle array . . .] 5[. . .] and they shall return back to the land at that time [. . .] 6[. . .] then they shall bring him before the prince of [the congregation . . .]

5:1[. . . just as it is written in the book of] Isaiah the prophet, "And [the thickets of the forest] shall be cut down 2[with an ax, and Lebanon with its majestic trees w]ill fall. A shoot shall come out from the stump of Jesse 3[and a branch shall grow out of his roots" *(Isa. 10:34–11:1)*. This is the] branch of David. Then [all forces of Belial] shall be judged, 4[and the king of the Kittim shall stand for judgment] and the prince of the community—the bra[nch of David]—will have him put to death. 5[Then all Israel shall come out with tim-brel]s and dancers, and the [high] priest shall order 6[them to cleanse their bodies from the guilty blood of the c]orpse[s of] the Kittim.[38]

The image of the militant, victorious royal messiah is consistent with the biblical picture of King David of old, and it is consistent with the imagery of the Davidic messiah in *Psalms of Solomon* 17–18. This figure is to "destroy the unrighteous rulers, to purge Jerusalem from Gentiles" (17:22). He will "smash the arrogance of sinners," "shatter all their substance with an iron rod," and "destroy the unlawful nations with the word of his mouth" (v. 24). Again we hear echoes of Isa. 11.

Qumran's expectation of a conquering royal messiah is not distinctive, but appears to be entirely consistent with Jewish messianic and eschatological traditions from the time of Qumran (as seen especially in the *Psalms of Solomon* 17–18), through the New Testament period, and on into the time of the rabbis.

The Royal Messiah and the Anointed Priest

The *Rule of the Congregation* (1QSa = 1Q28a) describes a banquet that will take place "when God will have begotten[39] the messiah" among

38. For defense of the proper restoration and rendering "[with timbrel]s and dancers," as opposed to "[by stroke]s and by wounds," as in G. Vermes, "The Oxford Forum for Qumran Research Seminar on the Rule of the War from Cave 4 (4Q285)," *JJS* 43 (1992): 88, see M. G. Abegg, "Messianic Hope and 4Q285: A Reassessment," *JBL* 113 (1994): 81–91, esp. 90. Recognition that the text is speaking about women playing timbrels and dancing (as in Exod. 15:20 and Judg. 21:23, where Israelite women beat timbrels and dance following victories over Israel's enemies) makes all the more implausible the notion that 4Q285 is talking about a slain prince. On the contrary, the prince slays the leader of the Romans, the women dance, and the priest gives orders pertaining to purification of the land in the aftermath of battle.

39. The most probable reading of 1QSa 2:11 is *yôlid* ("he will have begotten"), though other readings have been proposed, such as "he will have brought." The reference to a "messiah" who is "begotten" is an allusion to Ps. 2, v. 2 ("messiah") and v. 7 ("begotten"). This language is, of course, metaphorical and does not require a literal interpretation. The author of this text and its subsequent readers did not imagine that God would bring about the birth of the messiah through a virgin, as in later Christian theology, as expressed in the Matthean and Lukan infancy narratives. All that is being affirmed in 1QSa is that God will raise up his anointed one.

the Community of the Renewed Covenant. Because the priest enters first and the messiah enters afterward, this is understood by some to imply that the royal messiah is subordinated to the priestly messiah.[40] The pertinent passages (1QSa 2:11–21) read,

> [11]The procedure for the [mee]ting of the men of reputation [when they are called] to the banquet held by the Council of the Yahad, when [God] has fa[th]ered(?) [12]the messiah among them: [the priest,] as head of the entire congregation of Israel, shall enter first, trailed by all [13][his] brot[hers, the Sons of] Aaron, those priests [appointed] to the banquet of the men of reputation. They are to sit [14]be[fore him] by rank. Then the [mess]iah of Israel may en[ter,] and the heads [15]of the th[ousands of Israel] are to sit before him by rank, as determined by [each man's comm]ission in their camps and campaigns. Last, all [16]the heads of [the con]gregation's cl[ans,] together with [their] wis[e and knowledgeable men,] shall sit before them by [17]rank.
>
> [When] they gather [at the] communal [tab]le, [having set out bread and w]ine so the communal table is set [18][for eating] and [the] wine (poured) for drinking, none [may re]ach for the first portion [19]of the bread or [the wine] before the priest. For [he] shall [bl]ess the first portion of the bread [20]and the wine, [reac]hing for the bread first. Afterw[ard] the messiah of Israel [shall re]ach [21]for the bread. [Finally,] ea[ch] (member of) the whole congregation of the Yahad [shall give a bl]essing, [in descending order of] rank.

The order of blessings in the *Rule of Blessings* (1QSb = 1Q28b), whereby the "prince of the congregation" is blessed last, also is thought to imply a subordination of the royal messiah to the priestly messiah, but the order of blessings may suggest just the opposite. First to be blessed is the community itself (1:1–7), followed by a blessing for the anointed priest (2:22–3:21) and blessing for all of the priests, the sons of Zadok (3:22–5:17). The last blessing is for the prince (5:20–29). The prince's blessing at the end could be climactic, perhaps mirroring eschatology itself, in that the royal messiah has not yet appeared. There is no compelling reason to see the order of blessings as proof of the royal messiah's subordination to the priestly messiah.

Is the order of events or blessings in 1QSa and 1QSb evidence of the "subordination" of the royal messiah, or is it only appropriate deference to the high priest in his capacity as one who consults the Urim and Thummim to ascertain God's will and leading? There seem to be three basic options: (1) the royal messiah is subordinated to the anointed high priest, (2) the royal messiah dominates (as one might suppose in 4Q521,

---

40. On the royal messiah's subordination to the priestly messiah, see Collins, "Messiahs in Context," 224, 227.

or as in Christian Christology), and (3) neither the royal messiah nor the anointed high priest dominates the other, but they serve faithfully side by side, each respecting the other's duties and prerogatives.

In my opinion, the third option seems to match the evidence of the scrolls better than either of the first two. Accordingly, I do not think that Qumran's messianism is distinctive in any significant way. It envisions the restoration of the monarchy and the priesthood and so may properly be described as diarchic messianism, a restorative messianism that is rooted in Scripture and is entertained in other traditions (e.g., the *Testaments of the Twelve Patriarchs*).

It certainly is correct to say that the priestly role in the eschatological drama is enhanced, but I think it goes too far to speak of the subordination of the royal messiah to the anointed high priest. Qumran says little about the royal messiah because his function was not at issue. What was at issue was the role of the priest and the function of the temple cultus. Here the Community of the Renewed Covenant had grave concerns. Accordingly, we should not be surprised that the anointed priest receives so much attention and the anointed king so little, comparatively.

Conclusions

The evidence considered above justifies four principal conclusions:

1. Qumran is not preoccupied with messianism; the community presupposes it and utilizes it as part of the community's eschatology and hopes of restoration. When God finally "begets" the messiah and raises him up, he will play an important role in Israel's liberation. He will engage the Kittim (i.e., the Romans) in battle and quite possibly will himself slay the Roman emperor.

2. In comparison to Jewish messianism of late antiquity, Qumran's messianism is not distinctive in any significant way.[41] Qumran's temple-related concerns (touching calendar, matters of purity, and other halakic issues) are distinctive in aggregate, but their messianism is not. Of course, Qumran assumes that the awaited messiah, the "branch of David" and "prince of the congregation," will fully endorse and support the congregation's cultic reforms. However, the messiah is not subordinated

41. Christian messianism became distinctive in that the priestly and prophetic dimensions were subsumed under the royal heading. But the royal messianism of early Christianity was otherwise hardly distinctive from Jewish messianism, as has been rightly emphasized by W. Horbury, *Jewish Messianism and the Cult of Christ* (London: SCM Press, 1998).

to the anointed priest, nor are his functions in any way significantly different from Jewish messianic expectation. The awaited messiah is subordinated only in the sense that his appearance is tied to Qumran's eschatology. Of course, the anointed priest will not be subordinated to the messiah. Neither anointed figure will encroach upon the duties and authority of the other.

3. If Qumranian messianism is not distinctive, that does not mean that it was not important. The restoration of Israel, and the vindication of the Community of the Renewed Covenant that is a vital part of this restoration, will not and cannot take place until the "anointed of Israel" appears, whom God will raise up, or in the words of Ps. 2:7 echoed in 1QSa, whom God will "beget" among his faithful remnant, the "poor." The appearance of the anointed "prince of the congregation" will trigger the eschatological events, which will include the defeat of Rome, the purification and reestablishment of proper worship in Jerusalem, and healing and blessings for the faithful.

4. Qumran's messianism sheds important light on the context of Jesus' ministry and how his contemporaries may have perceived him and his proclamation of the kingdom. The coherence between 4Q521's messianic expectation and Jesus' reply to the imprisoned and questioning John the Baptist (Matt. 11:5 = Luke 7:22) is a significant example. Even a ministry of consolation—healing the sick, raising the dead, proclaiming good news to the poor—if understood in a messianic sense, would readily have conjured up images of a warlike messiah (as in 4Q285) who would drive out and defeat Israel's enemies. The transition, as depicted in the New Testament Gospels, from Jesus the healer to Jesus crucified on a Roman cross thus becomes more explicable.[42]

---

42. And thus, it is unnecessary to infer that the manner of Jesus' execution reflects a response to a violent, militant message; *pace* S. G. F. Brandon, *Jesus and the Zealots: A Study of the Political Factor in Primitive Christianity* (New York: Scribner's Sons, 1967); idem, *The Trial of Jesus of Nazareth* (New York: Stein and Day, 1968).

FIVE

Messiahs Here and There

A Response to Craig A. Evans

RICHARD S. HESS

The place of the messiah in the Dead Sea Scrolls has enjoyed a long discussion. In 1991 scholars were for the first time given access to all of the extant Qumran literature. The result has been a decade of study and publication on many fronts. Among these, there has been a renewed interest in the messianic texts at Qumran, especially with the supplement of the newly published texts related to the subject.

Most of the thirty-plus nonbiblical texts from Qumran that refer to the messiah, or "anointed one," support an understanding of the figure as a royal leader. This individual's kingly character is supplemented by a priestly one, and these are understood by most as two separate messianic figures.[1] Traditional texts with contemporary messianic applications, such as Gen. 49:10–11; Num. 24:17; Isa. 11:1–9, supplement the picture of this figure with numerous references to titles and epithets. Examples include "branch," "star," "prince," and "ruler." Further, im-

---

1. Karl Georg Kuhn, "The Two Messiahs of Aaron and Israel," *NTS* 1 (1954–55): 168–80. See, however, the qualifications of Martin G. Abegg Jr., "The Messiah at Qumran: Are We Still Seeing Double?" *DSD* 2 (1995): 125–44.

plicit messianic texts, such as Ps. 2:2, 7, prepare the way for the *Rule of the Congregation* to identify a figure who was "begotten" by God (1QSa 2:11–12). As Evans observes, the third and second centuries B.C. witnessed the emergence of an eschatological dimension to the messiah that previously was not identified in the Old Testament. Thus, the *Rule of War* identifies the "branch of David" as one who will kill the leader of the opposition (4Q285 5:4). All this Evans has well summarized and thereby provided readers with a useful introduction to the subject.[2]

In his paper presented here, Evans continues this discussion with full references to the messiah as presented in the Dead Sea Scrolls. The purpose of my response is to address issues on the horizon of the subject that supplement the foundational presentation already given. These will be directed in two areas. First, I will give brief consideration to the appearance of the term "messiah," its root in the Old Testament, and how this usage is reflected in its interpretation at Qumran. Second, I will review some of the recent theories regarding the figure of the messiah in the Dead Sea Scrolls.

As to the Old Testament background, this already has been discussed. It remains only to emphasize a few points of particular interest for the messianic texts of the Dead Sea Scrolls.[3] To begin, it is helpful to review the basic idea of the messiah, the anointed one, as found in the prebiblical West Semitic world of the second millennium B.C. There it is used at Emar to describe the anointing of the chief female religious functionary. In Syria, a pharaoh of Egypt anoints a local prince to make him the ruler of the region. Farther north, the Hittite king is anointed as both a priest and a king.

The combination of religious and royal purposes for anointing continues in the biblical texts. Thus, the use of the root and of the term "messiah" in the Pentateuch regularly applies to a priest when it refers to a person. Elsewhere in the Old Testament the overwhelming number of occurrences of the term refer to royalty, most often to Saul as the anointed one, or, less frequently, to David and members of his line. Although the prophet Elisha is anointed as well (1 Kings 16:19), this is a singular occurrence. Most frequently, the texts designate anointed individuals as rulers. Usually they are kings of Israel. After the destruction of Jerusalem and the cessation of kingship there, however, a figure such as Cyrus can be so designated (Isa. 45:1). It is in this later period of the return from exile that the prophet Zechariah brings together the two

2. Craig Evans, "Messiahs," *EDSS* 1:537–42.

3. See further on what is presented here in Richard S. Hess, "The Image of the Messiah in the Old Testament," in *Images of Christ Ancient and Modern*, ed. Stanley E. Porter, Michael A. Hayes, and David Tombs, RILP 2 (Sheffield: Sheffield Academic Press, 1997), 22–33.

themes of priest and ruler as anointed ones. In Zech. 4:14, in the context of a discussion of the priest and governor of the postexilic community, he designates the two "who are anointed" (*běnê hayyiṣhār*, "sons of the oil").[4] This is suggestive of the combination of a priest and a ruler within the theme of the messiah. Such a duality is testified in the occurrences of the root in the Old Testament. It therefore is no surprise to find it present in the writings of the Dead Sea Scrolls. As Evans has argued, the most likely interpretation of the Qumran literature is that a separate ruler and priest are intended. This fits well with the witness of the Old Testament.

Turning now to recent theories of the messiah at Qumran, I will examine briefly two that have been presented. These are of particular interest because each has been written about on a somewhat popular level, designed for wide circulation among the general public. Therefore, they are most likely to find their way into the broader discussion of the messiah at Qumran.

Michael Wise has attempted to apply the *Thanksgiving Hymns*, the legal material of 4QMMT, and other Qumran texts to the pharisaic-priestly controversy that reached violent proportions in Judea during the first half of the first century B.C.[5] He identifies the hymns with the community's Teacher of Righteousness, whom he believes to be the historical figure named Judah. Judah was described by Josephus as a priest of great learning and stature who rose to prominence in the controversies of that time. His persecution and subsequent (supposed) exile under Hyrcanus are developed in vivid detail as Wise presents his case for Judah as the first messiah in history, predating Jesus of Nazareth by a century. Thus, the *Damascus Document* is not a symbolic description of exile in the wilderness, but a literal presentation of the departure of Judah and his followers from Jerusalem and Judea to eke out a living as bandits in the harsh terrain south of the actual city of Damascus. The subsequent persecution and death of Judah in the years preceding the conquest of the region by Rome in 63 B.C. contained in it the seeds of a great messianic movement. Judah had predicted the Roman invasion of Jerusalem. It remained for his followers to point to the texts in which he had spoken such words, as interpretations of biblical prophetic writings. The result was a powerful upsurge in the movement that followed the words of the dead messiah. It brought about the enrollment of thousands of new disciples who eagerly awaited the promised second coming of Judah in the fortieth year after his death. When this failed to materialize, sometime about the

4. Ibid, 32.
5. Michael O. Wise, *The First Messiah: Investigating the Savior before Jesus* (New York: HarperCollins, 1999).

year 34 B.C., the result was the collapse of the movement. Subsequently, nothing more was written by members of the movement, who themselves disappeared by the turn of the era. The writings somehow found their way into the collection of the Qumran texts.

This hypothesis identifies the messiah as a respected religious leader who opposed the Pharisees and their political allies. However, the opposition was not successful, and the messianic figure, Judah, faced persecution, exile, and perhaps death at the hands of his opponents under the rule of Alexandra and Hyrcanus. The primary textual resources for interpreting the life of this figure are the Qumran hymns. Although there are other sources that he uses, Wise understands the central collection of these hymns as originally personal reflections of Judah concerning various stages in his life as a messiah.

Israel Knohl argues that the suffering and exalted figure described in one of the hymns from Qumran is best understood as Menahem, a respected Jerusalem scholar who flourished in the final decades before the turn of the era.[6] He would have been a member of the court of Herod the Great, who trusted him as an adviser on matters related to the Jews. At the same time, he belonged to a secret society of revolutionaries dedicated to the overthrow of Roman control. There is mention of Menahem in both the Mishnah and the Jerusalem Talmud. These references point to an attempt by this messiah to enlist the assistance of the Pharisees, led by Hillel, in an armed revolt against Roman power. However, Hillel rejected his plan and banished him from the presence of the Pharisees. Sometime subsequent to this, his followers understood that Menahem was killed, his body exposed to public scorn, and after three days he was resurrected. Knohl emphasizes the title "son of God" and other motifs that occur in Roman honorifics to the reigning emperor in the same period. He suggests that there was influence between Roman sources and those of Judaism in the first century B.C.

Both Wise and Knohl thus interpret texts from Qumran as bearing witness to a messiah before the time of Jesus. For both, this messiah flourished in the first century B.C., though at different times. Both identify the figure as a Jewish male who gained respect and influence at the highest levels of Jerusalem politics due to his understanding, interpretation, and teaching of the Jewish Scriptures. He also was a leader of a group of followers. These followers were banished, along with their leader, after a confrontation with Jewish authorities. For both Wise and Knohl, the leader experienced a time of defeat and eventual death in rel-

6. Israel Knohl, *The Messiah before Jesus: The Suffering Servant of the Dead Sea Scrolls* (Berkeley: University of California Press, 2000).

ative obscurity, and both writers regard this figure as the direct antecedent to the messianic self-understanding of Jesus of Nazareth.

For Wise, the background is a more general one in which his messiah, Judah, actually creates the category of messiah as a religious leader who ushers in the new age. Thus, Judah's teachings and ideas serve to provide essential background for the messianism of all later Jewish messiahs and especially for some of the ideas and teachings of Jesus. Wise sets his whole movement in the context of crisis cults. He examines such cults found throughout the world and uses common traits and problems found in these as his basis for filling in the gaps of the account as reconstructed from the Qumran literature.

Knohl, on the other hand, makes wider and more eclectic use of contemporary and later sources in establishing his case. Knohl seems to make less use of any model for reconstructing the life and ministry of his messiah, except for the Jesus of the Gospel accounts. One has the sense that he wishes to find in the Dead Sea Scrolls a theology and "gospel message" as close to those of the New Testament as possible.

As must be the case with these interpretations, they are as convincing as their sources are credible. This is the great weakness of both, and it remains a problem for any reconstruction of a historical messiah from the Dead Sea Scrolls. There simply is insufficient detail to allow a specific location of such a figure in what is known of the historical events of the first century B.C., or the century before or after. This problem cannot be resolved by creative application of anthropological models of crisis cult leaders, as Wise attempts, or by the wide-ranging use of Roman and later Jewish and Christian sources, as Knohl suggests. In both cases we are left with hypothesis and speculation as the glue that ties together disparate and vague allusions. It remains to be shown that any of the Qumran hymns, even those with first-person references, were intended to be read against the developments of Jewish history and to produce an actual picture of a messianic individual. Instead, it is clear that these hymns share many of the features of laments and praises that occur in the psalmic literature of Judaism and originate in the psalms of the Old Testament. Such poetry seems intentionally devoid of much in the way of specific historical references as a means to allow its greater application beyond one individual to a larger community of worshipers. Thus, the historical interpretations of this psalmic literature are subject to the same criticism of speculative reconstruction as the attempts by a biblical scholar to apply Ps. 51–72 to the sequence of events in the lives of David and Solomon narrated in the books of Samuel and Kings.[7] There, at least, the title of Ps. 51

7. Michael D. Goulder, *The Prayers of David (Psalms 51–72): Studies in the Psalter, II*, JSOTSup 102 (Sheffield: JSOT Press, 1990).

provides a hint as to a historical context. However, both the biblical psalms and those of Qumran lack a clear and compelling case for linking the various poetic allusions of their contents to historical figures and events. The very nature of the two completely different reconstructions of Wise and Knohl bears witness to the problematic nature of this exercise.

That is not to say that there is not much that is useful and can be learned from these two studies. Both promise more detailed and scholarly studies defending aspects of their conclusions, and these no doubt will provide a better understanding of their positions. At present, one of the most important observations that both reconstructions agree on is the application of the Qumran *Hymn of Self-Glorification* to messianic understanding in the century before Jesus of Nazareth. This hymn has been identified in at least four fragments and variants.[8] As an example, 4Q491c, frag. 1, lines 7–11 may be cited:

> [7][. . .] I am counted among the gods and my dwelling is in the holy congregation; [my] des[ire] is not according to the flesh, [but] all that is precious to me is in (the) glory (of) [8][. . .] the holy [dwel]ling. [W]ho has been considered despicable on my account? And who is comparable to me in my glory? Who, like the sailors, will come back and tell? [9][. . .] Who bea[rs all] sorrows like me? And who [suffe]rs evil like me? There is no-one. I have been instructed, and there is no teaching comparable [10][to my teaching . . .] And who will attack me when [I] op[en my mouth]? And who can endure the flow of my lips? And who will confront me and retain comparison with my judgment? [11][. . . friend of the king, companion of the holy ones . . . incomparable, f]or among the gods is [my] posi[tion, and] my glory is with the sons of the king.[9]

This collection of prophetic references includes allusions to the unique text of Isa. 53, the passage of the suffering servant. The psalmist of this Qumran text therefore identified with the suffering of that servant and, in the same breath, with the exaltation to the highest places of heaven, in the presence of God. This integration of both themes is a key text. Whether or not the composer was a messiah such as Wise and Knohl describe, the text, as it appears among the Dead Sea Scrolls, demonstrates an awareness of the importance of the suffering servant passage and its close tie to an exalted, perhaps divine, figure. This connection was present before the coming of Jesus and thus served as one source for the Gospel writers' understanding of his mission.

8. 1QH[a] 26 (top); 4Q427 7 I; 4Q471b 1–3; and 4Q491c 1.

9. Florentino García Martínez and Eibert J. C. Tigchelaar, eds., *The Dead Sea Scrolls Study Edition: Volume 2 (4Q274–11Q31)* (Leiden: Brill; Grand Rapids: Eerdmans, 2000), 980–81. Note that the brackets indicate reconstructions on the basis of other parallel fragments.

Part 3

THE MESSIAH IN THE NEW TESTAMENT

SIX

Messiah
in the New Testament

CRAIG L. BLOMBERG

To survey the theme of the messiah in the New Testament is a daunting task, not easily defined. Many might expect an exercise in biblical theology, that is, a focus on the distinctive contributions of each New Testament author or corpus to the varied portrait of Jesus with his many titles and functions. This task is important, but it has been done repeatedly and accurately, and clearly it requires more than one chapter of a book to accomplish in any detail.[1] Alternately, one might imagine a word study that takes into account every usage of the Greek term *Christos* ("Christ"), the translation of the Hebrew *māšîaḥ*, "anointed one." But the word occurs 531 times in the standard critical editions of the Greek New Testament, so even this narrower task would quickly become both tedious and repetitious.[2] This essay, then, will tackle something less ambitious but hopefully more significant, as it undertakes a little of both of the above tasks of biblical theology and lexical study but also defends a particular thesis with respect to the use of *Christos* in the New Testament that cuts sharply against the grain of much current scholarship.

1. The best recent example is Ben Witherington III, *The Many Faces of the Christ* (New York: Crossroad, 1998).
2. Contrast the abbreviated studies in the standard lexical tools; for example, Karl H. Rengstorf, "Jesus Christ, Nazarene, Christian," *NIDNTT* 2:330–48.

A generation ago it was widely held that New Testament theology developed in a fairly linear fashion, as the fledgling Jesus movement expanded from its Palestinian Jewish origins to a Hellenistic Jewish milieu and finally to a Hellenistic Gentile context. Christology in particular, it was believed, evolved slowly from a thoroughly Jewish view of Jesus the admired teacher and prophet to a Greco-Roman portrait of a divine son of God.[3] With a few notable exceptions,[4] this approach is now largely abandoned in favor of a far more nuanced summary of early christological developments. Today most scholars recognize elements of a very "high" Christology already within pre-Pauline creeds (e.g., Phil. 2:6–11; Col. 1:15–20), which probably emerged within the first decades after Jesus' life, and very "undeveloped" forms of referring to the Christ even in some of the latest New Testament literature at the end of the first century (e.g., the very Jewish uses of "messiah"—twice in Greek transliteration—in the Johannine Gospel and Epistles). Yet it is still widely assumed, across the major theological spectra, that *Christos* began as a title in the earliest stages of Christianity but quickly divested itself of this significance so that for much of apostolic Christianity it functioned as little more than Jesus' "last name."[5] It is this conclusion that this essay will challenge head-on.

Jewish Backgrounds

Previous chapters in this book have examined significant Old Testament and intertestamental uses of *māšiah* in some detail. Suffice it to summarize here by saying that the anthology of essays edited by James Charlesworth has demonstrated the diversity of expectations (and the occasional lack of any expectation) surrounding a messianic figure in pre-Christian Judaism,[6] while John Collins's major study has rehabili-

3. See Ferdinand Hahn, *The Titles of Jesus in Christology* (London: Lutterworth, 1969); Reginald H. Fuller, *The Foundations of New Testament Christology* (New York: Scribner's, 1965).

4. For example, P. M. Casey, *From Jewish Prophet to Gentile God* (Cambridge: Clarke, 1991); Georg Strecker, *Theology of the New Testament* (New York: de Gruyter, 2000).

5. For example, Leonhard Goppelt, *Theology of the New Testament*, 2 vols. (Grand Rapids: Eerdmans, 1981–82), 1:168–72; James D. G. Dunn, *Unity and Diversity in the New Testament*, 2d ed. (Harrisburg, Pa.: Trinity Press International, 1990), 41–45; George E. Ladd, *A Theology of the New Testament*, rev. and ed. Donald A. Hagner (Grand Rapids: Eerdmans, 1993), 139–41.

6. James H. Charlesworth, ed., *The Messiah* (Minneapolis: Fortress, 1992). See also Howard C. Kee, "Christology in Mark's Gospel," in *Judaisms and Their Messiahs at the Turn of the Christian Era*, ed. Jacob Neusner, William S. Green, and Ernest Frerichs (Cambridge: Cambridge University Press, 1987), 190.

tated the notion that a nationalist, militaristic messiah who was not necessarily more than a great man still reflected the perspective of at least a plurality, if not even a small majority, of first-century Jews.[7] We may not presuppose, as we turn to the New Testament, that, when Jesus or his first followers used the term "messiah," they could count on an agreed-upon meaning for it, but we may assume that many might well have looked for a warrior who would help Israel rid the land of the Romans. In both cases, whatever Jesus or the New Testament writers meant by "messiah" would have to be clarified; it could not simply be taken for granted as already understood.

The Historical Jesus

A huge body of literature attaches to the ongoing "third quest" for the historical Jesus, with respect to virtually every major theme or aspect of his life. The most explicit Christology in the canonical Gospels is also the most controversial, being attributed to the early church rather than to Jesus himself by all but the most conservative of scholars. Ben Witherington and N. T. Wright have broken fresh ground, among more conservative treatments, by stressing the more implicit christological teaching and behavior of Jesus in the context of the ongoing narratives of Jewish history.[8] Raymond Brown speaks for many "centrists" by contending that it is "implausible" that Jesus ever denied that he was the messiah, "very probable" that his followers thought of him as such during his lifetime, and "probable that Jesus never clearly or enthusiastically accepted the title in the sense in which both followers and opponents proposed it for him."[9]

To enter into this debate would require another extensive essay all its own. Nevertheless, at least one interesting connection with the development of New Testament Christology more generally emerges at this juncture. We will see that the vast majority of the uses of *Christos* on the pages of the four Gospels clearly are titular, an observation that does not readily support the theory of linear development unless most of those uses reflect actual incidents from the life of the historical Jesus.

7. John J. Collins, *The Scepter and the Star* (New York: Doubleday, 1995). See also I. Howard Marshall, "The Messiah in the First Century: A Review Article," *CTR* 7 (1993): 67–83.

8. Ben Witherington III, *The Christology of Jesus* (Minneapolis: Fortress, 1990); N. T. Wright, *Jesus and the Victory of God*, vol. 2 of *Christian Origins and the Question of God* (Minneapolis: Fortress, 1996).

9. Raymond E. Brown, *An Introduction to New Testament Christology* (New York: Paulist, 1994), 79.

On even conservative datings, the Gospels were written later than most or all of Paul's letters, and yet it is Paul, not the Gospels, that seems to shift to the use of "Christ" as a name. On the other hand, if the four evangelists are reflecting accurate usage from the lifetime of Jesus of Nazareth, it is possible that the linear theory still could be defended. Yet this is precisely not the combination of conclusions typically affirmed by adherents of a linear trajectory of development. What is more, as my study unfolds, we will see that this theory does not adequately account for the New Testament data in other respects either. With these preliminary remarks in mind, it is time to turn to the texts of the New Testament themselves to see what kind of uses of "messiah" emerge.

The Gospel of Mark

If even a significant fraction of this first written Gospel is historically accurate, the appropriate chronological starting point for this survey is Mark. This Gospel refers to Jesus in its very first verse as "Christ" and "Son of God." Neither attribution has the definite article in the Greek, but "Son of God" clearly is titular in meaning throughout Mark's work, so it is reasonable to assume that "Christ" is too.[10] This, in fact, is what subsequent usages bear out. Though occurring only six more times, five of these six occurrences are very strategically located and clearly titular in meaning, as Jack Kingsbury has stressed.[11]

Thus, after giving us ample illustration of Jesus' messianic ministry, Mark concludes the first "half" of his Gospel with the conversation between Jesus and the disciples on the road to Caesarea Philippi, in which Peter explicitly confesses him to be the Christ (Mark 8:29). Despite one strand of scholarship that claims that Jesus refused the title,[12] it seems best to understand his subsequent command to silence and teachings about the road to the cross (8:30, 31–38) as simply significant qualification of the conventional expectation surrounding the label. A suffering, dying messiah was still not in these Jewish disciples' purview.[13] A similar strategy best accounts for the exchange between the high priest and Jesus at his trial before the Sanhedrin. Asked if he

10. Cf. Phillip G. Davis, "Mark's Christological Paradox," *JSNT* 35 (1989): 11–12. We might also invoke Apollonius's corollary here: when both nouns in this kind of genitive construction are anarthrous, "both will usually have the same semantic force" (Daniel B. Wallace, *Greek Grammar beyond the Basics* [Grand Rapids: Zondervan, 1996], 250).

11. Jack D. Kingsbury, *The Christology of Mark's Gospel* (Philadelphia: Fortress, 1983).

12. For example, C. S. Mann, *Mark,* AB 27 (Garden City, N.Y.: Doubleday, 1986), 115.

13. R. Alan Cole, *Mark,* 2d ed., TNTC (Grand Rapids: Eerdmans, 1989), 61–62; William R. Telford, *The Theology of the Gospel of Mark* (Cambridge: Cambridge University Press, 1999), 35–38.

is "the Christ, the Son of the Blessed," Jesus replies, "I am," but immediately refers to the exalted "Son of Man" to illustrate the nature of his messiahship (14:61–62). It is almost certainly the latter claim that yields the response of "blasphemy," not the former.[14] In between these two appearances of *Christos,* we find the term also in 12:35, in which Jesus is demonstrating that the messiah cannot be merely a human "son of David" if that very king in a psalm traditionally ascribed to him speaks of the messiah as his Lord. Jesus' point is consistent with his redefinition at his trial, and his more indirect self-reference supports the authenticity of the episode.[15]

The other three uses of "messiah" in Mark prove less central but do not conflict with the patterns just noted. The oddest of these references is 9:41: "Anyone who gives you a cup of water in my name because you belong to Christ will certainly be rewarded."[16] Here is the one reference in Mark in which it would seem most natural to take the anarthrous "Christ" as equivalent just to a name, and probably a redactional reworking of an original saying of Jesus more akin to the parallel in Matt. 10:42, which lacks *Christos* altogether.[17] On the other hand, the genitive construction *Christou este* may account for the absence of the article on purely grammatical grounds, with *Christou* referring back to the clearly titular use in Mark 8:29, as Jesus demonstrates how to act consistently with a confession like Peter's.[18] The remaining two references in Mark are unambiguously titular: 13:21 warns against false messiahs (and not necessarily just those claiming to be Jesus),[19] while 15:32 presents the crowds taunting Jesus on the cross to come down if he is "this Christ, this king of Israel," the one they no doubt had hoped would turn into a political savior.[20]

The concept of messiah thus remains relatively undeveloped in Mark but should be interpreted by its collocation with other titles—"Son of God," "Son of David," "Lord," and "King."[21] It always is an accurate de-

---

14. See Darrell L. Bock, *Blasphemy and Exaltation in Judaism* (Tübingen: Mohr, 1998).

15. Cf. Marinus de Jonge, *Christology in Context* (Philadelphia: Westminster, 1988), 60–61.

16. Unless otherwise specified, all translations are taken from the NIV.

17. Werner G. Kümmel, *The Theology of the New Testament* (Nashville: Abingdon, 1973), 69; Hans Conzelmann, *An Outline of the Theology of the New Testament* (New York: Harper & Row, 1969), 129–30.

18. Robert H. Gundry, *Mark: A Commentary on His Apology for the Cross* (Grand Rapids: Eerdmans, 1993), 523.

19. Morna D. Hooker, *The Gospel according to Saint Mark,* BNTC (London: Black, 1991), 317.

20. Note G. B. Caird and L. D. Hurst, *New Testament Theology* (Oxford: Clarendon, 1994), 168: "For Mark 'Messiah' means 'King of Israel.'"

21. Edwin K. Broadhead, *Naming Jesus* (Sheffield: Sheffield Academic Press, 1999), 145–54.

scriptor but seldom an adequate one. Jesus is indeed God's anointed, through whose ministry of word and deed God is acting in history to establish his reign.[22] But it is only after his death and resurrection that one can fully understand the kind of messiah he was (9:9); hence the frequent injunctions to silence during his earthly ministry.[23]

The Gospel of Matthew

Matthew takes over four of Mark's eight uses of *Christos*. Three of these appear in passages that largely duplicate Mark's language and contents, although, interestingly, each seems to spawn an additional unparalleled use of the title in its larger context (cf. Matt. 24:23 with 24:5; 26:63 with 26:68; 27:22 with 27:17). In one instance, Matthew's parallel proves dramatically different from Mark, with Simon Peter's Matthean confession receiving Jesus' lavish praise (Matt. 16:16; cf. vv. 17–19). This, however, fits Matthew's heightened "Son of God" Christology as compared with Mark more generally.[24]

More telling perhaps are Matthew's several other unparalleled uses. Like Mark, Matthew uses "Christ" in his opening verse, again without the article. Again, too, the link with clearly titular but anarthrous predicates—"son of Abraham," "son of David"—confirms Matthew's intent, as do the articular uses of *Christos* in the genealogy immediately following (Matt. 1:16, 17).[25] The article at the beginning of 2:1 probably is resumptive, suggesting the sense, "Now the birth of *this* Jesus Christ" (i.e., the Jesus just identified as the messiah).[26] The traditional sense of the

22. Robert A. Guelich, "The 'Christ' of the Gospel: A Lesson from Mark's Christology," in *Perspectives on Christology*, ed. Marguerite Schuster and Richard Mueller (Grand Rapids: Zondervan, 1991), 16.

23. The vexed question of Mark's "messianic secret" lies beyond the scope of this paper, but for a representative sampling of scholarly perspectives, see Christopher Tuckett, ed. *The Messianic Secret* (Philadelphia: Fortress, 1983). For a very recent, succinct overview and conclusions consistent with my findings, see Craig A. Evans, *Mark 8:27–16:20*, WBC 34B (Nashville: Nelson, 2001), lxx–lxxii. On Mark's Christology more generally, see ibid., lxx–lxxx.

24. On which, see Jack D. Kingsbury, *Matthew: Structure, Christology, Kingdom* (Philadelphia: Fortress, 1975), though needing to be tempered with Donald J. Verseput, "The Role and Meaning of the 'Son of God' Title in Matthew's Gospel," *NTS* 33 (1987): 532–56. The balance seems to be captured correctly by Lidija Novakovic, "Jesus as the Davidic Messiah in Matthew," *HBT* 19 (1997): 148–91. For Novakovic (152–53), Matthew progressively redefines the Christ or Davidic messiah as the "Son of God."

25. R. T. France (*Matthew: Evangelist and Teacher* [Exeter: Paternoster, 1989], 281) notes that both the use of *legomenos* and the twofold occurrence of the definite article confirm that Matthew understood "Christ" as a title, even in the narrative portions of his writing.

26. Robert H. Gundry, *Matthew: A Commentary on His Handbook for a Mixed Church under Persecution*, 2d ed. (Grand Rapids: Eerdmans, 1994), 26.

predicted Jewish liberator is clear when Herod inquires of the religious leaders "where the Christ was to be born" (2:4).[27] Matthew 11:2 reflects a key usage of "messiah" in this Gospel, as John the Baptist sends some of his disciples to Jesus in response, literally, to "the works of the Christ." In replying to the question about his identity, Jesus points people to his miracles, couched in language that recalls Isa. 35:5–6 and the wonders that would accompany the messianic age. Finally, the oddest use of the title in Matthew probably is 23:10, where, as in Mark 9:41, Jesus uses the label in the third person, almost as if he were referring to someone else: "Nor are you to be called 'teacher', for you have one Teacher, the Christ." But the parallels with synonymous commands regarding "rabbi," "master," and "father" make it plain that "Christ" is still conceived of as a title.

It is surprising that most studies of "Christ" in the New Testament treat Matthew as if he had little to add to Mark.[28] Rather, it appears that the title is considerably more important to Matthew, as he employs it sixteen times (vs. seven in Mark). This is precisely what we would expect in the most Jewish of the four Gospels, and the titular sense is retained in every instance.[29] When one adds related concepts, most notably the eschatological prophet or the new Moses,[30] the christological database becomes larger still. Rudolf Schnackenburg overstates the matter only slightly when he concludes that *Christos* "is for Matthew the summary designation . . . for the bringer of salvation who comes out of Israel and goes his way through the cross and resurrection."[31]

The Gospel of Luke

A full-orbed assessment of Luke's theology will have to await my survey of Acts, but there are significant enough differences in Luke's christological emphasis in his Gospel from those in Acts to merit treating the two separately (and to suggest that Luke is not blurring the historical distinctions between pre- and post-Easter

27. On royal messianic imagery in Matthew more generally, see Brian M. Nolan, *The Royal Son of God* (Fribourg: Editions Universitaires, 1979).

28. An important exception is Goppelt, *Theology of the New Testament*, 2:216–24. For a good summary of the Christology of Matthew more generally, see Birger Gerhardsson, "The Christology of Matthew," in *Who Do You Say That I Am? Essays on Christology*, ed. Mark A. Powell and David R. Bauer (Louisville: Westminster John Knox, 1999), 14–32.

29. See Leon Morris, *New Testament Theology* (Grand Rapids: Zondervan, 1986), 126.

30. On which, see Dale C. Allison Jr., *The New Moses* (Minneapolis: Fortress, 1993), even if at times he overstates the case for Mosaic typology.

31. Rudolf Schnackenburg, *Jesus in the Gospels: A Biblical Christology* (Louisville: Westminster John Knox, 1995), 105.

theology).[32] Luke does not introduce Christology into his first verse, but Luke 2:11 functions as a programmatic introduction to his most important titles for Jesus: "Today in the town of David a Savior has been born to you; he is Christ the Lord." "Savior" (and related words for salvation) reflects Luke's most distinctive Christology, particularly in his Gospel; "Lord" reflects his most characteristic title, particularly in Acts.[33] The anarthrous "Christ" in 2:11 once again leaves the reader wondering about exact usage, but Luke 1–2 is dominated by imagery of the Davidic messiah, so the royal background should be apparent.[34] And a scant fourteen verses later, Luke describes Simeon as one whom God had promised would live until he had seen "the Lord's Christ," an allusion to 1 Sam. 24:6, in which David refers to King Saul as "the anointed of the Lord."

Ten additional uses of "Christ" in Luke confirm this word's consistent titular meaning. Seven of these occur in the narrative of Jesus' last week of life. Four of the ten parallel Mark and add little to our understanding of the term (9:20; 20:41; 22:67; 23:35), although the expression "the Christ of God" in 9:20 and 23:35 also harks back to the Old Testament language of "the Lord's [i.e., God's] Christ." The first remaining unparalleled use appears in 3:15, in which people begin to wonder if the Baptist is the messiah. In 4:41, Luke uses "the Christ" as a synonym for "the Son of God," as elsewhere in Mark and Matthew. In 23:2, *Christos* is explained for Luke's Gentile audience by the appositional *basileus* ("king").[35] Luke 23:39 affords a conceptual equivalent to the crowds' taunts, but now from a fellow criminal being crucified: "Aren't you the Christ? Save yourself and us!" The last two references appear in 24:26, in which we read that it was necessary for the Christ to suffer and die and to fulfill everything prophesied about him in all three divisions of the Hebrew Scriptures. This theme will recur repeatedly in Acts. One additional text in Luke merits mention, for even though it does not contain the noun "anointed one," it employs the cognate verb, "to anoint" (*chrio*). That text is 4:18, in which Jesus introduces his Nazareth "manifesto" with the quotation from Isa. 61:1 that "the Spirit of the Lord . . .

---

32. On which, see I. Howard Marshall, *Luke: Historian and Theologian*, 3d ed. (Exeter: Paternoster, 1988).

33. Cf. C. F. D. Moule, "The Christology of Acts," in *Studies in Luke-Acts*, ed. Leander E. Keck and J. Louis Martyn (Nashville: Abingdon, 1966), 159–85.

34. I. Howard Marshall (*The Gospel of Luke*, NIGTC [Grand Rapids: Eerdmans, 1978], 110) says that the verse implies "that Jesus is 'the Messiah (and) the Lord,'" perhaps even a savior who is Yahweh.

35. Ibid., 853. See also C. F. Evans, *Saint Luke*, TPINTC (London: SCM; Philadelphia: Trinity Press International, 1990), 74.

has anointed me." Luke unambiguously knows the Jewish background to *Christos* and preserves it throughout his Gospel.[36]

Thus, Luke expands on Mark's use of "messiah" to about the same degree as Matthew does. Again, this time responding to Christopher Tuckett, it probably goes too far to call it the most all-embracing christological title for Luke.[37] Nevertheless, it is a singularly important one, the significance of which Joseph Fitzmyer aptly captures: "For Luke the title *christos* used of Jesus designates him as God's anointed agent announcing himself as the bearer of a new form of salvation to mankind and its relation to God's kingdom among them in a new form."[38]

Q

It goes beyond the scope of this paper to assess the contents of every putative Gospel source, but because interest in Q remains at such a high level, at least two brief observations merit mention. On the one hand, despite Matthew's and Luke's considerably larger number of uses of "messiah" than in Mark, in no instance do Matthew and Luke make the same additions of the term. Put another way, if Q existed, it has left no traces of the occurrence of the word "Christ" as part of its contents. At first glance, this curious omission could suggest that the title was not part of the earliest Christian vocabulary for describing Jesus. On the other hand, Q is made up almost entirely of sayings material, and it includes no infancy, passion, or resurrection narratives, whereas the uses of "Christ" throughout the Gospels appear almost exclusively either in narrative passages or on the lips of characters other than Jesus. So we probably should not have expected to find "Christ" in Q, and its absence proves nothing about its tradition history.[39]

The Gospel of John

Given that John's Gospel differs from the Synoptics in so many respects, we might expect its use of *Christos* to be distinctive as well. As it

36. See de Jonge, *Christology in Context*, 100; Hans Conzelmann, *The Theology of Saint Luke* (London: Faber and Faber, 1960), 171.

37. Christopher M. Tuckett, "The Christology of Luke-Acts," in *The Unity of Luke-Acts*, ed. J. Verheyden (Leuven: Leuven University Press and Peeters, 1999), 161.

38. Joseph Fitzmyer, *The Gospel according to Luke I–IX*, AB 28 (New York: Doubleday, 1981), 199.

39. Cf. de Jonge, *Christology in Context*, 83: It is "extremely unlikely, however, that the communities in which the sayings of the Q collection were handed down knew no other traditions about Jesus' life, death, and resurrection/exaltation."

turns out, this is largely not the case. The term appears nineteen times in John, and with only a couple of exceptions the titular sense of each occurrence proves quite clear. John also is the only New Testament document to contain the actual transliteration in Greek (*messias*) of the Hebrew *māŝîaḥ*—twice, each time with explanation (1:41, 4:25).

John's first use of *Christos* comes naturally in his prologue (1:17), and it is one of the exceptional uses that could be interpreted just as a name: "For the law was given through Moses; grace and truth came through Jesus Christ." Because 1:1–18 forms the theological introduction to John, before the actual historical narrative begins in v. 19, it would be natural for John himself to use the later, common compound "name" of "Jesus Christ," even though this form reappears only once again in this Gospel.[40] But the conclusion that "Christ" has lost all its force as a title by the end of the first century cannot be assumed; we will have to evaluate that claim after we have surveyed the rest of the New Testament's usage. Certainly, as John himself continues writing, he provides almost no further support for this notion.

Instead, the conventional Jewish use of *Christos* dominates. John 1:20 and 25 find the Jewish authorities asking the Baptist if he is "the Christ" in conjunction with their questioning him about other titles too.[41] After Jesus appears on the scene, he is acclaimed with a barrage of titles, all of which boil down to early belief that he is the messiah (1:41).[42] Despite frequent claims that this presentation contradicts the Synoptics, those Gospels also reflect testimony to Jesus' exalted nature, beginning at his baptism (Mark 1:11 pars.).[43] Moreover, much later, John's Gospel itself will demonstrate that Jesus' followers have not well understood his identity throughout his ministry (16:29–30), which warns us not to read much distinctively Christian understanding into these early confessions.

The extended conversation between Jesus and the Samaritan woman leads to his own self-disclosure as the Jewish messiah to this unlikely prospective follower (4:25). Again, the difference with the apparently slow progression of the revelation of Jesus' identity in the Synoptics

40. We may not simply assume that the prologue was written first to provide a key for interpreting all crucial terminology recurring throughout John's Gospel. It may well be, with Ed L. Miller ("The Johannine Origins of the Johannine Logos," *JBL* 112 [1993]: 445–57), that the prologue was composed last on the basis of the contents of the rest of John's narrative, in which case the usage of any term in the body of the Gospel might largely determine its meaning in the prologue.

41. John's denial of being the Christ may have been included because of a Baptist-worshiping sect in existence already at the end of the first century.

42. On which, see Rodney A. Whitacre, *John,* IVPNTCS 4 (Downers Grove, Ill.: Inter-Varsity, 1999), 72–73.

43. Donald Guthrie, *New Testament Theology* (Leicester: Inter-Varsity, 1981), 244.

stands out. But the very fact that she is a Samaritan probably explains his openness; the Samaritans were looking more for a messianic teacher than for a military revolutionary.[44] Jesus' behavior also fits the consistent Synoptic pattern in which he reveals himself to "outsiders" to the Jewish establishment while remaining frustratingly cryptic with the upstanding, religious "insiders" (cf. esp. Matt. 11:25–30).[45]

The next several Johannine uses of "Christ" all reflect intra-Jewish debates readily conceivable in the first third of the first century. The crowds in Jerusalem wonder whether some of their leaders have come to believe in Jesus as the Messiah (7:26). The crowds themselves divide over whether he could be the Christ, because they think they know his origin, whereas one strand of messianic expectation looks for a "hidden messiah" to reveal himself suddenly (7:27). Still, his wondrous miracles appear messianic in nature (v. 31).[46] The debate soon progresses to the question of his birthplace; many think that Jesus came from Nazareth, not Bethlehem, where the Scriptures predicted the Christ would be born (7:41 [2x]).[47] John 9:22 plunges the reader into the vexed question of Jewish excommunication of synagogue members for "confessing Christ." After a period in which most scholars were convinced that such actions began only at the end of the first century, it is now far more common to find support for the historicity of this policy in and around Jerusalem already during Jesus' lifetime.[48] The anarthrous *Christos* is explained by the double accusative: "they confessed him [direct object] *as* Christ [predicate object]," a construction that makes it probable that the label continues to be viewed as a title.

The titular form unambiguously reappears in 10:24, as Jesus' opponents insist, "If you are the Christ, tell us plainly," a key text in showing that Jesus has not been as open with the Jewish leaders in John's Gospel as much as his preceding "I am" texts often have suggested to Christian readers.[49] Martha's confession in 11:27 retains the titular

44. Leon Morris, *Jesus Is the Christ* (Grand Rapids: Eerdmans, 1989), 75.

45. D. A. Carson, *The Gospel according to John*, PNTC (Grand Rapids: Eerdmans, 1991), 227.

46. On the expectation of a "hidden messiah" to emerge out of "nowhere," see Raymond E. Brown, *The Gospel according to John I–XII*, AB 29 (Garden City: Doubleday, 1966), 313.

47. But John's readers know better and can support the messianic identification (Leon Morris, *The Gospel according to John*, 2d ed., NICNT [Grand Rapids: Eerdmans, 1995], 380 n. 98).

48. See Stephen Motyer, *Your Father the Devil?* (Carlisle: Paternoster, 1997), 92–94, and the literature cited there.

49. A key text also linking John's presentation of Jesus with Mark's messianic secret. See further C. K. Barrett, *The Gospel according to St. John*, 2d ed. (London: SPCK, 1978), 378.

sense—"you are the Christ, the Son of God"—and sets the stage for John's purpose statement in 20:31 involving the identical titles.[50] John 12:34 reflects the intra-Jewish debate over whether or not the messiah was eternal; a majority seemed to think that he was.[51] Finally, the one other reference that seemingly breaks John's mold is 17:3, in which Jesus, in his high-priestly prayer, apparently refers to himself in the third person as "Jesus Christ." But more likely this is John's "targumic," explanatory insertion into Jesus' prayer (in a world without footnotes) and, like 1:17, reflects end-of-first-century usage.[52] Still, this conclusion does not demonstrate that John has abandoned the use of "Christ" as a title.

If John's Gospel is not substantially historical in nature, then the information reviewed above conclusively disproves any linear development of *Christos* away from its original Jewish usage, since almost all scholars agree that John wrote in approximately the 90s, toward the end of the formation of the New Testament documents.[53] One can, of course, postulate hypothetical early Jewish-Christian stages of John's community reflected in his language, but there is no actual external evidence to support this hypothesis. What both the internal and the external evidence of the Johannine Epistles do point to, however, is an antidocetic impulse in which John must stress the humanity of Jesus.[54] The more exalted, titular sense of "the Christ" does not obviously fit this redactional need and thus is better attributed to the actual people with whom the historical Jesus interacted. Theologically, Marinus de Jonge's conclusions concerning Johannine usage strikingly resemble the consensus views on Mark: "The Jewish statements about the messiah *either* point to a complete misunderstanding (7:27, 41b–42; 12:34) and are, therefore, ignored (7:41b, 42; 12:34) or reinterpreted fundamentally (7:27); *or* they represent an inadequate formulation of belief in Jesus (7:31), which is subsequently im-

50. Martha's understanding may not be nearly as full as her language at first glance might suggest; see Francis J. Moloney, *The Gospel of John*, SP 4 (Collegeville, Minn.: Liturgical Press, 1998), 327–31.

51. For a survey of texts, see Morris, *John*, 532. An important exception describing a mortal messiah appears in 2 Esdr. 7:28, 30.

52. So even as conservative a commentator as Ben Witherington III (*John's Wisdom* [Louisville: Westminster John Knox, 1995], 269).

53. D. Moody Smith (*The Theology of the Gospel of John* [Cambridge: Cambridge University Press, 1995], 86–87) observes, "No Gospel stands at a greater remove from such [conventional Jewish nationalist messianic] hope and expectation than John; but at the same time no Gospel is more clearly in touch with Jewish, traditional roots." See also Paul N. Anderson, *A Christology of the Fourth Gospel* (Tübingen: Mohr, 1996), 20 n. 6.

54. On which, see Udo Schnelle, *Antidocetic Christology in the Gospel of John* (Minneapolis: Fortress, 1992).

plicitly corrected."[55] Finally, "Christ" is not the most fundamental title for John, even if the more expansive Christology of the rest of his Gospel does link it with a very elevated view of Jesus.[56]

The Book of Acts

We return now to Luke's work. *Christos* continues to play an important role, appearing twenty-five times in Luke's second volume. While Darrell Bock perceives an overall shift from messiah to prophet to servant to Lord throughout these two books, Mark Strauss observes that messiah reemerges in Acts with considerable significance.[57] Variations in the form in which "Christ" appears, however, for the first time occur often enough to merit categorizing.

In eight contexts, *Christos* is unambiguously titular. Acts 2:31 speaks of the resurrection of the Christ in the context of the quotation of a messianic psalm (Ps. 16:10). Acts 2:36 announces Jesus' exaltation after that resurrection and his reenthronement as both "Lord and Christ."[58] The same pair of titles recurs in 4:26, quoting another messianic psalm (Ps. 2:2) and echoing the use in Luke's Gospel of "the Lord's Christ." In 8:5 Philip preaches "the Christ" to the Samaritans; in 9:22 the newly converted Saul demonstrates to Jews in Damascus that Jesus is "the Christ." Three times we read that the Christ had to suffer (3:18; 17:3; 26:23; recall Luke 24:26). In six of these eight passages the audiences clearly are Jewish; in the other two (8:5; 26:23) the speakers can assume knowledge of Jewish beliefs about the messiah (among the Samaritans and with Herod Agrippa II).[59]

On the other hand, Acts presents eight additional texts that employ the compound form "Jesus Christ." Is this the beginning of Christian usage of this expression as a mere name? Probably not, because six of the eight references appear in the formula "the name of Jesus Christ" (2:38; 3:6; 4:10; 8:12; 10:48; 16:18), in which the genitive noun in con-

---

55. Marinus de Jonge, *Jesus: Stranger from Heaven and Son of God* (Missoula, Mont.: Scholars Press, 1977), 85.

56. Contra John F. O'Grady, *According to John: The Witness of the Beloved Disciple* (New York: Paulist Press, 1999), 18–19.

57. Darrell L. Bock, *Proclamation from Prophecy and Pattern*, JSOTSup 12 (Sheffield: JSOT Press, 1987); Mark L. Strauss, *The Davidic Messiah in Luke-Acts*, JSNTSup 110 (Sheffield: Sheffield Academic Press, 1995).

58. Contra the view that takes this text as supporting adoptionism, see C. K. Barrett, *A Critical and Exegetical Commentary on the Acts of the Apostles*, 2 vols., ICC (Edinburgh: Clark, 1994–98), 2:lxxxv.

59. Richard N. Longenecker, *The Christology of Early Jewish Christianity* (London: SCM, 1970), 74–75.

struction could account for the anarthrous form all by itself.[60] After all, 2:38 appears almost immediately after the titular use in 2:36, which surely would govern the meaning of the later verse (cf. also 8:12 after 8:5). The other two uses of the compound form are "Jesus Christ heals you" (9:34) and "peace through Jesus Christ" (10:36), which prove equally formulaic and could have been modeled on the form of "the name of Jesus Christ" references. The latter text also goes on immediately to call Jesus "Lord of all," further suggesting that titles are being predicated of him.

In six instances, Luke precedes the name "Jesus" with "Christ" but not in the normal compound form ("Christ Jesus") that Paul regularly employs. Instead, we read that God will send "the Christ . . . even Jesus" (3:20);[61] that the disciples proclaimed the Christ to be Jesus (5:42); that Paul explained "that this is the Christ, Jesus" (17:3); and that the Christ was Jesus (18:5, 28). In each of these last four texts, the NIV (like many translations) reverses the order of the proper nouns, thus masking the original constructions. The only anarthrous use of "Christ" in these six texts comes in 24:24 in the expression that Paul "spoke about faith in Christ Jesus." But this is not yet Paul's famous *en Christō*; rather, Luke writes *eis Christon Iēsoun pisteōs*, which could just as readily yield the translation "faith directed toward the Christ, [that is,] Jesus," following the pattern of all of the rest of Acts' compounded forms in this sequence. The lack of the article could stem from the use of "Christ" as the object of the preposition and have no further linguistic significance.[62]

Finally, there are three passages in Acts that utilize the triple form "Lord Jesus Christ" (11:17; 15:26; 28:31). This form recurs frequently in later New Testament texts as well, but tellingly, the form "Lord Christ Jesus" never appears. If "Christ" and "Jesus" were interchangeable as simply names for the same person, this pattern would be inexplicable. But if the authors of Scripture recognized "Christ" as a title, then it makes sense that they would consistently begin with one title ("Lord"), immediately identify by name who that Lord was, and then predicate a second title of him.[63] Given that thus far Luke uniquely and consistently has used "Lord" and "Christ" together in other texts as a

60. Here, Apollonius's canon could come into play: "in genitive phrases both the head noun and the genitive noun normally have or lack the article" (Wallace, *Greek Grammar beyond the Basics*, 239).

61. Contra the view that takes 3:20 to refer to an entirely future first appearance of the messiah, see Mark A. Powell, *What Are They Saying about Acts?* (New York: Paulist Press, 1991), 42–43.

62. Wallace, *Greek Grammar beyond the Basics*, 247.

63. See Martin Hengel, *Between Jesus and Paul* (Philadelphia: Fortress, 1983), 68–69.

pair of titles for Jesus, it is most probable that he continues to do so in these three passages.[64]

Nearly seventy years ago, Henry Cadbury argued that Luke's use of *Christos* throughout Acts was consistently titular.[65] More recent scholarship almost uniformly has disagreed,[66] but the present survey discloses no reason for not preferring Cadbury to the current consensus. As in Luke's Gospel, throughout Acts "Christ" remains a title for the anticipated Jewish liberator, now identified as Jesus, who in turn has partially redefined the messianic role. More generally, as one proceeds through the two volumes, one encounters a Jesus who moves from humanity through resurrection and exaltation to heavenly lordship.[67] Less sequentially, Luke's Christology portrays Jesus as "a deity who waits on tables"—he is both God and suffering servant, as well as messiah.[68]

The Epistles of Paul

However much scholars are willing to grant that a majority of the uses of *Christos* in the Gospels and Acts remain titular, there is almost unanimous agreement that a large percentage of Paul's texts retain little if any of the historic, Jewish significance of this noun.[69] A cursory scan of the data quickly explains this consensus. The term appears approximately 380 times in the Pauline Epistles.[70] Paul twenty-two times uses the compound form "Jesus Christ" when nothing in the contexts re-

64. See Guthrie, *New Testament Theology*, 247

65. Henry J. Cadbury, "The Titles of Jesus in Acts," in *The Acts of the Apostles*, ed. F. J. Foakes-Jackson and Kirsopp Lake, *The Beginnings of Christianity*, part 1 (London: Macmillan, 1920–33), 5:358.

66. For example, Ben Witherington III, *The Acts of the Apostles: A Socio-Rhetorical Commentary* (Grand Rapids: Eerdmans, 1988), 150. Cf. Donald L. Jones, "The Title Christos in Luke-Acts," *CBQ* 32 (1970): 67–76; Stephen S. Smalley, "The Christology of Acts Again," in *Christ and the Spirit in the New Testament*, ed. Barnabas Lindars and S. S. Smalley (Cambridge: Cambridge University Press, 1973), 79–93.

67. George W. MacRae, "'Whom Heaven Must Receive until the Time': Reflections on the Christology of Acts," *Int* 27 (1973): 165.

68. H. Douglas Buckwalter, "The Divine Saviour," in *Witness to the Gospel: The Theology of Acts*, ed. I. Howard Marshall and David Peterson (Grand Rapids: Eerdmans, 1998), 119.

69. Cf. scholars as otherwise diverse as Guthrie, *New Testament Theology*, 248; Goppelt, *Theology of the New Testament*, 1:67; Kümmel, *Theology of the New Testament*, 154; Strecker, *Theology of the New Testament*, 94; and Victor P. Furnish, *Jesus according to Paul* (Cambridge: Cambridge University Press, 1993), 37.

70. The count is approximate because numerous textual variants make uncertain the original reading—with or without "Christ" in compound forms—in a number of texts. My overall generalizations, however, are not affected, so I have followed UBS[4] (= NA[27]) in every case.

quires "Christ" to be anything besides another name for Jesus. On fifty-eight additional occasions "Jesus Christ" is combined with "Lord" to create the forms "the/our Lord Jesus Christ" or "Jesus Christ the/our Lord," although thirty-six of these come after nouns in the genitive and another eight in formulaic expressions with "grace and peace," so that one suspects that certain grammatical constructions alone often trigger certain specific ways of referring to Jesus. In eighty-two instances Paul employs the form "Christ Jesus," but no other New Testament writer ever uses this expression. When one sets the lists of all the Pauline references to "Jesus Christ" (with or without "Lord") and "Christ Jesus" side by side, both cover the waterfront of major Pauline doctrines in which Jesus is mentioned, with understandable emphasis on Jesus' death, resurrection, and parousia. No demonstrable difference in topics or meanings emerges from such a comparison.

Even more telling are the approximately 220 uses of *Christos* in Paul all by itself in an even broader range of contexts. In almost every case one could substitute "Jesus" for "Christ" with no apparent loss of meaning. It is true that almost half of these stand-alone uses of "Christ" are articular, but numerous parallel expressions occur both with and without the article, suggesting that the presence or absence of "the" was almost indiscriminate, as at times seems the case with other proper nouns or names.[71] As examples of the interchangeability of anarthrous and articular forms, we could mention "body of (the) Christ," "(the) Christ according to the flesh," "day of (the) Christ," "in/into (the) Christ," "word of (the) Christ," "(the) Christ is the head," "glory of (the) Christ," "through (the) Christ," and "servants of (the) Christ."

On the other hand, a surprisingly strong case can be made against the notion that the titular sense of "Christ" in Paul usually disappears. No less than eighteen separate arguments cumulatively move us in this direction.

1. Almost all scholars agree that Rom. 9:5 is the one passage in all of Paul where clearly the titular sense of *Christos* is preserved: "Theirs [from the Jews] are the patriarchs, and from them is traced the human ancestry of [lit., 'the'] Christ, who is God over all, for ever praised! Amen."[72] So at least it is clear that Paul knew the word's historic meaning, a reasonable inference from his Jewish background anyway.

---

71. For an excellent chart representing various theological statements predicated of "Christ," "Jesus Christ," or "Christ Jesus" in Paul, see Marion L. Soards, "Christology of the Pauline Epistles," in *Who Do You Say That I Am?* ed. Powell and Bauer, 90–93. Soards then distills fifty-two theological statements that he believes can be deduced from these uses and presents them in their logical narrative sequence (93–97).

72. See Joseph A. Fitzmyer, *Paul and His Theology*, 2d ed. (Englewood Cliffs, N.J.: Prentice-Hall, 1989), 51; Furnish, *Jesus according to Paul*, 37; Strecker, *Theology*, 93.

2. In a seminal study,[73] frequently cited approvingly,[74] Nils Dahl added a number of other uses of "Christ" in Paul likely to retain the original titular sense: 1 Cor. 10:4; 15:22; 2 Cor. 5:10; 11:2–3; Phil. 1:15–17; 3:7; Rom. 1:2–4. James Dunn plausibly adds Rom. 15:3, 7, and 19;[75] worth consideration, too, are 1 Cor. 1:13; 11:3, 5; 12:12; Eph. 5:2, 23, 24, 25, 29.

3. The wordplay in 2 Cor. 1:21 (". . . you stand firm in Christ [*Christon*]. He anointed [*chrisas*] us . . .") shows that Paul knew and utilized the original meaning of *Christos* as an "anointed one" and presumably expected his readers to understand it.[76]

4. N. T. Wright suggests a considerably larger minority of Pauline passages in which the titular sense is at least as natural as a mere name, including a number of Paul's "in Christ" usages, because he understands these as "incorporative." That is, just as ancient kings were bound together with their people, Wright thinks that many of Paul's references to Christ are to "the messiah" to whom his followers are attached and who functions as their representative. An extended discussion of Philem. 6 affords a plausible illustration of this tendency.[77]

5. If it is the case, as it seems to be, that the anarthrous and articular uses of *Christos* normally are interchangeable, and given the approximately equal balance in frequency of the two forms, it is just as persuasive to argue that the titular use carries over to anarthrous forms as that the nominal use carries over to articular forms.

6. If one then asks why the variation in forms exists, the answer in a sizable majority of instances seems to be purely grammatical, syntactical, or idiomatic. Dahl, for example, observed,

> The genitive *tou Christou* is placed after an articular noun and, on the contrary, only *Christou* is used after an anarthrous noun. The article is used with the dative when it is not governed by a preposition. Otherwise, *Christos* is used most frequently without an article; where the article is

73. Nils A. Dahl, "The Messiahship of Jesus in Paul," repr. in *The Crucified Messiah* (Minneapolis: Augsburg, 1974), 40, 171.

74. For example, A. M. Hunter, *The Gospel according to St. Paul* (Philadelphia: Westminster, 1966), 64; James D. G. Dunn, *The Theology of Paul the Apostle* (Grand Rapids: Eerdmans, 1998), 198; Leander E. Keck, "'Jesus' in Romans," *JBL* 108 (1989): 445.

75. Dunn, *Theology of Paul the Apostle*, 198.

76. N. T. Wright, *The Climax of the Covenant* (Edinburgh: Clark, 1991), 48–49; contra Jerome Murphy-O'Connor (*The Theology of the Second Letter to the Corinthians* [Cambridge: Cambridge University Press, 1991], 24), who notes the wordplay but makes both terms equivalent to the name "Christ," whereas Wright sees them both meaning "the Anointed One."

77. Wright, *Climax of the Covenant*, 41–55.

used it is to be explained as an anaphora. In an analogous fashion the forms *Iēsous* and *ho Iēsous* are also alternated.[78]

The choice of the proper noun or nouns also seems often governed by grammar. Wright examines the frequencies of "Jesus," "Jesus Christ," "Christ Jesus," "Christ," and "Lord Jesus Christ" after the prepositions *en, eis, syn,* and *dia,* noting a variety of interesting patterns. Particularly striking are that *en* almost never occurs with "Jesus," *dia* almost never with "Christ," and *eis* always with "Christ" but never with "Jesus" or "Lord."[79]

7. But if it is potentially the case that all anarthrous forms of "Christ" by itself could still preserve at least some of the original titular meaning, then the same, at least theoretically, must be true for all the compounded forms of "Christ" with "Jesus" and/or "Lord."

8. This theoretical possibility actually becomes probable when we observe that certain formal features likewise account for the variation between "Jesus Christ" and "Christ Jesus," and between both forms and the triply compounded "Lord Jesus Christ." Again, citing Dahl,

> As a rule a simple form, either "Christ," "the Christ," or "the Lord," stands as the subject of a sentence. Those complete, liturgical-sounding forms, such as "(our) Lord Jesus Christ" are used primarily in the genitive and in prepositional phrases and occur frequently at the end of a sentence. Moreover, Paul always writes *(ho) kyrios (hēmōn) Iēsous Christos,* but if the name "Lord" follows he alternates between "Jesus Christ" and "Christ Jesus." Furthermore, Paul obviously avoids the dative form, *Iēsou,* which is identical with the genitive; for that reason Christ is placed before Jesus in dative constructions. Paul says *en Christō Iēsou,* but on the contrary *dia Iēsou Christou.*[80]

For whatever reason, furthermore, certain key Pauline expressions seem only or largely to be joined with one kind of reference to Jesus and not another. "Faith," "proclamation," "revelation," and "Spirit" always go with "of Jesus Christ" (6x), while "slave," "servant," "soldier," "minister," "apostle" (except for Titus 1:17), and "prisoner" go with "of Christ Jesus" (13x).

9. The very reversibility of "Christ Jesus" and "Jesus Christ" in remaining contexts suggests that "Christ" remained a title rather than a proper name, inasmuch as neither Jewish nor Greco-Roman practice normally varied the sequence of two or three proper names joined to-

---

78. Dahl, "Messiahship of Jesus in Paul," 38–39.
79. Wright, *Climax of the Covenant,* 44–45.
80. Dahl, "Messiahship of Jesus in Paul," 38.

gether. "Pontius Pilate" never was written as "Pilate Pontius," nor was "Simon son of John" written as "son of John Simon." If a Roman had a triple name—for example, Lucius Porcius Festus—the three names always would appear in that sequence.[81]

10. Paul recognizes the fundamental role of the early Christian confession "Jesus is Lord" (see esp. Rom. 10:9; cf. 1 Cor. 12:3; Phil. 2:11), but nowhere writes "Christ is Lord," as we would expect if "Christ" were merely an alternate, interchangeable name for Jesus.[82]

11. Some scholars have argued that *Christos* as a title in a Greco-Roman world would have proved virtually meaningless, akin to naming a person in modern English and then attaching the label "Rubbed" or "Smeared."[83] But Paul's letters, like the rest of the New Testament, are filled with quotations, allusions, and echoes of the Old Testament,[84] and early Christian catechesis regularly taught Jewish backgrounds to Gentile converts, so that even Christians unfamiliar with the Jewish meaning of "messiah" would have quickly learned it. As Thomas Schreiner elaborates,

> As a Jew, Paul would continue to recognize the titular associations of the term. He speaks of "Jesus Christ" and "Christ Jesus" so often because one of the foundations of Paul's worldview is that Jesus is the promised Messiah. No extended defense of such a view was needed since the messianic status of Jesus was apparently well accepted in all his churches.[85]

12. A contemporary analogy shows how little exposure probably would have been needed for outsiders to the Jewish meaning of the term to catch on to it. In many charismatic Christian circles today, "anointed" has become a common adjective to apply to a speaker who has been powerfully used by God, perhaps exhibiting the more directly supernatural spiritual gifts. This is not a standard usage of the word in popular, secular culture, but one needs to hear the term only a handful of times in certain churches to understand its meaning from the context.

81. S. Vernon McCasland, "Christ Jesus," *JBL* 65 (1946): 377–83.

82. Dahl, "Messiahship of Jesus in Paul," 38.

83. For example, Martin Hengel, *Studies in Early Christology* (Edinburgh: Clark, 1995), 2; Richard N. Longenecker, "A Realized Hope, A New Commitment, and a Developed Proclamation: Paul and Jesus," in *The Road from Damascus*, ed. Richard N. Longenecker (Grand Rapids: Eerdmans, 1997), 34.

84. The three categories are those made famous particularly by Richard B. Hays, *Echoes of Scripture in the Letters of Paul* (New Haven: Yale University Press, 1989).

85. Thomas R. Schreiner, *Paul: Apostle of God's Glory in Christ* (Downers Grove, Ill.: InterVarsity, 2001), 77. See also Ben Witherington III, *Paul's Narrative Thought World* (Louisville: Westminster John Knox, 1994), 134.

13. An ancient analogy from Paul's own vocabulary may be even more directly relevant. In more than 90 percent of its 121 Pauline uses, *nomos* fairly clearly refers to *the* Hebrew Scriptures (or *the* first five books of Moses) whether it is anarthrous or articular.[86] One can account for much of the variation by the same kind of grammatical patterns noted with *Christos*, but in other cases the choice of form seems unmotivated. Yet the law in view remains quite definite, even though, again, non-Jewish Christians would have had to be taught its meaning.

14. A perusal of a Hebrew concordance shows that the Hebrew word for "law," *tôrâ*, equally frequently alternates between articular and anarthrous forms, often due either to grammatical structures in which they are embedded or to what seems to be merely stylistic variation.

15. *Christos* in the LXX, like the underlying *māšîaḥ* in the Hebrew Scriptures that it regularly translates, exhibits similar variation. Yet no one argues that either of these terms ever functions as a proper name in either language.

16. Paul's writings reflect the earliest known Christian documents, with the possible exception of James. Frequently, especially in passages referring to "Christ," he relies on even older, often creedal or liturgical phrases or confessions. The earlier the original uses of "Christ," the more likely the Jewish, titular background would have been preserved whether or not later usage followed a linear trajectory of development.[87]

17. As we have already seen with John's Gospel, and as will recur with the Johannine Epistles and Revelation, the titular sense continues to dominate even end-of-the-first-century Christian writings. This makes one doubt whether the background and original meaning of *Christos* ever could have been lost during so early a time and in so large a swath of the Roman Empire as the writings of Paul reflect.[88]

18. Finally, the fact that the name "Jesus" appears all by itself only thirteen times in the entire Pauline corpus, each time in a context in which the historical Jesus (or continuity with the historical Jesus) is implied, suggests that Paul does not feel free simply to insert the earthly name for the man from Nazareth any time he is referring to his risen Lord. Conversely, it makes sense that "Christ" is not a name he can arbitrarily substitute for "Jesus."[89]

86. Douglas J. Moo, "'Law,' 'Works of the Law,' and 'Legalism' in Paul," *WTJ* 45 (1983): 73–100.

87. See Werner Kramer, *Christ, Lord, Son of God* (London: SCM, 1966). Kramer also notes the substantial percentage of Pauline uses that may be traceable to pre-Pauline material (19–64).

88. Cf. Wright, *Climax of the Covenant*, 42.

89. On the lack of interchangeability between "Jesus" and "Christ," at least in two major Pauline Epistles, see Keck, "'Jesus' in Romans"; Murphy-O'Connor, *Second Letter to the Corinthians*, 143.

It is difficult, therefore, to believe that the titular sense of *Christos* ever was entirely lost in any Pauline reference or that it ever became diluted into merely a name rather than a reference to the Jewish messiah.[90] It would appear that this could have happened only later in a purely Hellenized form of Christianity almost entirely divorced from its Jewish roots, a situation that, sadly, did characterize much of the church from the mid-second century onward.[91] It remains to be seen if it intruded already into any of the other New Testament documents not yet surveyed.

One other topic calls for attention before we turn to those later writings. In light of the debate over the authorship of 2 Thessalonians, Ephesians, Colossians, and the three Pastoral Epistles, it is interesting to ask whether significant, distinctive patterns in the use of *Christos* emerge in any of these disputed letters. In fact, two noteworthy distinctives do arise. First, in 2 Thessalonians, eight of the nine references to *Christos* appear in the expression "Lord Jesus Christ." But this could reflect the predominant focus on the parousia in 2 Thessalonians, the most common New Testament context for the use of this elaborate imperial title.[92] First Thessalonians, moreover, also contains distinctive patterns that Paul does not preserve elsewhere, as "Lord" and "Jesus" occur considerably more often than "Christ" (10x, 24x, and 16x respectively). It may be, then, that in his earliest two letters (on the assumption of the authenticity of 2 Thessalonians), Paul simply had not yet established consistent linguistic usage.[93]

The second distinctive pattern involves the Pastorals. In 1 Timothy, twelve of fifteen uses of "Christ" appear in the expression "Christ Jesus;" in 2 Timothy, eleven of twelve uses do the same. Intriguingly, despite numerous other stylistic parallels among all three Pastorals, in Titus only one of the four uses reflects this sequence. But in three instances, Titus also employs the title "Savior" in conjunction with "Christ" (1:4; 2:13; 3:6), perhaps combating the Hellenistic predilection for identifying other saviors, not least the emperor.[94] So it could be argued that the

90. Note Herman Ridderbos, *Paul: An Outline of His Theology* (Grand Rapids: Eerdmans, 1975), 50–51: "However much the name Christ in the Pauline usage seems to have acquired the sense of a proper name, this does not mean that this designation has lost official historic-Israelitic significance. Paul proclaims Christ as the fulfillment of the promise of God to Abraham, as the seed in which all the families of the earth shall be blessed (Gal. 3:8, 16, 29), the eschatological bringer of salvation whose all-embracing significance must be understood in the light of prophecy (Rom. 15:9–12), the fulfillment of God's redemptive counsel concerning the whole world and its future."

91. Hengel, *Between Jesus and Paul*, 72.

92. Ibid., 68 n. 93.

93. Ibid., 66.

94. Ibid., 65.

distinctive statistics for 1 and 2 Timothy, in conjunction with the other well-known stylistic and linguistic peculiarities of this corpus, support at least the hypothesis of a different amanuensis who was given a fair amount of freedom to write in his own words, if not deutero-Pauline authorship altogether.[95] On the other hand, given that no other New Testament writer besides Paul ever uses "Christ Jesus," perhaps a dramatically increased frequency of this title in these two epistles reflects Paul's hand all the more as he attempts to emphasize the messiahship of Jesus.

As for Ephesians and Colossians, the term *Christos* appears somewhat more frequently than in comparably sized Pauline writing elsewhere (45x and 25x, respectively). But the frequency clearly seems dictated by the contents, with the emphasis in these two letters on the supremacy of (the) Christ.[96] And no other obvious, distinctive patterns of linguistic usage emerge.

Theologically, it is certainly true that "Christ," even if still somewhat titular, is used so often in Paul that it takes its meaning almost entirely from who Jesus was and is and from the nature of his salvific activity.[97] As C. K. Barrett explains,

> Of Christology we learn most from hints dropped at random as other subjects are developed. Paul and his contemporaries were not able to take over a ready-made doctrine of the Messiah. . . . [Paul began] with the fact of Jesus, who refuses to be neatly filed away in a Jewish pigeon-hole labeled "Messiah"; on this basis Paul proceeds to revise and rewrite the hopes, categories, and exegesis of Judaism.[98]

But the distinctive background of the term, as over against other titles, is by no means entirely effaced. Building on Wright's study of the "corporate Christ" in Paul, David Wenham summarizes, "Whereas 'Son of God' suggests Jesus' relationship to the Father and 'Lord' his relationship to the world and to individuals, 'Christ' suggests his relationship to Israel and to the church."[99]

95. Perhaps the most sensitive, detailed analysis of both continuities and discontinuities between Paul and the Pastorals appears in I. Howard Marshall, *A Critical and Exegetical Commentary on the Pastoral Epistles*, ICC (Edinburgh: Clark, 1999).

96. See Andrew T. Lincoln and A. J. M. Wedderburn, *The Theology of the Later Pauline Letters* (Cambridge: Cambridge University Press, 1993), s.v. "Ephesians" and "Colossians." See also H. Wayne House, "The Doctrine of Christ in Colossians," *BSac* 149 (1992): 180–92.

97. Fitzmyer, *Paul and His Theology*, 51.

98. C. K. Barrett, *Paul: An Introduction to His Thought* (Louisville: Westminster John Knox, 1994), 103.

99. David Wenham, *Paul: Follower of Jesus or Founder of Christianity?* (Grand Rapids: Eerdmans, 1995), 121.

The Epistle to the Hebrews

Christos occurs thirteen times in Hebrews. Ten of these are the simple form "Christ," six of which are introduced with the definite article. The remaining three references involve "Jesus Christ." The contexts of the term reflect the larger christological emphases of this letter. The dominant theme in these verses is Jesus as high priest and once-for-all sacrifice by virtue of his death (5:5; 6:1; 9:11, 14, 24, 28; 10:10).[100] "Christ" also is linked to Jesus' exalted sonship (3:6)[101] and eternality or "constancy" (13:8),[102] and to believers' roles as sharers of him (3:14), suffering disgrace for his sake (11:26) and doing what is pleasing through him (13:21).

As with Paul's usage in Rom. 9:5, there is one striking, almost certainly titular reference to "Christ" in Hebrews in 11:26. Speaking of Moses, the author writes, "He regarded disgrace for the sake of [lit., 'the'] Christ as of greater value than the treasures of Egypt." Given the Old Testament context, this passage surely is referring to the messiah in the abstract rather than to Jesus personally.[103] "We have come to share in [lit., 'the'] Christ" (3:14) almost exactly matches Wright's "incorporative" texts in Paul, in which the messiah is closely bound up with his people. The passages that use "Christ" with the article in the contexts of Jesus' suffering and death (5:5; 9:14, 28) make us think of Luke's emphasis on the need for the messiah to suffer and can thus readily be taken as titular too. "The word of the Christ" (NIV: "the teachings about Christ") parallels Paul's exclusively articular use of the expression "the gospel of the Christ" (Rom. 15:19; 1 Cor. 9:12; 2 Cor. 2:12; 9:13; 10:14; Gal. 1:7; Phil. 1:27; 3:18; 1 Thess. 3:2). All the articular uses of *Christos* in Hebrews should, therefore, be understood as titular.[104]

As with Paul, then, given that the theology taught in the contexts of the anarthrous uses seems indistinguishable from that of the articular uses, one may inquire whether it is probable that the meaning of these latter six texts carries over to the other seven, equally intelligible as titular or nontitular, rather than arguing from the more ambiguous to the less ambiguous passages. And if James Schaefer's thesis proves

100. William L. Lane (*Hebrews 1–8*, WBC 47A [Dallas: Word, 1991], cxli) observes, "The evidence of 5:5–10 indicates that the writer formulated the conception of Jesus as high priest on the basis of a messianic interpretation of Pss. 2, 110, and 116."

101. On which, see Barnabas Lindars, *The Theology of the Letter to the Hebrews* (Cambridge: Cambridge University Press, 1991), 35.

102. Craig R. Koester, *Hebrews*, AB 36 (New York: Doubleday, 2001), 104.

103. Philip E. Hughes, *A Commentary on the Epistle to the Hebrews* (Grand Rapids: Eerdmans, 1977), 495–96.

104. So also Strecker, *Theology of the New Testament*, 614.

plausible, as it seems to, that pre-Christian Jewish expectation of an ideal messianic priest informs a large part of the imagery of Hebrews,[105] then we should place all the more weight on the clearer uses of "Christ" as messiah as determinative for the entire collection of references. Certainly, it appears difficult to agree with Paul Ellingworth that in this letter "the traditional title 'Christ' is not developed in any distinctive way."[106]

The Epistle of James

Often the Christology of James is alleged to be almost nonexistent. The only appearances of *Christos* in this letter come in 1:1 and 2:1 in the formulaic expressions "James, a servant of God and of the Lord Jesus Christ" and "believers in our glorious Lord Jesus Christ." Of course, if one expands to survey beyond explicit names or titles, one discovers an emphasis on allusions to the teachings of Jesus as both sage and prophet. Jesus as "the Lord" heals, forgives, and judges.[107] And if *tēs doxēs* in 2:1 is taken as an appositional genitive, one may translate "our Lord Jesus Christ, who is (the) Glory," that is, the *shekinah* presence of Yahweh himself.[108] But the simple descriptive genitive "glorious Lord Jesus Christ" seems more probable.[109]

If our focus remains on *Christos* itself, then there is little more to say. Still, given our observations in studying Luke and Paul about the fixed order of titles in the expression "Lord Jesus Christ," some measure of the original titular sense of "Christ" seems to be preserved here.[110] And if one dates James early and takes the references in the letter to a Jewish-Christian audience literally,[111] then both time and milieu strongly favor the preservation of the meaning of "messiah."

105. James R. Schaefer, "The Relationship between Priestly and Servant Messianism in the Epistle to the Hebrews," *CBQ* 30 (1968): 359–85.

106. Paul Ellingworth, "Jesus and the Universe in Hebrews," *EvQ* 58 (1986): 338.

107. Robert B. Sloan, "The Christology of James," *CTR* 1 (1986): 3–29. See also John Reumann, "Christology of James," in *Who Do You Say That I Am?* ed. Powell and Bauer, 128–39, for a shorter but similarly helpful summary.

108. So Michael J. Townsend, "Christ, Community and Salvation in the Epistle of James," *EvQ* 53 (1981): 116–17.

109. So Peter H. Davids, *The Epistle of James*, NIGTC (Grand Rapids: Eerdmans, 1982), 106; Douglas J. Moo, *The Letter of James*, PNTC (Grand Rapids: Eerdmans, 2000), 101.

110. Ralph P. Martin, *James*, WBC 48 (Waco: Word, 1988), 7.

111. See the standard New Testament introductions for the debate. For a good representative defense of both of these views, see D. A. Carson, Douglas J. Moo, and Leon Morris, *An Introduction to the New Testament* (Grand Rapids: Zondervan, 1992), 414–15.

1 Peter

The first letter attributed to Peter contains twenty-two uses of *Christos*. More as in Paul and less as in Hebrews and James, "Jesus Christ" again appears frequently (8x). "Lord Jesus Christ" comes only in 1:3 in introductory material. As with both Paul and Hebrews, the simple form "Christ" is the most common (13x), but only three times does the article precede it (3:15; 4:13; 5:1). All three of these references, however, make good sense if one translates "the messiah." The most literal translation of the relevant portion of 3:15 is "sanctify the Lord as the Christ," with *ton Christon* as the predicate portion of a double accusative.[112] In other words, "set apart Jesus [to whom 'the Lord' refers] as the Messiah." (If "Christ" is a mere name, this becomes an inexplicable redundancy.) First Peter 4:13 and 5:1 both speak of "the sufferings of [lit., 'the'] Christ," again harking back to the parallel expressions in Luke recognized as unambiguously titular. As John Elliott states it, "This formulation reflects an older stratum of tradition in which *the Christ* still functioned as a title for Jesus as *the Messiah*."[113]

Interestingly, there are no uncompounded uses of the name "Jesus" anywhere in 1 Peter. Thus, it is not possible, as with Paul, to suggest that "Jesus" alone was used when emphasis fell clearly on the historical Jesus; perhaps in 1 Peter, "Christ" really has become a substitute name. Yet, of the ten anarthrous uses of the uncompounded *Christos*, four likewise deal with his sufferings (1:19; 2:21; 3:18; 4:1), suggesting no change of meaning from the articular references in 4:13 and 5:1. Another four texts use "Christ" without the article, following the prepositions *eis* or *en* (1:11; 3:16; 5:10, 14), which, as we saw in Paul, almost always triggered the anarthrous form on grammatical grounds alone. And the remaining two are genitive forms in construction (1:11; 4:14), which regularly in Paul, though with slightly more common exceptions, also lacked the article. In a similar vein, the eight uses of "Jesus Christ" scarcely seem random. Six occur as genitives in construction (1:1, 2, 3, 7, 13; 3:21), and the other two are objects of the preposition *dia* (2:5; 4:11). The sole use of "Lord Jesus Christ" (1:3), as often elsewhere, appears in a formulaic expression. Once again, grammar rather than meaning seems to have dictated the use of a particular way of referring to Jesus throughout this epistle.

Assessing the meaning of "Christ" in 1 Peter, then, depends to a large extent on one's starting point and the cumulative force of the evidence thus far surveyed. If it is reasonable to begin with unambiguous usages

112. Paul J. Achtemeier, *1 Peter*, Hermeneia (Minneapolis: Fortress, 1996), 232.
113. John H. Elliott, *1 Peter*, AB 37B (New York: Doubleday, 2000), 775, 820.

and use them to help interpret more ambiguous forms (rather than vice versa), then there are no usages of *Christos* in this letter that could not preserve some nuances of its original meaning as "messiah." As for a summary of 1 Peter's Christology more broadly, Peter Davids's two-point summary proves both representative and accurate:

> The first is that the majority of the references to Christ are to his suffer-ing. This is clearly because he is the model of suffering for the Christians. Perhaps no book in the New Testament makes this aspect of his life so clear. The second fact is that the believers are related to God through or in Christ.[114]

2 Peter and Jude

With most scholars, I will treat these two short epistles together be-cause of their similarities and probable literary interdependence. In 2 Peter the statistics shift again. Seven of nine uses of "Christ" come in the expression "Lord Jesus Christ," for which we have found good rea-sons to take as titular. This conclusion is reinforced by the observation that in three of these seven triple forms and in one of the two remaining double forms ("Jesus Christ"), "Savior" also is inserted into the immedi-ate context (2 Pet. 1:1, 11; 2:20; 3:18). The only other passage in the en-tire New Testament with all four words "Savior," "Lord," "Jesus," and "Christ" linked together is Phil. 3:20. The reference in 2 Pet. 1:1 also predicates of Jesus Christ that he is "our God" as well as "Savior." Strik-ingly, there is no use of "Christ" that appears all by itself, nor, as also noticed in 1 Peter, is there any independent use of "Jesus."

Clearly, then, 2 Peter promotes a very high Christology,[115] even though this little book often is neglected in studies of New Testament Christology overall. The distinctive language again may be countering the claims made for various Hellenistic savior-gods and Roman emper-ors.[116] Perhaps the false teachers whom the letter more directly ad-dresses also were making inflated claims for themselves, but their doc-

114. Peter H. Davids, *The First Epistle of Peter*, NICNT (Grand Rapids: Eerdmans, 1990), 23. See further Paul E. Davies, "Primitive Christology in 1 Peter," in *Festschrift to Honor F. Wilbur Gingrich*, ed. Eugene H. Barth and Ronald E. Cocroft (Leiden: Brill, 1972), 115–22; Earl Richard, "The Functional Christology of 1 Peter," in *Perspectives on First Peter*, ed. Charles H. Talbert (Macon, Ga.: Mercer University Press, 1986), 121–39.

115. See Simon J. Kistemaker, *Exposition of the Epistles of Peter and of the Epistle of Jude*, NTC (Grand Rapids: Baker, 1987), 226–27.

116. Ralph P. Martin, "2 Peter," in *The Theology of the Letters of James, Peter, and Jude*, by Andrew Chester and Ralph P. Martin (Cambridge: Cambridge University Press, 1994), 159.

trinal emphases are notoriously hard to pin down because the epistle focuses almost exclusively on their moral errors.[117] At the very least, we may conclude, with Donald Guthrie, that "the messianic office is certainly never in question, even if the form has become stereotyped."[118]

The probable literary dependence of 2 Peter on Jude is reinforced by the virtually identical distribution of lexical data on "Christ" in the two letters. Jude three times uses the exalted "Lord Jesus Christ" (vv. 4, 17, 21), and once, after *dia*, uses "Jesus Christ our Lord" (v. 25). The other two appearances of *Christos* come in v. 1 with the common form "Jesus Christ." In v. 4, we learn that the false teachers were in fact denying Jesus' sovereign lordship, even if, again, the rest of the letter focuses primarily on their immorality.[119] Pheme Perkins thinks that the use of "Lord" and "Savior" throughout these two small letters is largely "honorific," in recognition of "the divine benefactor to whom Christians must remain loyal."[120] Ralph Martin believes that the Christology of Jude may be summed up under the twin emphases of Jesus' judgment and mercy.[121] In no instance is the uniformly titular nature of "Christ" that we have discovered thus far challenged.

The Epistles of John

If the theory of linear development from a Jewish titular "Christ" to a Hellenistic "second name" for Jesus has any merit, one would expect the strongest evidence for the latter stage to appear in the Johannine Epistles and in Revelation. These quite likely are the latest New Testament documents, and they are free from the references to the historical Jesus that make analysis of John's Gospel more complicated. But, in fact, clearer evidence emerges in these final texts for an unambiguously titular "Christ" than in all the previous New Testament Epistles surveyed. Countering apparently docetic and probably protognostic false teachers

117. Thus, the two most detailed recent attempts to identify the false teachers behind 2 Peter both make persuasive cases for philosophical schools that were diametrically opposed to one another! Identifying the Epicureans is Jerome H. Neyrey, *2 Peter, Jude*, AB 37C (New York: Doubleday, 1993); identifying the Stoics is J. Daryl Charles, *Virtue amidst Vice: The Catalog of Virtues in 2 Peter 1*, JSNTSup 150 (Sheffield: Sheffield Academic Press, 1997).

118. Guthrie, *New Testament Theology*, 250.

119. On the relationship between the two errors, see Richard Bauckham, *Jude, 2 Peter*, WBC 50 (Waco: Word, 1983), 40.

120. Pheme Perkins, "Christ in Jude and 2 Peter," in *Who Do You Say That I Am?* ed. Powell and Bauer, 154.

121. Ralph Martin, "Jude," in *Letters of James, Peter, and Jude*, by Chester and Martin, 77.

in and around Ephesus,[122] 1 John 2:22 proclaims starkly, "Who is the liar? It is whoever denies that Jesus is the Christ. Such a person is the antichrist—denying the Father and the Son." Likewise, 5:1 declares, "Everyone who believes that Jesus is the Christ is born of God, and everyone who loves the father loves his child as well." These texts mesh well with the central purpose of John's Gospel: to convince people that Jesus was the Christ and the Son of God (John 20:31). The other articular use of "Christ" appears in 2 John 9 in the expression "the teaching of [lit., 'the'] Christ," which parallels the "word of the Christ" and "gospel of the Christ" expressions in Hebrews and Paul respectively.

In eight other instances the letters of John refer to "Jesus Christ." Three of these involve the identical confession of 2:22 and 5:1, insisting that Jesus came "in the flesh" (1 John 4:2; 2 John 7) and "by water and blood" (probably referring to his baptism and death as signs of his genuine humanity).[123] Four describe Jesus as the "Son" (1 John 1:3; 3:23; 5:20; 2 John 3) and thus are taken most naturally as linking one title ("Son") with another ("Christ"). The sole remaining use is found in 1 John 2:1, in which Jesus Christ is called "the righteous" by a substantive adjective in apposition to "Christ," again turning both words into virtual titles.

Stephen Smalley probably captures the best balance in summarizing the overall Christology of these epistles. For former Jews easily prone to exaggerate the humanity of Jesus, John insists on the preexistence of the Christ, holy and pure, waiting to return in glory at the end of the age. For former pagans tempted to overemphasize Jesus' divinity, John stresses the Christ's real humanity, life and death. For both groups, John presents a Christology that "holds in tension the truth that Jesus is both one with God and one with man."[124] John does not include all this information in every one of his statements of what believers must acknowledge and confess, but each stands as a synecdoche—one key part of the entire theological formulation that is presupposed throughout.[125] And indisputably, John uses *Christos* in a manner that far exceeds "Jesus" as merely a "last name."

The Book of Revelation

Finally, we come to the end of the New Testament. Clearly, an exalted Christ dominates this apocalypse. In his visions John sees Jesus

---

122. See Colin G. Kruse, *The Letters of John*, PNTC (Grand Rapids: Eerdmans, 2000), 15–27.

123. So Daniel L. Akin, *1, 2, 3 John*, NAC 38 (Nashville: Broadman & Holman, 2001), 195–97.

124. Stephen S. Smalley, *1, 2, 3 John*, WBC 51 (Waco: Word, 1984), xxvi.

125. Raymond E. Brown, *The Epistles of John*, AB 30 (New York: Doubleday, 1982), 352.

as a powerful conqueror, just avenger, and slain sacrificial deity who returns in splendor and authority, most notably in his glimpses of the heavenly Christ and in the hymns of praise to Christ as God (esp. in Rev. 1; 4–5; 11–12; 15–16; 19). In short, Jesus as the Christ is a lion who also is a lamb (cf. esp. 5:5–6).[126] Two unambiguously titular uses of *Christos* hark back to Lukan reliance on Old Testament imagery: "the kingdom of the world has become the kingdom of our Lord and of his Christ" (11:15), and "now have come the salvation and the power and the kingdom of our God and the authority of his Christ" (12:10).[127] Revelation 20:6 matches these uses, substituting "the" for "his": God's people "will be priests of God and of [lit., 'the'] Christ." This makes it likely that the reference just two verses earlier, "they came to life and reigned with [lit., 'the'] Christ," also is titular.[128] All four texts present Jesus as God's "anointed," now publicly demonstrated in that role for all to see as he returns and establishes the full, final reign of God.[129]

The other three passages involving *Christos* in Revelation use the familiar form "Jesus Christ," and all three appear in John's introduction. Two employ the genitive form in construction (1:1, 2); the other follows the preposition *apo* (1:5). Thus, grammatical reasons no doubt account for the usage; we need not postulate nominal rather than titular meaning simply because of the anarthrous form.[130] Interestingly, "Jesus" all by itself returns with some frequency in Revelation (9x). As in Paul, a

126. Excellent overviews of the Christology of Revelation appear in Donald Guthrie, *The Relevance of John's Apocalypse* (Grand Rapids: Eerdmans, 1987), 37–64; Graeme Goldsworthy, *The Gospel in Revelation* (repr., Exeter: Paternoster, 1994), passim. For fascinating studies of the possible influence of Jewish reflection on exalted angels on the Christology of Revelation, see Peter R. Carrell, *Jesus and the Angels: Angelology and the Christology of the Apocalypse of John* (Cambridge: Cambridge University Press, 1997); Loren T. Stuckenbruck, *Angel Veneration and Christology* (Tübingen: Mohr, 1995). For a study of the son of man, lamb, and divine warrior images, see Thomas B. Slater, *Christ and Community: A Socio-Historical Study of the Christology of Revelation*, JSNTSup 178 (Sheffield: Sheffield Academic Press, 1999).

127. For Old Testament background and a demonstration of the messianic nature of both of these references, see David E. Aune, *Revelation 6–16*, WBC 52B (Nashville: Nelson, 1998), 639.

128. David E. Aune, *Revelation 17–22*, WBC 52C (Nashville: Nelson, 1998), 1000.

129. Marinus de Jonge, "The Use of the Expression ΧΡΙΣΤΟΣ in the Apocalypse of John," in *L'Apocalypse Johannique et l'Apocalyptique dans le Nouveau Testament*, ed. J. Lambrecht (Louvain: Leuven University Press, 1980), 278.

130. Nor is there any need to resort to a hypothesis about the composition of Revelation in two stages, only one of which understood the titular usage of "Christ," as proposed by Sarah A. Edwards, "Christological Perspectives in the Book of Revelation," in *Christological Perspectives*, ed. Robert F. Berkey and Sarah A. Edwards (New York: Pilgrim, 1982), 139–54.

case can be made for deliberate emphasis on or continuity with the historical Jesus in these absolute uses (1:9 [2x]; 12:17; 14:12; 17:6; 19:10 [2x]; 22:16), especially when one notices that a majority of them refer to the "testimony of Jesus," that is, the revelation of God's word that the historical Jesus initiated and still continues.[131]

That *Christos* remains titular throughout Revelation also is reinforced by the observation that imagery of a Davidic messiah permeates the book even when explicit titles are missing.[132] So also, the use of an antichrist figure (given the use of that label in John's letters and his more detailed description of the figure in the Revelation) demonstrates that John envisions an archenemy of God's messiah. It makes little sense to think of "antichrist" as merely a personal name, and so "Christ" is not likely to be one either.[133]

Conclusions

Even this comparatively limited survey, focusing almost exclusively on uses of *Christos* per se, reflects the profound depth and breadth of New Testament Christology more generally: Mark's so-called messianic secret, Matthew's heightened Son of God Christology, Luke's emphasis on the scriptural requirement that the messiah must die, Paul's rich presentation of Jesus' person and work from which most systematic theologies derive their overarching categories, Hebrews' portrait of the messiah's priesthood, 1 Peter on exemplary suffering, 2 Peter and Jude countering Greco-Roman savior models, the Johannine Epistles against docetic schismatics, and the exalted judge of the Book of Revelation.

In the midst of all this diversity we must not lose sight of a fundamental unity of thought. David Wenham best sums up the unifying features of New Testament theology more generally under the headings "context, center, community and climax." With respect to Christology in particular, he includes, under the "center" of New Testament thought, the claim that "Jesus was the Spirit-filled messiah of Israel and the Son of

131. G. K. Beale (*The Book of Revelation*, NICNT [Grand Rapids: Eerdmans, 1999], 183–84) notes, "The genitive phrases . . . could imply that God and Jesus are the subject of the revelations (so most commentators). But the genitives may also express the idea that these visions are 'about' God and Jesus (cf. the passages mentioned in the comments on v 1, esp. 1:9; 6:9; and 20:4, where the same genitive phrase may include both a subjective and objective sense)."

132. Richard Bauckham, *The Theology of the Book of Revelation* (Cambridge: Cambridge University Press, 1993), 66.

133. See Guthrie, *New Testament Theology*, 250.

God."[134] This summary comports well with my findings about the consistent use of "Christ" throughout the New Testament documents.

But the more focused nature of the present survey allows us to argue also for a very specific thesis about the New Testament use of *Christos*. This thesis proves quite surprising in view of the largely contrary state of current scholarship on the topic. Stated in brief: *There is no unambiguous evidence to demonstrate that "Christ" in any of its 531 New Testament uses ever "degenerated" into a mere second name for Jesus.* Clear titular uses appear in every New Testament subcorpus. The dates of the documents in which they appear most frequently exclude any attempt to argue for a linear development of "messiah" in first-century Christianity away from its Jewish backgrounds into a purely Hellenistic form. Outside of the Gospels and Acts, a majority of the uses of "Christ" are susceptible to either a titular or a nominal interpretation. But if we proceed from the unambiguous to the ambiguous uses in each corpus (rather than vice versa, as so many seemingly do), we will conclude that some vestige of titular meaning remains attached even to all the anarthrous and compound forms. In fact, a majority of the uses of "Christ" without the article in the New Testament can be explained on grammatical grounds alone, suggesting that we should not read into those uses assumptions about the loss of messianic meaning.

If for no other reason than the sheer number of appearances of "Christ" in them, the Pauline Epistles prove the hardest corpus for which to defend my thesis consistently, yet even there a surprisingly detailed case appears for a uniformly titular interpretation. That is not to say that in the majority of anarthrous uses of "Christ" or "Jesus Christ" in the epistles (both Pauline and non-Pauline), the New Testament writers consciously were stressing Jesus' role as Jewish messiah; it is simply to argue that Jesus' messiahship remains both presupposed and implied, and that the Jewish background never was entirely forgotten. It would appear that one must turn to post–New Testament, post-first-century, purely Greco-Roman Christian documents for the earliest unambiguous uses of a purely nominal *Christos*. Obviously, our contemporary culture, both inside and outside the church, regularly does treat "Christ" as Jesus' "last name"—when it is not blaspheming it by using it, even more thoughtlessly, as profanity. It would appear, then, that we face a considerably uphill battle if we wish to reeducate people as to how Jesus was *the Christ*, the promised Jewish liberator, who in his life, death, and resurrection also redefined the messianic role into something far more wonderful and powerful than anyone had ever anticipated.

134. David Wenham, "Appendix: Unity and Diversity in the New Testament," in *A Theology of the New Testament*, by Ladd, 712.

SEVEN

Christos: Jewish Title or Hellenistic Name?

A Response to Craig L. Blomberg

WILLIAM W. KLEIN

At the outset, I extend profuse thanks to Professor Craig Blomberg for his precise, clearly written, and surprising essay. Why surprising? Not in its scope, thoroughness, and grasp of the secondary literature; we have come to expect that from Dr. Blomberg's work in many facets of New Testament studies—and even beyond that specific domain—and this essay evidences all of these. His essay is surprising in that it takes head-on one of those allegedly "assured results" and shows that the consensus is not as incontrovertible as some might have thought. That is, if his thesis can be sustained, then the consensus needs revision. One cannot doubt Blomberg's courage in this systematic search for the best understanding of these issues. What issues? To that we now proceed.[1]

1. I am making the conscious decision not to engage in any analysis of the secondary literature either to confirm or challenge Professor Blomberg's uses of it. Since his own approach is dominantly exegetical, employing the literature only to document the state of the discussion and, usually, to support his own analyses, I will respond in kind by addressing the nature of his argumentation and his uses of the New Testament texts.

Evaluating all the occurrences of the Greek term *Christos* on the pages of the New Testament, what do we discover? Does the term retain its titular sense growing out of its origin in a Jewish milieu, or has it come to function as the equivalent of another proper name for Jesus? That is, should we understand "Jesus Christ" (or "Christ Jesus") as "Jesus (the) Messiah" ("Messiah Jesus") or on the analogy of "Pontius Pilate"? In brief, this is the question that Professor Blomberg tackles in his article. Many Gospel scholars defend the theory that uses of the term *Christos* trace a linear (i.e., temporal) development from Jewish title to mere name as one moves through the pages of the New Testament and into the following centuries. Blomberg challenges the dominant view that for much of apostolic Christianity, *Christos* functioned predominantly as Jesus' "last name." So although the subapostolic era and beyond may well reflect uses of *Christos* as a proper name, Blomberg concludes that in the New Testament itself, "there is no unambiguous evidence to demonstrate that 'Christ' in any of its 531 New Testament uses[2] ever 'degenerated' into a mere second name for Jesus." What is more, he argues against the view that there was a "linear development of 'messiah' in first-century Christianity away from its Jewish backgrounds into a purely Hellenistic form."

He has thrown down the gauntlet! In claiming that there is *no* unambiguous evidence, he appears to adopt a precarious position, for if we can find even one instance, then we will have forced him to back down. Surely, it will be easy to discover one instance! Then he will need to frame his case more in terms of a "dominant" pattern of Jewish title rather than merely Hellenistic name. To be fair, Blomberg does not imagine that in every instance where they used *Christos*, New Testament writers consciously were stressing or even aware of Jesus' role as Jewish messiah, but only that "the Jewish background never was entirely forgotten." So perhaps the question becomes whether he has so formulated the terms of the issue that no evidence is sufficient to overturn his case. That is to say, how might we ever know with certainty for each of the occurrences that the Jewish background was or was not entirely forgotten? How much overturns his case "entirely," and how would we demonstrate that a "Jewish background" was completely absent? Blomberg has created a rather slippery enterprise, given that all the New Testament writers were Jews (with the likely exception of Luke). Could any Jew ever write *Christos* and not have Jewish background inform the term? If Blomberg simply assumes that the answer

2. Blomberg's statistics indicate a total of 531 occurrences; my counting is 529. Clearly, this discrepancy cannot impact the results of his analyses, for if his case holds for 531, it will hold for fewer instances.

to that question is no, then his essay could have been considerably shorter! What evidence would he like to see to show that the Jewish background was completely absent? He never tells us. Rather than this tack, Blomberg takes the positive approach in the essay. He attempts to show that Jesus' role as the Messiah underlies every use of *Christos* in the New Testament, even in those instances in which the naming sense predominates. How convincing is his case? In short, it is convincing in most instances, though not in all. I hope that what follows will promote further dialogue and research.

Blomberg proceeds to assess the use of *Christos* in each portion of the New Testament, and the first paragraph of his study of Mark identifies an essential element of his methodology: is the use of *Christos* titular or not? This method poses a problem, I believe. At times, after showing that a specific use is titular, he moves on as if that alone proved his case.[3] In addition, in his study of the Synoptic Gospels, it appears to him that showing a titular use in one Gospel (e.g., Mark) assures that when another writer takes over those uses (assuming Markan priority), they will be titular there as well. But is a titular use enough to show a "Jewish background" for *Christos?* That is, how does Blomberg know that underlying every "titular use" is some semblance or even hint of a Jewish messianic understanding? Would use of the title "procurator" demonstrate the user's acquaintance with its Roman background?[4] In a Greco-Roman world of many political and religious figures with a plethora of titles, can we presume that every user of a title understood its background or even a hint of it? Or to use a modern example, do we suppose that all citizens of the United Kingdom understand the original background when they hear a reference to one of such hereditary titles as duke, marquis, earl, viscount, or baron? Samuel Fuller made a Western movie, *The Baron of Arizona* (1950), that used the title "baron," but can we expect that typical moviegoers would understand or even recognize any European origin for it? So I wonder if Blomberg might need to refine his methodology somewhat; he may need to prove more than merely that instances of *Christos* are titular.[5] What other features in the

---

3. In many instances, however, Blomberg does more than show a use to be titular, and there his case is very strong. That is, where a use of *Christos* is both titular and evidences other contextual clues to its Jewish or messianic connection, Blomberg's case proves unassailable.

4. In fact, countries as diverse as the Dominican Republic and Azerbaijan use that title today.

5. Even his impressive case of eighteen arguments pointing to the titular use of *Christos* in Paul is not sufficient, in my mind, to prove a Jewish provenance for the title. Space prohibits a detailed assessment of each of these eighteen arguments. I found several of them unconvincing or subject to alternative explanations. That does not negate their overall effect, with which I agree: for Paul, the titular use predominates.

context must coincide with the titular use to prove the case? At times, he brings in such additional evidence (e.g., concerning Matt. 11:2), but not always.

I have a related methodological question growing out of Blomberg's arguments concerning the use and nonuse of Greek articles. He adopts the premise that when *Christos* has the article, it is likely to be titular, whereas anarthrous uses could potentially not be titular.[6] So, for example, when Acts uses the compound "Jesus Christ" where no article occurs (with "Christ"), Blomberg feels that he must account for the article's absence so as to defend that *Christos* is titular. And when he can explain anarthrous uses grammatically, he seems relieved, for then they can be put in the classification of titular. He takes this same approach repeatedly throughout the article. Clearly, this fits with his program of finding titular uses, but I fail to follow the grammatical argument here. In speaking of the Pauline material, he says, "The presence or absence of 'the' was almost indiscriminate, as at times seems the case with other proper nouns or names." So I am puzzled why he feels the need to account for whether titles are articular or anarthrous. Again, for me, the question is not so much whether *Christos* is titular (with or without the article), but whether in the titular uses Blomberg can demonstrate a messianic connection. What is more, in Greek, articles regularly occur with names.[7]

I will use a specific example to highlight another methodological question. In various places Blomberg identifies formulaic expressions, such as "Lord Jesus Christ" (by my count, there are sixty-two occurrences). As I read through the article, he seems either to dismiss summarily the potential of the naming sense (e.g., he says, "Thirty-six of these come after nouns in the genitive and another eight in formulaic expressions with 'grace and peace,' so that one suspects that certain grammatical constructions alone often trigger certain specific ways of referring to Jesus") or to identify them as titular (and therefore, messianic) by definition. Though grammatical forces can at times determine certain linguistic collocations of words, I don't think that this phenomenon removes the need to ask in these instances whether or not *Christos* has a naming or messianic semantic value. Grammatical considerations

6. Is Professor Blomberg thinking too much along the lines of English uses of definite articles, whereby "I love Christ" and "I love the Christ" clearly convey different senses? The Greek uses of articles do not always make this distinction. This makes me wonder, therefore, if I am missing his point. In any case, I think he needs to delineate more clearly what semantic value he believes the presence or absence of the Greek article conveys.

7. For a few representative examples, see "Jesus" (Matt. 4:1, 17; 10:5; 12:15); "Joseph" (John 1:45); "John" (Matt. 3:13; John 1:28; Mark 9:38); "Peter" (Matt. 16:22; 17:1, 24; 26:40).

alone do not obviate semantic values. These certainly require more individual analysis, but could it be that the title is "Lord" and that "Jesus Christ" functions as a compound name, at least in some instances? If so, we might have a start on a list of potentially unambiguous uses of *Christos* as merely a name in the New Testament. There are other places in which Blomberg's study of grammar seems to trump semantics—prepositional phrases that require or eschew articles and genitival constructions, to name two. Grammar may dictate how to formulate certain constructions, but still we must assess other factors to determine the semantic values of the terms so joined.

In a number of texts, concepts in the context determine the presence of "messiah" for Blomberg. This occurs most observably with the idea of suffering. For example, he quotes Davids approvingly: "The first is that the majority of the references to Christ are to his suffering." Does the fact that authors say "Christ suffered" in effect denote that they mean in every instance "messiah suffered"?[8] Though we may establish on other grounds that an essential component of the meaning of "messiah" for the Jews (and Jesus) resides in the role of suffering, and even that *Christos* is the Greek translation for the Hebrew *māšîaḥ* ("anointed one"), the point at issue is whether it can be employed as the equivalent of a proper name even within the time frame of the New Testament writings. Paul does say in 1 Thess. 4:14 that "Jesus died" (though, admittedly, this is a unique combination). In Heb. 9:25–26 the author refers to Jesus as the priest who suffers. Suffering is not a necessary criterion to establish a messianic title. A similar phenomenon occurs in Blomberg's treatment of Luke. Since in the citation of Isa. 61:1–2, Luke's text employs *kyrios* (Luke 4:18), "Luke unambiguously knows the Jewish background to *Christos* and preserves it throughout his Gospel," avers Blomberg. First of all, here Luke is quoting the LXX; and second, does this not beg the question as to whether Luke can use it as a name in places? If Luke quotes Isa. 61:1–2, does this require the conclusion that all of his uses of *Christos* are messianic? That may be a stretch in logic. In short, how can Professor Blomberg merely assert that all of these are ambiguous at best?

Beyond these initial observations, I will select some examples or arguments that he employs that appear to me to be less convincing, in the hopes of engaging in more dialogue with Professor Blomberg about these instances and, therefore, the viability of his conclusion as stated.

---

8. Here we might consider another occurrence of the phrase "sufferings of Christ," in 2 Cor. 1:5: "For just as the sufferings of Christ are abundant for us, so also our consolation is abundant through Christ." It is far from clear that these occurrences of *Christos* have messianic overtones, but Blomberg assures us that they do because they occur with "sufferings" in the first instance.

That is to say, though I think that his case is mostly convincing, I would like to see more evidence to support it in several examples, or else get him to soften his claim that all the uses of *Christos* are Jewish (messianic) or ambiguous.

Unless I am missing something, Blomberg admits that John 1:17 is an exceptional example "that could be interpreted just as a name," and he never fully rescues it from that category. He warns rightly that we cannot merely assume that *Christos* has lost its titular force by the time of the writing of John's Gospel. But neither can we assume that because it occurs as a title in other places, it is likely to be a title here (since he maintains that there are *no* unambiguous uses). He must show positively that in John's affirmation "grace and truth came though Jesus Christ" we have more than a name. What is ambiguous about this use?

Also in his discussion of John's Gospel, Blomberg makes a perplexing assertion: we are not to read too much distinctively Christian understanding into the early confessional material, because Jesus' followers did not well understand his identity throughout his ministry. This begs us to view the Gospel in a way that is too one-dimensional, as if it reflected only the precise historical nuances and understandings that the disciples would have had during the period of Jesus' ministry.[9] John is composing this book some sixty years later! Perhaps as editor he is adopting a later Christian understanding, especially in view of his Asian readers who may have little Jewish background. Whatever misunderstandings the disciples may have had at the earlier stage, John is not likewise misguided as he writes (e.g., see John's postresurrection reflections indicated in 2:21–22; 12:4, 16). Blomberg allows for John's "'targumic,' explanatory insertion" of "Christ" at 17:3. Why is Blomberg confident that 1:17 and 17:3 are titular if, as he admits, they reflect end-of-first-century usage? My point here is merely that this is a matter to be more expansively argued, not merely asserted. He ought not merely assign them to the category of ambiguous instances.

Blomberg notes that *Christos* occurs some 380 times in Paul's writings. I wonder what to make of such admissions (in speaking of the Pauline data) as these: "Paul twenty-two times uses the compound form 'Jesus Christ' when nothing in the contexts requires 'Christ' to be anything besides another name for Jesus," and "In almost every case one could substitute 'Jesus' for 'Christ' with no apparent loss of meaning." If there is no question that "Jesus" is a name, does not this substitution suggest that "Christ" can function strictly in the same way? So while the titular sense might predominate, he allows in such statements

9. I am not disputing his case for the historicity of John's Gospel, but am arguing that here he appears not to account sufficiently for the role of its editor.

as these that the naming sense may (often) occur. Where is the evidence to posit a Jewish semantic component to them? They do not seem to be ambiguous.

I lodge a final question. First, it pertains to Blomberg's explanation of the uses of "Lord Jesus Christ" in 2 Thessalonians (assuming Pauline authorship). He seems to want to let Paul (or perhaps himself) off the hook for using a naming sense by pleading, "Paul simply had not yet established consistent linguistic usage." But this is precisely the kind of maneuvering that will not do in the kind of case that Blomberg seeks to build. It seems to me that the issue is precisely not one of idiolect. Blomberg's argument rests on the semantic value of *Christos* as a Jewish (messianic) title, not whether Paul (or the author) eventually comes to use it that way. If Paul can use it in a nontitular way, then the "Jewish background" clearly is not part of the essential semantic makeup of the word in that use. So we possibly gain some more unambiguous instances.

Correspondingly, in treating the uses in Hebrews, Blomberg argues that "probably" the meaning of the six articular, titular, messianic priest uses of *Christos* should carry over to the anarthrous uses that might be either titular or nontitular. This is arguably probable, though far from certain, and so perhaps adds a few others to the category of the unambiguous. The discussion of 1 Peter raised questions as well, where he argued that the clearer references to Jesus' messianic role in certain uses of *Christos* demand that we carry over that sense to the more ambiguous forms. Yet is "messiah" really that clear in all the articular uses? Though 1 Pet. 4:13 and 5:1 speak of "the sufferings of [lit., 'the'] Christ," must we assume that this refers to messiah? As noted above, articles regularly occur with proper names. If we could speak of the sufferings of Jesus (and use it as a name), could not Peter so speak of Christ?

The cumulative case that Blomberg constructs is formidable. His painstaking analyses of the data make it extremely difficult, if not impossible, for anyone still to assert that *Christos* has lost its titular sense during the period of time during which the New Testament was written. Nor can one merely assume a clearly definable and linear development within the New Testament of the movement from *Christos* as a Jewish title to a purely Hellenistic name. Has he made an overwhelming case for seeing on the pages of the New Testament a thoroughly Jewish Jesus in his Jewish context as the promised Jewish liberator? By all means, yes. But has Professor Blomberg proved his case "that Jesus' messiahship remains both presupposed and implied, and that the Jewish background never was entirely forgotten" in every use of the term *Christos?* I think not.

Methodologically, Blomberg starts from the Jewish and messianic origin of *Christos*. He then puts the burden of proof onto his opponents. He asks them to show one unambiguous example of a use of *Christos* in which the Jewish messianic sense has been lost to a purely Hellenistic naming sense. But given that the evidence clearly shows that in the second century and beyond, that was precisely what developed (as Blomberg admits), he also has the burden to show that no instance in the New Testament has yet reached that point. That he did not do. Often, he assumed ambiguity. As I said at the outset, these terms by which he has framed his discussion make proof a rather slippery commodity. I do not agree that he has shown that in all instances the Jewish background was "presupposed," "implied," and "never . . . entirely forgotten." And assigning the label "ambiguous uses" will not resuscitate those instances whose Jewish background cannot be clearly demonstrated.

Part 4

THE MESSIAH
IN LATIN AMERICAN
THEOLOGY

EIGHT

Jesus' Messianism: A Proposal and an Assessment from Latin America

Gerardo A. Alfaro González

Latin America is a place where many messiahs have made their appearance. Five hundred years ago, the white Spaniard riding on a stallion with his armor and sword seemed in the eyes of the Indians to be the *Tonatiou*, the white god, whom their prophecies had foretold. With all his glory and power, it did not take long for the Amerindians to realize that the cross and sword of the Spaniard were instruments to be used not to bring them salvation, but a history of enslavement and death.

New hopes were brought to Latin America when the *Próceres*, the so-called fathers, proclaimed independence from Spain in the 1800s. However, the majority of the people very soon would discover that the freedom promised for all was only a new strategy for a new elite to take over the control of the continent. The master had changed, but the slaves were the same.

Finally, another example of what we could consider historical messianism was implemented by the liberal governments during the nineteenth century and the beginnings of the twentieth.[1] Simón Bolívar is one of the most famous liberals of this era and was even proclaimed the *Liberator*. Before dying, he expressed his famous and revealing words, "We have plowed in the sea, America is ungovernable." Even if these words were overly pessimistic about the liberal achievements of the time, they faithfully described the general frustration of many people in our countries. As many other "messianic" examples of the twentieth century have shown, Latin American reality is in crisis, and the question is, Is there hope?[2] A similar question, one especially important for those of us who call ourselves Christians, is, How does Jesus' messianism relate to our reality?

My purpose in this paper is to examine and briefly assess, from my own Latin American perspective, one of the most important theological proposals that links the previous two questions and offers an answer to them. I have chosen Jon Sobrino's[3] work for various reasons. First, early on in the development of liberation theology, Sobrino became an important representative. Alfred Hennelly, for example, believes that Sobrino's theological methodology is the best articulated within all liberation theology.[4] Second, while Leonardo Boff and Juan Luis Segundo also are key figures, for various reasons their christological influences have waned. On the other hand, scholars recently have shown special interest in Sobrino's Christology.[5] This interest corresponds to his own continuous production of christological writings. Third, for decades Latin American theologians have searched for a christological method that would enable them to present Jesus Christ in a way that is both contextually relevant and faithful to Scripture and Christian tradition. When compared to more innovative Christologies, such as those of Segundo and Boff, Sobrino's thought appears closer to both classical Roman Catholic and Evangelical theologies. In what follows, I try to summarize Sobrino's thought on Jesus' messianism, and then I offer a brief assessment.

1. See Pablo Deiros, *Protestantismo en América Latina* (Nashville: Caribe, 1997), 15–33.

2. See Emilio A. Núñez and William D. Taylor, *Crisis and Hope in Latin America: An Evangelical Perspective*, rev. ed. (Pasadena, Calif.: William Carey, 1996).

3. Jon Sobrino is a Spanish Jesuit theologian who has lived in El Salvador since 1957. He is professor of theology at the University of Central America (UCA) in El Salvador.

4. Alfred Hennelly, "Theological Method: The Southern Exposure," *TS* 38 (December 1989): 709–35.

5. For example, Susan Brooks Thistlethwaite, "Suffering: Different Faces and Reactions: Response to Jon Sobrino," in *Pluralism and Oppression: Theology in World Perspective*, ed. Paul Knitter (Lanham, Md.: University of America Press, 1991), 179–87; Rufus Burrow, "Archbishop Romero: Memories and Reflections," *JRT* 48 (spring 1992): 85–89; Harold Hatt, "The Dialogue of Theology and Film," *Encounter* 51 (spring 1990): 103–23; Peter Sedgwick, review of *Jesus the Liberator*, by Jon Sobrino, *Theology* 98 (April 1995): 128–29.

Sobrino on Jesus' Messianism

In order to understand Sobrino's proposal, I have divided this discussion into three main sections. The first section deals with how Sobrino conceives the fundamental historical backgrounds of the term "messiah." The second summarizes his convictions about the development of the title in the early church. The third section explains the theological task that Sobrino proposes in order to appropriate and apply the significance of Jesus' messianism especially to Latin America.

Backgrounds for the Term "Messiah"

The Messiah in the Old and New Testaments

According to Sobrino, the term "messiah" in the Old Testament is an expression that mainly reflects the popular hope for liberation; "it does bespeak a primordial relation to a people's hope of liberation."[6] Of course, this hope was expressed primarily in terms of the kingdom of God, but it also was thought to be related to a public and political leader. This leader, at the beginning, was supposed to save the people as a particular group, and therefore he was conceptualized as the anointed king who was promised an eternal kingdom. However, history proved this expectation wrong, and as a result, the messiah gradually was understood to be an eschatological figure. It is only later, in the context of the exile, that the messiah is conceived as someone who will restore the kingdom, defeat the Gentiles, and promote true religion. The messiah will appear as the just king who will defend the weak and will achieve reconciliation and fraternity. Even throughout the different phases of this development, the crucial meaning of "messiah" was maintained: the messiah would be someone who would solve the problem of injustice and oppression.[7]

By the time of Jesus, the term had taken on a variety of meanings and expectations. In fact, in some contexts it was unclear whether it was God himself or the messiah who would defeat Israel's enemies by means of mighty deeds and wonders. Was the future messiah a peaceful priest or a mighty warrior? Nevertheless, in the midst of all this conceptual plurality, Sobrino believes that there was a common factor: the messiah was considered to be a historical figure, not a mythical, cosmic, or ce-

6. Jon Sobrino, "Systematic Christology: Jesus Christ, the Absolute Mediator of the Reign of God," in *Systematic Theology: Perspectives from Liberation Theology: Readings from "Mysterium Liberationis,"* ed. Jon Sobrino and Ignacio Ellacuría (Maryknoll, N.Y.: Orbis, 1996), 129.

7. Jon Sobrino, *La Fe en Jesucristo: Ensayo desde las Víctimas* (San Salvador: UCA Editores, 1999), 262–63.

lestial one.[8] For this reason, his earthly mission would be to set up a historical and political kingdom.[9] Therefore, he indeed was considered to be a public, political figure. The important point to be underlined here, once again, is that according to the popular belief, the messiah would be the answer to the people's hope. He would act to transform Israel's oppressive situation.

Jesus' Own Awareness

What about Jesus himself? It is obvious that he lived in the midst of strong messianic expectations. He himself aroused some of those expectations, and it is very probable that the people could have thought that he was the one to come. The *titulus* on the cross shows that the people might have thought that he believed himself to be the messiah, or at least that they would want him to be. "It is clear that Jesus aroused some popular hope, and to describe that hope, the most adequate word, in that context, was 'messiah.'"[10]

On the other hand, we have no evidence that Jesus considered himself as the messiah king. In fact, apart from the cleansing of the temple, his actions were very different from those of the Zealots.[11] For example, according to John 6:15, Jesus rejected the opportunity of being crowned king. All this is true, but we also have to keep in mind that it is not absolutely clear that Jesus firmly rejected being identified as the messiah.[12] Even in the trials he is highly ambiguous. There is no way to determine in those trial passages whether Jesus is saying that he is or is not the messiah.[13] In other words, apparently he let the people entertain messianic ideas about him. "The conclusion is that we cannot say with certainty whether Jesus considered himself as the messiah." For Sobrino, the "messianic secret" will be interpreted later in different ways,

8. Ibid., 264.

9. Jon Sobrino, "Jesús, el Reino de Dios: Significado y Objetivos Últimos de su Vida," *Christus* 45 (1980): 17–25.

10. Sobrino, *La Fe en Jesucristo*, 264.

11. In *Jesucristo Liberador*, Sobrino is more inclined to see Jesus closely connected to the Zealots. Sobrino perhaps is influenced here by Ignacio Ellacuría, another Jesuit and liberation theologian, who was murdered in El Salvador (Jon Sobrino, *Jesucristo Liberador: Lectura Teológica de Jesús de Nazaret* [San Salvador: UCA Editores, 1993], 212–18; cf. Ignacio Ellacuría, *Freedom Made Flesh: The Mission of Christ and His Church*, trans. J. Drury [Maryknoll, N.Y.: Orbis, 1976], 60–69).

12. This is another significant and recent change in Sobrino's opinion. In *Jesucristo Liberador*, he affirmed, "Jesus refuses the title of Messiah, which Peter has called him, referring to himself instead as Son of Man" (151). No nuances are provided.

13. Sobrino seems to be unclear whether the reasons for Jesus' death given by the Synoptics are historical or redactional. He switches back and forth (see *Jesucristo Liberador*, 195–211; idem, *Christology at the Crossroads: A Latin American Approach*, trans. J. Drury (Maryknoll, N.Y.: Orbis, 1978), 179–235.

but this he makes clear: "The important fact for our reflection here, however, is that as a whole, the Gospels show, on the one hand, that Jesus did not understand himself as a messiah king, but, on the other, that the people related him, somehow, to the hopes that they usually related to a messiah."[14]

The Development of the Title in the New Testament

But if that is the case, why is it that all the strata of the New Testament call Jesus the messiah? Sobrino reminds us that Matthew, Mark, Luke, and all the writings of the New Testament speak naturally of Jesus as the messiah. How is it that they all came to associate Jesus with the messiah? In order to answer this question, Sobrino appropriates Ferdinand Hahn's four-stage theory, according to which the title "messiah" was not applied to Jesus from the very beginning, but as a result of a process of theological reflection. The theory can be summarized as follows: (1) the title was given to Jesus only when associated with the "Son of Man," who would come in the parousia; (2) the messiah was related to the resurrected and exalted one, and if Jesus was the exalted Lord, then he should be the messiah; (3) the messiah is related to the passion narratives; and (4) the messiah is related to Jesus' earthly life, focusing especially on his miracles.[15] Sobrino thinks that a big change in the conception of salvation came to pass at the third step. Jesus brought salvation not in the Old Testament sense, but mysteriously through the cross. Moreover, when Jesus' miracles were incorporated into the term "messiah," the term itself then was being loaded with elements not present in its Jewish conception.[16]

Sobrino acknowledges the problem of judging the exegetical accuracy of this theory. Nevertheless, he accepts its conclusion: "messiah" was an inclusive term to describe the whole reality of Jesus (his earthly past, his present, and his future), and was an honorific title that "focused on the unique reality of Jesus."[17] That is why the title came to be used coextensively with Jesus himself. However, two important things occurred as this process went on. The first was that the kingdom was separated conceptually from the messiah. The second was that the messiah began to be described mainly in terms of his being the "Son of God"

14. Sobrino, *La Fe en Jesucristo*, 265.
15. Ferdinand Hahn, *The Titles of Jesus in Christology: Their History in Early Christianity*, trans. Harold Knight and George Ogg (New York: World, 1969); Sobrino uses the German original, 1963.
16. Sobrino, *La Fe en Jesucristo*, 267.
17. Sobrino, *Jesucristo Liberador*, 41.

rather than in terms of his historical work. Both changes were the result of the delay of the parousia.[18]

According to Sobrino, as the title "Christ" came to be used as a proper name for Jesus, it also began to lose its historical meaning, namely, that of being the expression of the hope of oppressed peoples. After the resurrection, the first Christians acknowledged Jesus as savior, and upon this basis they gave him the title "messiah." Thus, the meaning of "messiah" was now heavily dependent on that new concept of salvation that the first Christians were trying to formulate. Since salvation was now seen as primarily something future and related directly to the individual forgiveness of sins, the hopes for a historical salvation fell progressively into oblivion.[19] The people, as a historically collective reality, who were the original addressees of the messianic hopes were no longer the focus of this salvation. It is the individual or, at most, the church that now takes the place of importance. Of course, the process might be seen as having theological and historical reasons. On the one hand, the resurrection itself implied a concentration on an individual, the person of Jesus. On the other hand, historically, the small size of the first Christian communities made them feel insignificant for the task of changing the world, thus contributing to the fading of the messianic hopes of the poor.

Something similar happened to the relationship between "messiah" and "Son of God." The latter was identified very soon in the process as the most distinctive Christian designation for Jesus.[20] In other words, the most intimate reality of Jesus comes to be described as *filiation*, the sacrament of the Father, the historical presence of God in this world, and this is thought to be the most important thing that could ever happen in history. This way of focusing on the mediator's person, though part of the good news, has frequently forgotten the most important element in describing Jesus' identity.[21] He is related to God not only in ontological terms, but also in historical terms. He is concerned not only with his vertical, but also with his horizontal, relationship to God. This relationship is mediated through his commitment to the will of God— the coming of the kingdom.[22] And the best title to express this transcendental dimension in Jesus is "messiah." This is an important observation, especially when we notice that after centuries of Christian theology some believers think that God is absolutely happy just because his mediator, Jesus, showed up in human history, and now it is not so cru-

---

18. Sobrino, *La Fe en Jesucristo*, 270–74.
19. Ibid., 271–72.
20. On christological titles, see Sobrino, *La Fe en Jesucristo*, 213–31.
21. Jon Sobrino, *Jesus in Latin America* (Maryknoll, N.Y.: Orbis, 1987), 29–53.
22. Sobrino, *Christology at the Crossroads*, 41–61.

cial whether or not his creation dies in corruption without experiencing the kingdom.[23] "Messiah" recovers the biblical meaning of Jesus' identity, through which it is clear that God is not pleased with the world as it is. God is concerned with the utopian or messianic hope of his kingdom on earth. Neglecting this whole dimension in favor of a Christology of the person of Jesus is a major mistake that not only violates the original meaning of "messiah," but also cuts short the hope of those who desperately need it. As a result, we have proclaimed a Jesus who, being called the Christ, has no messianic importance for the deprived and the oppressed, those who most need it.[24]

The "Re-Messianization" of Jesus

One of the severe criticisms that Sobrino raises against Christian theology in general and especially against postmodern Christian theology has to do with its accommodation to and indulgence in presenting a Jesus with no messianic import whatsoever.[25] In the so-called First World, Sobrino says, there is no place for utopias, messiahs, or messianisms. There is a notorious deficit of leaders who may want to maintain the hope for the poor. Perhaps this has been reinforced by the dangers of messianisms (paternalisms, populisms, dictatorships, etc.) that recent history has proved real.[26] However, the conclusion, according to Sobrino, is that just as years ago secularization questioned the content of the title "Son of God" for referring to the deity, postmodernity today is questioning, objectively, the title of "messiah" for referring to utopias and popular hopes. Nonetheless, the poor of this world, that immense major part of humanity, need utopias— or messianic hopes, by whatever name we may call them. This may be as simple as considering life and dignity as being possible.

Thus, in order for theology to correct the serious mistake of a Jesus without his messianic implications, Jesus has to be "re-messianized." The fact that Jesus was not a militarist and violent messiah should not lead us to forget that he wanted to configure the *polis* in the direction of the kingdom of God. We have to keep in mind that even if Jesus used neither political nor military power, he did use the power of love, of truth, and of witness to transform his reality.[27]

We also should resist the temptation to separate the notion of messiah from "the oppressions and the hopes of human beings in society, those who are poor and victims"; theology should strive to maintain the

---

23. Sobrino, *Jesucristo Liberador*, 121–34.

24. Sobrino, *La Fe en Jesucristo*, 267–68; idem, *Christology at the Crossroads*, 269–70.

25. Sobrino, *Jesucristo Liberador*, 12–17.

26. Sobrino, *La Fe en Jesucristo*, 264.

27. Sobrino, *Jesus in Latin America*, 152–54.

salvific relationship between the messiah and the popular majorities.[28] And in order to do this, some methodological steps should be taken. For example, when coming to understand the meaning of "messiah," we have to define "messiah" in terms of Jesus, and not the other way around, Jesus in terms of "messiah." In other words, we should not say that Jesus is the messiah, but that the messiah is Jesus. In fact, the titles we use for Jesus are secondary. "What matters is that Jesus expresses the heart of the messianic hopes of the poor in the Old Testament. . . . The Synoptics show this by presenting Jesus in essential relationship with the kingdom of God."[29] This is so because, even without considering the titles, in the Gospels Jesus resembles "the just and partial king" of Isaiah, who wants to establish justice and righteousness and who exercises mercy toward the weak and denounces the oppressor. Today we need to repeat what the Gospels did for their time and context. We need to recover the essential meaning of "messiah" lest we maintain the contradiction of using "Christ" (messiah) as the most common designation for Jesus and at the same time continue to cut short any suggestion about biblical messianism, which is hope for the poor and exploited.[30]

Liberation theology has tried to overcome this contradiction by applying to Jesus the title of "liberator."

> The faith of Latin American Christians and the Christology of liberation have restored the meaning of the title Messiah. With the title "Liberator" they want to capture the center of the most original sense of the title: Someone will appear in history who will bring salvation to the poor and the oppressed; a just king will appear who will set free the popular majorities from bondage.[31]

For Sobrino, this is not reducing the image of Jesus to an ideological icon. On the contrary, naming Jesus as the liberator provides the possibility of developing a Christology whose starting point may be Jesus' liberating messianism.[32] In Sobrino's view,

> The image of "Christ the liberator" restores the essence of the title "Messiah," which though maintained for centuries, has by now lost any sense of historical or popular messianism. The title "Christ the liberator" picks up a history which was more or less broken off after the first generation of Christians.[33]

28. Sobrino, *La Fe en Jesucristo,* 276–77.
29. Ibid., 277.
30. Sobrino, "Systematic Christology," 137.
31. Sobrino, *La Fe en Jesucristo,* 278.
32. Sobrino, "Systematic Christology," 131.
33. Sobrino, *Jesucristo Liberador,* 36 n. 12.

Another decisive element in recovering Christ's messianism has to do with what Sobrino calls the "messianic mystery." When we turn to Jesus of Nazareth, we find the unthinkable fact that he is a "crucified messiah."[34] For Latin American theology this has serious implications, both positive and negative. First, a crucified messiah is someone who crucifies magical, mechanical, or egocentric messianisms.[35] This is what the temptation stories express.[36] Second, a crucified messiah confronts us brutally with something scandalous: the *mysterium iniquitatis*. The world persecutes and kills the best messiahs, those who bring about its salvation, whether individuals like El Salvador's Archbishop Romero, or movements like the Nicaraguan revolution. Both are implacably and mercilessly persecuted to the point of making them disappear. In this concrete and painful way, the crucified messiah reminds us that the real issue with Jesus' messianism is not a "messianic secret," but a *messianic mystery:* "the true messiah, the defender of the poor's hope, ends up on a cross."[37]

Summary

In this short description of Sobrino's work on Jesus' messianism we have discovered at least three general points:

1. "Messiah" is a title that was given to Jesus after the resurrection to express the salvific significance of his life, and, from the poor's perspective, the title was the objectification of their hopes for a more just world.
2. When the title was applied to Jesus as a proper name, it absorbed Jesus' singular historicity, but at the same time it began to lose its original and historical characteristics, especially those related to the hopes of the poor.
3. In order to correct this "de-messianized" Jesus, theology should insist on the need that the poor have for utopias and messianisms. It also should recover the messianic meaning that "Christ" has in the Bible. And finally, it should be aware of the mysterious nature of a world that crucifies all those who, like Jesus, embody true messianism.

34. Ibid., 220.

35. Sobrino does not tell us what is he referring to with these adjectives, but probably he has in mind developmental projects such as those implemented in the recent past and in the present by economic liberal and neoliberal ideologies (see Sobrino, *La Fe en Jesucristo*, 14–16).

36. Sobrino, *Jesus in Latin America*, 182; Ellacuría, *Freedom Made Flesh*, 54–60.

37. Sobrino, *La Fe en Jesucristo*, 280.

Assessment

Personal

I begin my appraisal of Sobrino's work by underlining my own geographical and social origins. I was born in El Salvador, Central America. And as far as I can trace back its history, my family has experienced all the ordeals of a typical peasant family in our country. Extreme poverty, social injustice, hunger, and violent death are some of the critical circumstances that my close family has experienced. In other words, while some theologians nowadays discuss whether or not they should place themselves among the poor, I did not have to choose. I have lived with them; I am one of them. I consider this issue very important for two reasons. First, liberationists have been quick to dismiss as uncommitted and irrelevant evaluations coming from European and North American theologians whose personal and social experiences have not been those of poverty and injustice. Such criticism, however, cannot be directed at those of us who have been born and raised in the same oppressive realities as they have. We have no need to identify with the poor, because we are the poor. And we too have come to follow and experience Jesus' liberating power, yet from a somewhat different perspective. Second, so-called First World thinkers typically reveal a limited perception regarding theological productivity in Latin America. It seems that for them, liberation proposals are the only valuable contributions coming from the Latin American culture of more than five hundred million people and thirty-five countries.[38] Unfortunately, over the past three decades Latin American theology has become largely synonymous with liberation theology. By the same token, many in Latin America itself have come to believe that liberation Christology is the final paradigm, both in theological method and in content. But is this true? In my opinion, the need persists to keep looking for new ways of expressing an authentically Latin American Christology—one that is, at the same time, faithful to Holy Scripture and classical Christian tradition. This assessment is motivated by the conviction that much remains to be done in clarifying a biblical Latin American messianology.[39]

Having said this, where should we start to evaluate Sobrino's proposal? I suggest that because of the space limitations, it is best to focus on four of his major methodological points: the role of reality, the role of the historical Jesus, the role of Christian tradition, and the role of the biblical narratives.

38. See Deiros, *Protestantismo en América Latina.*
39. I am using "Christology" and "messianology" interchangeably.

The Role of Reality

Contrary to what seems to be the case in latitudes where discussion about Jesus' messianism is only a scholarly debate or food for polemical talk shows that do not directly affect politics or social issues, Sobrino's approach to Jesus' messianism seriously considers Latin American reality. Serious consideration of reality in our context, of course, means more than the number and quality of bibliographical notes. It may make the difference between life and death.[40] For Sobrino, however, reality is not just the context in which we apply our biblical and theological knowledge. Nor is it just the complex web of epistemological presuppositions that we bring to our hermeneutical tasks. Reality for Sobrino is, above all, the place where revelation is discerned, where we find God's word for the present. Revelation in history, moreover, has its "privileged places." Sobrino believes that place to be embodied in the poor. It is in the poor where the new image of Jesus is found. Our understanding of Jesus' messianism will depend a great deal on agreeing with him in this axiom of faith. As a matter of fact, his whole discussion of Jesus' messianic role begins with the assumption that messianism is a function of the liberating hopes of the poor. However, he does not stop to discuss whether or not this is indeed the case. We end up with the impression that the issue has been solved beforehand.[41] Of course, this way of seeing Jesus will affect, from the very beginning, our assessment of him and his messianic mission. Liberation Christologies, nonetheless, will refuse to accept that their christological conclusions are simply subjectivistic or capricious fabrications of what really happened. Thus, they will appeal to historical studies for support. The historical Jesus is, then, presented as "the starting point" of Sobrino's Christology.

The Role of the Historical Jesus

Sobrino's way of seeing reality revolves, according to him, around the historical Jesus. As I am correcting this paper in San Salvador, it is 11:30 P.M., December 23, 2000, and Sobrino is being interviewed on television. In his evaluation of the history of Christianity he repeatedly insists that his main concern is how Christianity has lost sight of Jesus'

40. In 1989 seven Jesuits were assassinated in El Salvador, among them Ignacio Ellacuría, another brilliant theologian and a very close friend of Sobrino. Sobrino had left the night before to give some lectures overseas.

41. Wright's comments on Juan Luis Segundo also apply to Sobrino: "The conclusions, though very different from the normal dogmatic ones, seem to have been at least outlined in advance; the detailed historical work has not really been taken with full seriousness" (N. T. Wright, *Jesus and the Victory of God*, vol. 2 of *Christian Origins and the Question of God* [Minneapolis: Fortress, 1996], 26).

historical perspective on society and reality. However, I have argued elsewhere that Sobrino's historical Jesus is deeply controlled by his theological convictions and that his historical methodology is not strong enough to sustain his major proposals.[42] In fact, I believe that his treatment of Jesus' messianism is a good example of this. First of all, if we take Sobrino's bibliographic sources, we find only a couple of quotations from Oscar Cullmann and one from Ferdinand Hahn, two important but, in the opinion of some experts, outdated works. There is a total silence regarding the overwhelming amount and richness of recent historical research.[43] The information provided by these fresh historical studies could help to nuance, supplement, and correct some of Sobrino's affirmations. For example, is it true that all the messianic expectations at the time of Jesus considered the messiah as a historical and political figure who would establish his kingdom on earth?[44] Is it true that the notion of messianic miracles was not present in Jewish messianic expectations?[45] How would Jesus' messianism be related to Israel's messianic hopes as a nation?[46] Among other reasons, Sobrino's historical Jesus seems to be not Jewish enough, because Sobrino does not consider this particular issue seriously. If the historical Jesus has the preponderant place Sobrino assigns to him in Christology, then a more detailed and meticulous work on historical research is needed.

Another example demonstrates even more clearly the method Sobrino uses to understand Jesus' messianism. When discussing Jesus' own awareness, Sobrino focuses both on the way the Gospels present Jesus and how people would have seen him. However, he fails to dis-

42. Gerardo A. Alfaro, "Análisis y Evaluación del Jesús Histórico en la Cristología de Jon Sobrino" (Ph.D. diss., Dallas Theological Seminary, 2000).

43. See, for example, Craig A. Evans, "The Historical Jesus and Christian Faith: A Critical Assessment of a Scholarly Problem," ChrSchR 18, no. 1 (1988): 48–63; E. P. Sanders, Jesus and Judaism (Philadelphia: Fortress, 1985); Ben F. Meyer, The Aims of Jesus (London: SCM, 1979); James H. Charlesworth, Jesus within Judaism: New Light from Exciting Archaeological Discoveries (Garden City, N.Y.: Doubleday, 1988); John P. Meier, A Marginal Jew: Rethinking the Historical Jesus, 3 vols. (New York: Doubleday, 1991–2001); John Dominic Crossan, The Historical Jesus: The Life of a Mediterranean Jewish Peasant (San Francisco: HarperSanFrancisco, 1991). The same critical observation has been made by, among others, John P. Meier, The Mission of Christ and His Church: Studies in Christology and Ecclesiology (Wilmington, Del.: Glazier, 1990): 56–57; Michael L. Cook, "Jesus from the Other Side of History: Christology in Latin America," TS 44 (1983): 273–74.

44. See Gerd Theissen and Annette Merz, The Historical Jesus: A Comprehensive Guide, trans. John Bowden (Minneapolis: Fortress, 1998), 533–37.

45. See Meier, Marginal Jew, 2:617–1038; Ben Witherington III, The Many Faces of the Christ: The Christologies of the New Testament and Beyond (New York: Crossroad, 1998), 11–23.

46. See Scot McKnight, A New Vision for Israel: The Teachings of Jesus in National Context (Grand Rapids: Eerdmans, 1999).

cuss the awareness Jesus has of himself. This is very interesting, since Sobrino is fond of basing his conclusions on the evolution of Jesus' own thinking regarding God and the kingdom—by the way, an outdated methodology in Jesus-research studies. Nevertheless, according to his own method, I believe, it would be relatively easy to think of Jesus himself developing a messianic vocation, since he was able to develop even more difficult conceptions, such as those of God and the kingdom.[47] However, Sobrino is content with leaving the discussion in terms of how the people might have understood Jesus and how the Gospels present him.[48] Properly speaking, the historical Jesus is far from being the starting point of Sobrino's concept of messianism. Once again, the important thing for him at the moment is how Jesus *could* be perceived in the past and how he might be today. After all, the historical data is not crucial.

This last point opens the whole discussion about the role of the historical Jesus in Christology, but this is too big an issue to be treated here.[49] My main concern at this point is that Jesus' historical messianism in Sobrino's work has not been dealt with as deeply as it could be in the present. For example, historically, a strong case can be made for Jesus' considering himself to be the messiah, performing symbolic deeds, and telling stories not only about the kingdom of God, but also about his role as king, summoning Israel to follow him and to choose his messianic way for defeating evil forces.[50] Today, it is not as easy as it was three decades ago to state the problem of the development of Christology only in terms of the proclaimer becoming the proclaimed.[51] A real continuity between the kingdom and the king, it can be argued, predates the Easter experience.[52] Could it be said, then, that focusing on the king is not per se a betrayal of the kingdom? Actually, it could also

47. See Wright's proper remarks on the difference between doing psychology on Jesus and asking historical questions about him (*Jesus and the Victory of God*, 479–81).

48. Another interesting observation here is that Sobrino, otherwise very interested in interpreting Jesus' actions, does not discuss at all any of Jesus' symbolic actions and deeds.

49. See Alfaro, "Análisis y Evaluación del Jesús Histórico," 16–150; Evans, "The Historical Jesus and Christian Faith."

50. See Wright, *Jesus and the Victory of God*, 477–539; McKnight, *A New Vision for Israel*, 1–14.

51. See James D. G. Dunn, *The Christ and the Spirit*, 2 vols. (Grand Rapids: Eerdmans, 1998), 1:78–95; R. T. France, "Development in New Testament Christology," in *Crisis in Christology: Essays in Quest of Resolution*, ed. William R. Farmer (Livonia, Mich.: Dove Booksellers, 1995), 63–82.

52. See Marinus de Jonge, *God's Final Envoy: Early Christology and Jesus' Own View of His Mission* (Grand Rapids: Eerdmans, 1998), 59–69. Obviously, I am not arguing that all scholars are in agreement on this topic (e.g., the "Jesus Seminar"). What I am saying is that Sobrino neither discusses nor proves his case.

be argued that focusing on him is obeying his summons to follow him and discover in him the true meaning of his kingdom and, in fact, of his messiahship.[53] This would significantly change Sobrino's proposal regarding not only his historical Jesus, but also his hypothesis on the development of the theology of "messiah."

The Role of Christian Tradition

In general, Sobrino understands the history of theology in quite a negative fashion. On the specific topic of messianism, he sees it as a continuous deviation from its origins. In fact, Sobrino thinks that it has only been since the Latin American Episcopal Conferences of Medellín (1968) and Puebla (1979) that we can speak of a true return to the beginnings of the messianic movement of Jesus.[54] This extremely negative way of understanding the history of the title "messiah" is, I think, a logical result of the old history-of-religions school, in which "later" is synonymous with "deteriorated" or at least "qualitatively different." Of course, we cannot deny that in some areas or periods of the church Jesus' divinity has evaporated his humanity, and that, as a result, in those times Christian theology has become almost historically docetic.[55] We should ask, however, whether this line of thought is enough to encompass the whole Christian tradition concerning the title "messiah." In fact, I propose that at times other models also have been present,[56] and that in order to have a complete and correct messianology (Christology), there has to be an interplay among them. Moreover, development in christological history should not be seen necessarily as a departure from its origins, but as an organic process of unfolding—the organic development of the seed into the plant—and as a process that is needed to balance one-sided extremes.[57] Is that not what the very title "crucified mes-

53. See R. T. France, "The Church and the Kingdom of God: Some Hermeneutical Issues," in *Biblical Interpretation and the Church: The Problem of Contextualization*, ed. D. A. Carson (Nashville: Nelson, 1985), 40–41; Meyer, *Aims of Jesus*, 29–37.

54. Sobrino, *Jesucristo Liberador*, 36 n. 12

55. See Alister McGrath, "Christology: On Learning from History," in *Who Do You Say That I Am? Christology and the Church*, ed. Donald Armstrong (Grand Rapids: Eerdmans, 1999), 69–90.

56. See H. Richard Niebuhr, *Christ and Culture* (New York: Harper & Row, 1951); James M. Gustafson, *Christ and the Moral Life* (Chicago: University of Chicago Press, 1968); Jaroslav Pelikan, *Jesus through the Centuries: His Place in the History of Culture* (New York: Harper & Row, 1985).

57. See Alan R. Crippen II, "The Biblical Christ in a Pagan Culture," in *Who Do You Say That I Am?* ed. Armstrong, 92–100; Dunn, *Christ and the Spirit*, 1:388; France "Development in New Testament Christology"; Mark A. Noll, *Adding Cross to Crown: The Political Significance of Christ's Passion* (Grand Rapids: Baker, 1996); Samuel Escobar, "La Búsqueda de una Cristología Misionológica en América Latina," in *De la Misión a la Teología* (Buenos Aires: Kairos, 1998), 7–42.

siah" suggests? Following Keck's advice, then, I suggest that we should not go ahead with our historical Christologies without reworking a more balanced point of view concerning Christian tradition.[58]

Methodologically, moreover, it is important to take notice that when describing the history of the title "messiah," Sobrino uses a very complex historical hypothesis. In fact, I would say that this type of hypothesis is too complex to be considered historically reliable.[59] About this type of hypothesis, Wright says

> I think, in point of fact, that the mental gymnastics required to sustain this train of thought are themselves an indication that the truth is simpler, and that Paul, in company with all other very early Christians actually known to us (as opposed to those invented by ingenious scholars), believed that Jesus was indeed the true Messiah, and held that belief as a central identifying mark.[60]

The major problem here is that Sobrino takes for granted his hypothesis without any biblical, historical, or other bibliographical supports.

The Role of the Biblical Narratives

I conclude my assessment of Sobrino's understanding of Jesus' messianism by making some hermeneutical observations related to the biblical text and our Latin American reality. One of the most important features of Sobrino's Christology is its narrative style. I believe this to be one of the most powerful tools that this Christology has used to penetrate the ears of Latin Americans. The reason is found, I think, not only in that it recovers the basic biblical pattern of "telling stories,"[61] but also in that it captures the way our cultures express and share their most intimate realities and experiences.[62]

58. Leander E. Keck, "The Historical Jesus and Christology," *PSTJ* 19 (spring 1976): 21.

59. There is, I believe, another difficulty with Sobrino's logic in explaining the development of the title "messiah." On the one hand, he seems to favor the idea that Jesus did not consider himself to be the messiah, but that it was the church that assigned this title to him. On the other hand, he says that it was the same church that began to lose grasp of the real meaning of the title. Finally, he says that we have to "re-messianize" Jesus. If we follow his logic, "re-messianize" Jesus would not mean going back to the historical Jesus himself, but to the church that gave him that title! This sounds too Bultmannian for me.

60. Wright, *Jesus and the Victory of God*, 486.

61. See John Goldingay, *Models for Scripture* (Grand Rapids: Eerdmans, 1994); idem, *Models for the Interpretation of Scripture* (Grand Rapids: Eerdmans, 1995); Francis Watson, *Text and Truth: Redefining Biblical Theology* (Grand Rapids: Eerdmans, 1997).

62. See Manuel Luis Escamilla, *Cultura del Mestizaje*, Colección V Centenario (San Salvador: Ministerio de Cultura, 1987), 19–20.

In Sobrino's work, "messiah" is neither a title that Jesus receives nor his majestic surname. It is not the abstract data or category into which Jesus is supposed to fit. On the contrary, "messiah" has flesh and blood. It is the name Jesus receives inside a particular plot—a liberating story in which he sides with the poor and opposes the rich, in which once again we can reenact our own lives in the midst of that vital battle. It is precisely here where his use of the Gospels is conspicuous. The Gospels provide the narrative pattern, and his historical Jesus provides the story line and the argument.[63] The *stories* of the Gospels, each of them with its differences and particularities, do not appear in Sobrino's account. It seems that the only value these stories have is that of being stories. Their specific thrust as literary units is of no value whatsoever. This, of course, corresponds to Sobrino's existential conception of the nature of the Scriptures. They are mainly "some people's reflected faith before God."[64] The continuity between those people's faith and that of some Latin American Christians is found in that Jesus is the same object upon which their reflection is focused. It is in this context that Sobrino understands the formulation of new titles for Jesus, such as "liberator." Considering this fact, I suggest that there is a substantial discrepancy between Sobrino and some Latin American Evangelicals, myself included.[65]

Like Sobrino, I believe that in order to understand Jesus' messianism we need to have a solid grasp of the historical context of Jesus' appearance (I would say, one even more solid than that which Sobrino offers). But at the same time, I would add that we, as Latin American Evangelicals, have to study the canonical Gospels as units in their final form and allow their stories to rule over our new designations of Jesus. In other words, before *calling* Jesus anything, we have to *follow* Jesus—to use one of Sobrino's maxims—through the lenses of the evangelists. Reading Mark, for example, will guide us not only to call Jesus the messiah, but also to understand what the disciples and the other characters of the story did not realize during Jesus' earthly career: Jesus is the messiah, not primarily because he proposes himself as the fulfillment of the people's hopes, but because he proposes a distinctive agenda and hope that no one wants to appropriate, except him. Jesus appears as someone who not only condemns social and religious injustice and offers a singular liberation, but also as someone who rebukes other pseudoliberating methods. Jesus

63. Cf. Luke T. Johnson, *The Real Jesus: The Misguided Quest for the Historical Jesus and the Truth of the Traditional Gospels* (San Francisco: HarperSanFrancisco, 1996), 141–66.
64. Jon Sobrino, "Jon Sobrino: Análisis de los 2000 años de Cristianismo," television interview, San Salvador, 23 December 2000.
65. Cf. C. René Padilla, "Cristología y Misión en los Dos Terceros Mundos," *BolTeol* 8 (December 1982): 39–59.

condemns not only social and spiritual oppressions, but also, by means of his own liberating agenda, the alternative liberating methods of his society (Mark 9:40; Matt. 12:30; Luke 9:50; 11:23).[66] So, in order to be able to give Jesus any other title, such as "liberator," or to extrapolate any other theological analogy,[67] we have to be sure first that the title or analogy does not surrender the content of the Gospels' normative stories.

Conclusion

Latin America needs Jesus the Messiah. For Christian theologians, that is a given highlighted by our past and recent history. Sobrino is right when pointing to some Christologies that have been unable to relate faith and history—for example, Jesus' messianism and Latin America. According to Sobrino's own proposal, Jesus' messianism is a function of the poor's hope for liberation. Historically, this is the most crucial factor that theology has to recover, since the historical Jesus leaves us only at an impasse. Christian tradition continually has blocked this understanding, and until this is realized, Jesus' messianism will continue to be trivialized by so-called First World postmodern cultures and scholars.

Sobrino also is right when underlining the need for a messianology that deals with concrete, this-world problems, and especially with *the* problem of extreme poverty and its causes (something that many times is relegated to a secondary role within a parenthesis!). To be sure, systematic Christology can be informed by Sobrino's narrative eloquence, thematic perspicacity, and contextual relevance.

However, for all its illuminating and crucial practicality, Sobrino's proposal seems to run in the wrong track. In my opinion, Sobrino's messianology faces the following tasks: (1) the role and the use of the historical Jesus has to be clarified, corrected, and defended more adequately; (2) the role of Christian tradition needs a more carefully critical appreciation; and (3) the normative role of the Gospel stories has to be acknowledged and confronted with theological derivations. Of course, a messianology could be upheld only by an axiom of faith. Nevertheless, in that case there is no substantial way to determine whether such a messianology is Christian, or if it belongs to the already long list of false messianic pretenders.

66. See Jack D. Kingsbury, *Conflict in Mark: Jesus, Authorities, Disciples* (Minneapolis: Fortress, 1989), 95–103; Frank J. Matera, *New Testament Christology* (Louisville: Westminster, 1999), 11–26.

67. Not just the true messiah was crucified. Crucifixion was inflicted also on those who from a biblical perspective were false messiahs (e.g., the two rebels crucified with Jesus and the hundreds of other crucifixions at the time).

NINE

Reflections on Jesus as Liberator

A Response to Gerardo A. Alfaro González

Karen H. Jobes

I thank Professor Alfaro and the organizers of this conference for giving me the opportunity to reflect upon the two big questions that Professor Alfaro has raised: (1) Does the gospel of Jesus Christ give hope of liberation to the poor and oppressed of Latin America? and (2) How does Jesus' identity as the messiah relate to the reality of Christians living in poverty and oppression? I have appreciated this opportunity to learn more about the situation in which our brothers and sisters in Christ live in Latin America and specifically about the theological proposal of Jon Sobrino. Professor Alfaro has assessed four of Sobrino's major methodological points: (1) the role of reality, (2) the role of the historical Jesus, (3) the role of Christian tradition, and (4) the role of the biblical narratives.

I share Professor Alfaro's interest in these points and others as well. Since my personal history has not included poverty, injustice, and oppression, I wish to affirm some of the broader concerns that motivate liberation theology before turning to specific issues. I agree that it is wrong and ungodly for the powerful to use God's Word to justify and confirm the enslavement and oppression of other human beings for self-serving ends that preserve the status quo. I also affirm that God's ultimate will is for people to live in dignity and well-being, articulated, for instance, by the prophet Micah, who said that a time would come when all would live under their own vines and fig trees, and no one would make them afraid (Mic. 4:4). Although I believe that the Bible teaches that this ideal will not be fully realized until the parousia of Jesus Christ, I also believe that because Jesus' death and resurrection have inaugurated the messianic age, Christians are to conduct themselves in this life in accord with the characteristics of the eschaton to whatever extent they are able. Therefore, issues of economic justice and freedom from oppression are appropriate priorities to consider in evaluating public policy. I affirm that one cannot separate right thinking about Jesus from following Jesus, and that following Jesus is not limited to some religious aspect of one's inner life but embraces all of one's life, including one's political views. I admire the courage of Christians in Latin America who pursue the ideals of the kingdom, in some cases at the cost of their lives. My own complacency has been chastened by their stories.

I affirm Professor Alfaro's goal of defining Latin American theology more broadly than liberation theology and in ways that are faithful to Scripture and classical Christian tradition, as it seems that much contemporary theology pays too little attention to Scripture and to the voice of Christians from ages past. I will respond to Professor Alfaro's assessment of Sobrino's theological proposal by directing my remarks particularly to two points: (1) the role of the poor in the kingdom of God as understood by Latin American theology, and (2) the role of Jesus as the messiah in the Latin American context.

The Role of the Poor in the Kingdom of God

Alfaro confirms Sobrino's claim, "The major fact in Latin America is the massive, unjust poverty that threatens whole populations with death."[1] Given that reality, it seems quite appropriate to make the plight of the poor the focus of one's theological task. In such a setting one does not have the luxury of avoiding the question of what it means for a Christian to follow Jesus the Messiah in the face of great suffering.

Faced with such a situation, the privileged place of the poor must be a matter of praxis, or application, whereas Sobrino makes the experi-

1. Jon Sobrino, "Central Position of the Reign of God in Liberation Theology," in *Systematic Theology: Perspectives from Liberation Theology: Readings from "Mysterium Liberationis,"* ed. Jon Sobrino and Ignacio Ellacuría (Maryknoll, N.Y.: Orbis, 1996), 44.

ence of the poor the locus of contemporary revelation that defines his theological center. As Alfaro observes, "Reality for Sobrino is, above all, the place where revelation is discerned, where we find God's word for the present" (163). Alfaro also observes Sobrino's "existential conception of the nature of the Scriptures," from which Sobrino privileges experience over the normativity of the biblical text (168).

Because of Sobrino's concept of revelation, he does not give the poor merely a privileged status, but claims that theirs alone is the kingdom of God, and therefore that the program of Jesus was to bring the utopian conditions of the kingdom to realization in the lives of the poor and oppressed. Alfaro has observed that Sobrino supports his agenda by a rather selective use of the New Testament. Sobrino apparently understands the first beatitude as found in Luke 6:20, "Blessed are you who are poor, for *yours* is the kingdom of God," to be an absolute and delimiting statement.[2] There are at least two exegetical problems with any theology that absolutizes the poor as the recipients of the kingdom.

First, Sobrino does not discriminate between the poor who are believers in Christ and those who are not. Whatever liberating hope the messianic expectation of Israel offered, it always was limited to God's elect people and never was a message of liberation for the masses of oppressed people in general apart from their inclusion in the covenant. There may have been an openness to Gentiles joining God's covenant nation, but the extent of God's liberating program was delimited by the boundaries of his chosen people. As messiah, Jesus commands the church to preach the gospel actively to peoples of all nations, tribes, and languages, who are invited to find liberation within it by embracing faith in Christ. And so a theology of liberation that delimits the kingdom of God in terms of the experienced reality of the masses tends to imply soteriological inclusivism, if not outright universalism.

On the other hand, Latin American liberation theologians are working in countries in which virtually all have been baptized into the Roman Catholic church and are therefore at least nominal believers in Christ, if not devout and practicing. In such a setting, Sobrino's assumption that all of the poor of Latin America are the recipients of the kingdom might be appropriate. Nevertheless, to be true to the New Testament, any liberation theology must clearly recognize that one does not participate in the benefits of the kingdom of God by virtue of one's poverty apart from faith in Jesus Christ.

This is not to say that Christians should attend only to the poor within the church and ignore the poverty and suffering of those masses of people who are outside. Christians are to be merciful like their Father in

2. Ibid., 55.

heaven, who causes the sun to rise on both the evil and the good, and sends rain to fall upon both the righteous and the unrighteous (Matt. 5:45). Christians are to do good to all people, but especially to those who belong to the family of believers (Gal. 6:10). Christians should work to leave this world a better place for all peoples. But whatever socioeconomic liberation the oppressed of this world may come to experience in this life, what profit is it to them if they gain the world but lose their own souls? Even the most effective sociopolitical liberation is but an illusion of well-being if those who enjoy it do not also know Jesus the Messiah as their Lord who has atoned for their sin. The fact that the poor and oppressed often have been the victims of the sin of powerful others does not mean that they are not themselves sinners, just as are all human beings, and in that sense the poor are no different from their oppressors.

Second, in absolutizing the poor, Sobrino gives no exegetical defense for what the word "poor" in Jesus' beatitudes means, and perhaps he too rigidly defines it in reference to the socioeconomically poor. In comparison to the first beatitude in Luke, its Matthean parallel blesses the poor in spirit as the recipients of the kingdom (Matt. 5:3). Some might argue that "poor" and "poor in spirit" in this context are synonymous because those who live in poverty are by definition also poor in spirit (an assumption that should be challenged). To the contrary, one could argue that spiritual poverty is found especially rampant among the wealthy of our world who seek to satisfy with money what can be satisfied only by Christ. Sobrino seems to take this one beatitude out of context and does not relate it to the several other subsequent statements or to the overall purpose of Jesus' sermon.

Elsewhere in Luke, Jesus makes a similar statement about the recipients of the kingdom when he says, "Let the little children come to me, and do not hinder them, for the kingdom of God *belongs to such as these*" (Luke 18:16). Using the same logic that Sobrino applied to the first beatitude to justify his theology, it would seem that Jesus also teaches that only children are the recipients of the kingdom. But Jesus goes on to explain in the next verse that only those who become *like* a little child will enter the kingdom of God (Luke 18:17), and similarly one could argue against Sobrino that only those who become like the poor— that is, not depending on worldly wealth for their merit—will enter the kingdom. Neither the poor nor children are being absolutized in Jesus' statements about who enters the kingdom of God.

The first beatitude, which plays such a central role in Sobrino's thinking, would nevertheless be good news to those living in poverty because Jesus announces that their socioeconomic status, which had disqualified them from so many benefits in their society even to the extent of marginalizing their humanity, will not disadvantage them at all in the kingdom of God. The kingdom of God is theirs to enjoy, along with all who recognize their own spiritual poverty regardless of the balance in their bank account.

And so while I affirm the locus of the poor as essential for the praxis of Latin American liberation theology, I challenge a claim that the kingdom of God is revealed only among the oppressed and impoverished and cannot be understood or appropriated apart from that situation. In fact, the idea that the sociological experience of a group defines the truth sounds much like the postmodernism that Sobrino rejects when the kind of truth it concludes is used against the poor and oppressed.

The Role of Jesus as the Messiah

Professor Alfaro rightly argues that Sobrino's reconstruction of the historical Jesus "is deeply controlled by his theological convictions" and that his historical and exegetical methodology is insufficient to sustain his major theological points (164). As Professor Alfaro observes, in Sobrino's historical reconstruction the messianic expectation at the time of Jesus was for a public, political figure who would solve the problem of Roman injustice and the oppression of Israel by setting up a historical and geo-political kingdom (155–56). Furthermore, Sobrino claims that Jesus himself viewed his own mission in these terms. In support of Alfaro's critique of Sobrino's method, I challenge this understanding of Sobrino's historical Jesus on several fronts as well.

Sobrino's Selective Use of the New Testament

As Professor Alfaro has shown, Sobrino's existential conception of the nature of revelation leads him to pay little attention to the normativity of the Gospel texts in their particularities, which means that Sobrino lays little exegetical groundwork for the foundation of his theology. Moreover, no liberation Christology that wishes to be received as truly Christian can be based on the foundation of the Synoptic Gospels alone. Sobrino rejects most of the New Testament as irrelevant for his understanding of the historical Jesus because he believes that even during the time of the later New Testament writers, the character of Jesus' messianism already was being reinterpreted in transcendent categories that were not true to the historical Jesus' self-understanding as a political messiah. According to Sobrino, the very term "messiah" in its Greek form, *Christos*, was a title given to Jesus after the resurrection that came to describe the whole unique reality of Jesus and that subsumed any sociopolitical agenda under philosophical and timeless categories. The transcendence of the risen Christ swallowed up the political agenda of the historical Jesus as liberator of the oppressed in the thought of the developing church and, according to Sobrino, now must be recovered. Transcendence for Sobrino apparently means such a heavenly understanding of Jesus that it is no earthly good, at least for his purposes. Therefore, the church must rediscover what the term "messiah" would have meant in Jesus' view of his own mission before his death. Jesus must be "re-messianized."

One can question whether Sobrino's rejection of virtually all but the Synoptic Gospels for understanding the mission of the messiah simply means that Sobrino's own reconstruction of the historical Jesus trumps any biblical data that would contradict it. For instance, Sobrino claims that the kingdom that Jesus proclaims is to be fully realized in this world and that Jesus himself acted subversively to achieve it, most particularly in his "attack" on the temple. This subversion was recognized by the Jewish religious establishment and by Pilate, who saw Jesus as "a menace to established society, and for that he must die."[3] By rejecting the relevance of John's Gospel, for instance, Sobrino neglects Jesus' statement in John 18:36, in which Jesus seems to be correcting any politically subversive perception of himself by explaining to Pilate, "My kingdom is *not* of this world. If it were, my servants would fight to prevent my arrest . . ." (TNIV, emphasis added). Sobrino would argue that John's Gospel was written during that time when the church's reflection on Jesus was being too heavily influenced by Greek philosophy. However, even Sobrino's canon, the three Synoptic Gospels, which he assumes preserve the earlier and more reliable picture of the messiah, presents data that would at least question Sobrino's reconstruction of Jesus as a political liberator. To cite just one example, when Jesus is arrested, he complains, "Am I leading a rebellion, that you have come out with swords and clubs to capture me?" (Matt. 26:55 TNIV // Mark 14:48 // Luke 22:52). While there may be some debate about how to understand Jesus' words, his question is understood to require a negative answer, challenging Sobrino's reconstruction of Jesus' self-understanding as a political reformer.

Most New Testament scholars probably would challenge Sobrino's claim that there was a single unified messianic expectation among first-century Palestinian Jews and that Jesus' self-perception of his mission was as the Jewish leaders and Pilate saw him. Alfaro is right to criticize Sobrino on his neglect of the complexity of these claims as revealed by recent New Testament scholarship (164). For instance, Marinus de

3. Sobrino, "Central Position of the Reign of God," 53.

Jonge argues that Jesus indeed saw himself as the messiah of the Davidic dynasty; however, "This was not always correctly understood by his followers and was definitely misunderstood by his opponents; this misunderstanding led to his crucifixion as 'king of the Jews,' a political messiah."[4] James Charlesworth claims, contrary to Sobrino, "Jesus' message was certainly apocalyptic and eschatological; but it was not messianic"—at least as messianic would have been understood by the masses of first-century Palestine.[5] In fact, most New Testament scholars see Jesus as presented in Mark's Gospel as redefining the term "messiah" through his teaching and the nature of his miracles. Frank Matera writes, "Mark would define messiahship in terms of Jesus, rather than define Jesus in terms of messiahship. Although Jesus does not fulfill traditional messianic expectations, his life and ministry are the norm for defining what it means to be God's anointed one."[6]

Sobrino's reconstruction of the mission of the historical Jesus apparently suffers from one fatal flaw that eviscerates his theology of its practical value. (Though perhaps I fail to see its value because I am looking through Anglo presuppositions.) If Jesus indeed saw himself as a liberator whose goal was to free his fellow first-century Jews from Roman oppression, evidently he failed in his mission. Jesus did not liberate anyone socially, economically, or politically from the rule of Rome. Those who followed Jesus experienced disenfranchisement and persecution, and many followed him to horrific executions. Jesus did not prevent Jerusalem from being destroyed, or thousands of innocent, poor, and oppressed Jews from being slaughtered. In fact, Sobrino's reconstruction of the historical Jesus looks quite similar to Albert Schweitzer's: Jesus thought that he would inaugurate the reign of God that would liberate Israel from its oppression. He failed, but he died trying, and so should we! Sobrino rightly observes (as Alfaro summarizes it) "the mysterious nature of a world that crucifies all those who, like Jesus, embody true messianism" (161). Is this the gospel, the good news, that should be held up as a role model for the suffering Christians of Latin America? Does not the resurrected Jesus have to come into play in order to make sense of the historical Jesus as the messiah and liberator? Can the kingdom of God truly be understood apart from the transcendence of its resurrected king? I, for one, think not.

4. Marinus de Jonge, "The Christological Significance of Jesus' Preaching of the Kingdom of God," in *The Future of Christology: Essays in Honor of Leander E. Keck*, ed. A. J. Malherbe and W. Meeks (Minneapolis: Fortress, 1993), 12.

5. James H. Charlesworth, "From Messianology to Christology: Problems and Prospects," in *The Messiah*, ed. J. H. Charlesworth (Minneapolis: Fortress, 1992), 5.

6. Frank J. Matera, *New Testament Christology* (Louisville: Westminster John Knox, 1999), 25.

Sobrino apparently sees the resurrection as having an exclusively future, eschatological character, whereas the reign (or kingdom) of God he understands to have a more present reality and significance that is of greater practical value. Sobrino writes, "With all its power to express the ultimate meaning of history, with all of its radical hope, the resurrection does not have the same capacity [as the kingdom of God] to show how one should live in history."[7] Such liberation theology never can truly liberate if it excludes the relevance of the resurrection for understanding the person and mission of the historical Jesus and the practical value of that understanding for living in history.

What Does the Reality of the Resurrected Messiah Mean for Liberation Efforts Today?

I conclude my remarks by more directly addressing the two big questions that Professor Alfaro raised: (1) Does the gospel of Jesus Christ give hope of liberation to the poor and oppressed of Latin America? and (2) How does Jesus' identity as the messiah relate to the reality of Christians living in poverty and oppression? Taking the New Testament in its entirety indicates that Jesus himself taught that the sociopolitical structures of this world are so depraved that they cannot merely be fixed, but must be destroyed. This seems to be a major point of texts such as the parable of the wheat and the weeds in Matt. 13 and the Olivet discourse. The Book of Revelation, that revelation of Jesus of "what *must* soon happen" (ἃ δεῖ γενέσθαι ἐν τάχει), most eloquently speaks of the need for a new creation to replace this one oppressed by the forces of evil. The true liberation of the poor and oppressed awaits the return of the messiah as king of all kings over the earth. This suggests two implications for Christian efforts to liberate the poor and oppressed in the name of Jesus Christ today.

First, it sets the whole effort in a realistic light that tempers attitudes of idealism or triumphalism. Work as we might, whatever liberation and social justice that is achieved will fall far short of what is needed and of what God has deemed necessary to do for his reign to be fully realized. History has shown that even where the oppressed gain power, they all too easily become the oppressors, and the cycle continues. By both the testimony of Scripture and the experience of history we are forced to admit that the task of liberation in its fullest expression is the sole responsibility of Jesus the Messiah when he returns.

7. Sobrino, "Central Position of the Reign of God," 41–42.

However, it would be wrong to allow this truth to make us complacent and uncaring toward those who suffer injustice and oppression. For as Professor Alfaro has reminded us,

> The fact that Jesus was not a militarist and violent messiah should not lead us to forget that he wanted to configure the *polis* in the direction of the kingdom of God. We have to keep in mind that even if Jesus used neither political nor military power, he did use the power of love, of truth, and of witness to transform his reality. (159)

Because by his death and resurrection Jesus the Messiah has achieved the ultimate liberation of his people from sin and death, Christians live an ultimate reality that cannot be touched by the worst that oppression and poverty have to offer. It is this ultimate reality toward which all of history is moving. And while history is moving toward this end, Jesus the Messiah has commissioned his church to be busy bringing his liberating message to all nations, where he will be working with us even until the end of the age (Matt. 28:18–20). Therefore, this is no time for complacency or for hopelessness and despair.

As both Alfaro and Sobrino underscore, it is not enough to think that just because Jesus "showed up in human history" that God is content with the status quo (158–59). The reign of God over the nations was inaugurated some two thousand years ago through the death and resurrection of Jesus, and that was intended to have real effects mediated through the lives of his followers. As one of Sobrino's fellow Jesuit priests, Michael Cook, has eloquently put it, "Jesus' resurrection did not terminate the historical process by removing it from human history but rather unleashed into history the power of Christ's Spirit as a call and challenge to each succeeding generation."[8] And therefore, as the church commits itself to the reign of God that was inaugurated with the resurrection of Jesus Christ and that will be fully realized at his return, it can work with the confidence that the kingdom will be mediated, however imperfectly and partially, through its efforts because the risen Christ—not the historical Jesus—is with us. Remember Zacchaeus, the tax collector who had used his power to increase his wealth through extortion of the poor and powerless. His genuine encounter with Jesus compelled him thereafter to use his material resources to assist the poor whom he once had cheated (Luke 19:1–10). The efforts of the church committed to kingdom work will continue to multiply such liberations in the here-and-now that will bear testimony to the truth of that ultimate, future liberation of the world from sin and death that is found in Christ Jesus alone.

8. Michael L. Cook, "Jesus from the Other Side of History: Christology in Latin America," *Theological Studies* 44 (June 1983): 276.

Index of Scripture
and Other Ancient Writings

Index of Modern Authors

189

49171049R00116

Made in the USA
Lexington, KY
27 January 2016